If ever we need a laugh and a pick-me-up this super book is just the tonic. You'll be hard pressed to put it down. It's a showcase of the work of the talented Southend Standard cartoonists of the mid-1930s - smart, analytical and topical at the same time. Although the cartoons were created 90 years ago many would not be out place today. The images have been drawn from the Southend Standard archives, a newspaper ancestor of the Essex Echo. It's wonderful that we now have a readable and entertaining collection in the form of this book - guaranteeing these supreme cartoons will never be forgotten.

Emma Palmer
Chief Features Writer
Essex Echo

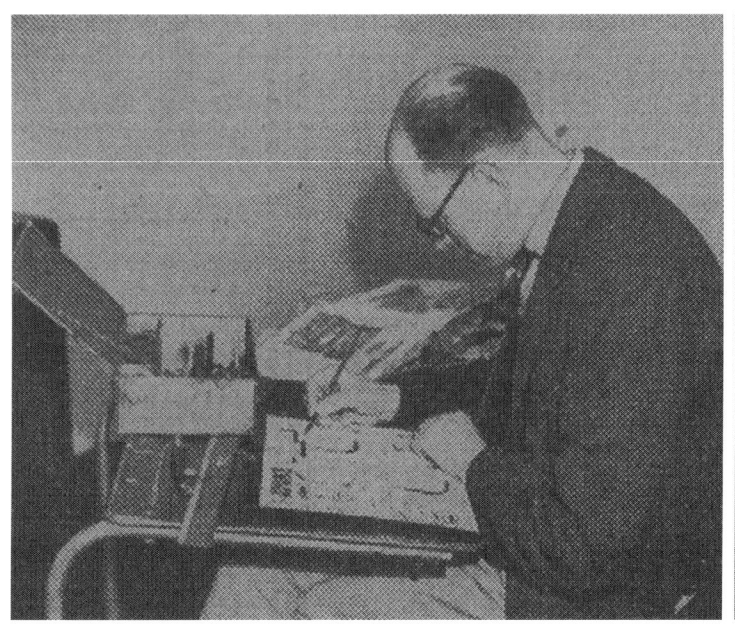 

Stan Harvey in 1939 *Fred Naughten at work in 1937*

ESSEX HUNDRED PUBLICATIONS

ONCE UPON A TIME IN SOUTHEND AND DISTRICT

Original Drawings by Fred Naughten and Stan Harvey

With additional text by Andrew Summers

Essex Hundred Publications

www.essex100.com   ask@essex100.com

**Once Upon a Time
in Southend (and District)**
Andrew Summers
© Copyright Andrew Summers

This edition first published March 2021

All rights reserved.

No part of this book may be reprinted or reproduced or utilised in any form or by any electronic, mechanical or other means, now known or hereafter invented, including photocopying and recording, or in any information storage or retrieval system, without the permission in writing from the publishers.

British library cataloguing in Publication Data,
A catalogue record for this book is available from The British Library.
ISBN 978-0-9931083-9-6

Typeset by Hutchins Creative Limited
Printed by 4edge Publishing
22 Eldon Way Eldon Way Industrial Estate
Hockley Essex SS5 4AD

*To cartoonists everywhere and especially
Stan Harvey and Fred Naughten.*

May their images live forever.

*With especial thanks to Glenis Summers
and John Debenham
for proof reading, checking historical facts
and making helpful suggestions.*

*This publication would not have been possible without the generous access of the
Newquest Media Group to their archive newspapers.*

Contents

9. .... Illustrations

11. .... Introduction

13. 1936

51. 1937

89. 1938

127. 1939

159. .... Conclusion

160. .... Andrew Summers

161. .... Also Available

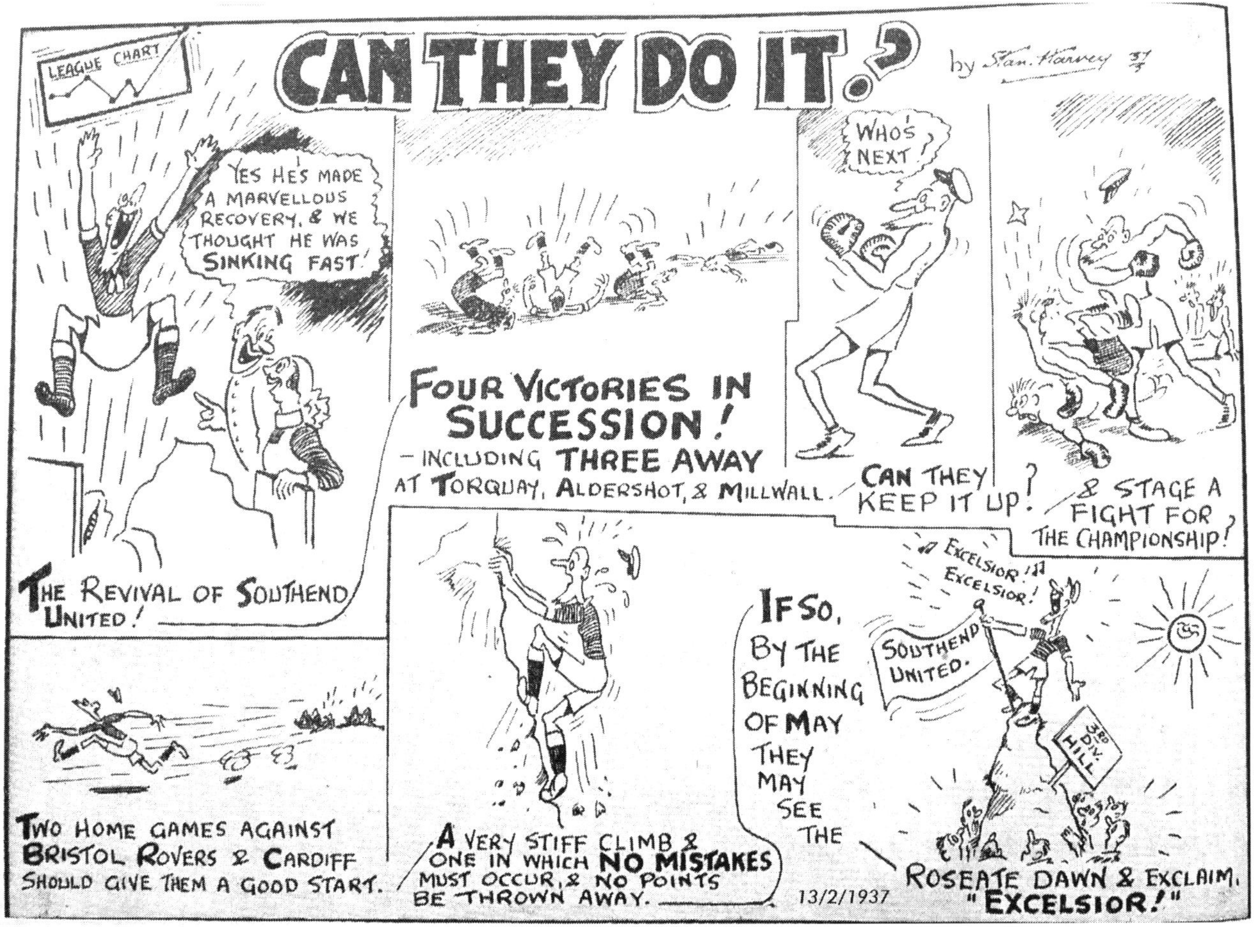
CAN THEY DO IT?
by Stan. Harvey 37
LEAGUE CHART
YES HE'S MADE A MARVELLOUS RECOVERY, & WE THOUGHT HE WAS SINKING FAST
THE REVIVAL OF SOUTHEND UNITED!
FOUR VICTORIES IN SUCCESSION!
- INCLUDING THREE AWAY AT TORQUAY, ALDERSHOT, & MILLWALL.
WHO'S NEXT
CAN THEY KEEP IT UP?
& STAGE A FIGHT FOR THE CHAMPIONSHIP?
TWO HOME GAMES AGAINST BRISTOL ROVERS & CARDIFF SHOULD GIVE THEM A GOOD START.
A VERY STIFF CLIMB & ONE IN WHICH NO MISTAKES MUST OCCUR, & NO POINTS BE THROWN AWAY.
IF SO, BY THE BEGINNING OF MAY THEY MAY SEE THE
EXCELSIOR!!! EXCELSIOR!
SOUTHEND UNITED.
3RD DIV. HILL
ROSEATE DAWN & EXCLAIM, "EXCELSIOR!"

13/2/1937

Illustrations

Excepting the following, all the images shown are the original works of Fred Naughten or Stan Harvey.

Pages 15, 80, 110
The Southend Pictorial Telegraph

Page 70
Heritage Plaque, Royal Terrace, Southend-on-Sea (Essex100)

Page 78
Joscelynes Beach, Liz Summers

Pages 140, 154
Southend-on-Sea & County Pictorial

Fred Naughten. Carnival season – The earliest recorded procession (about 936BC)

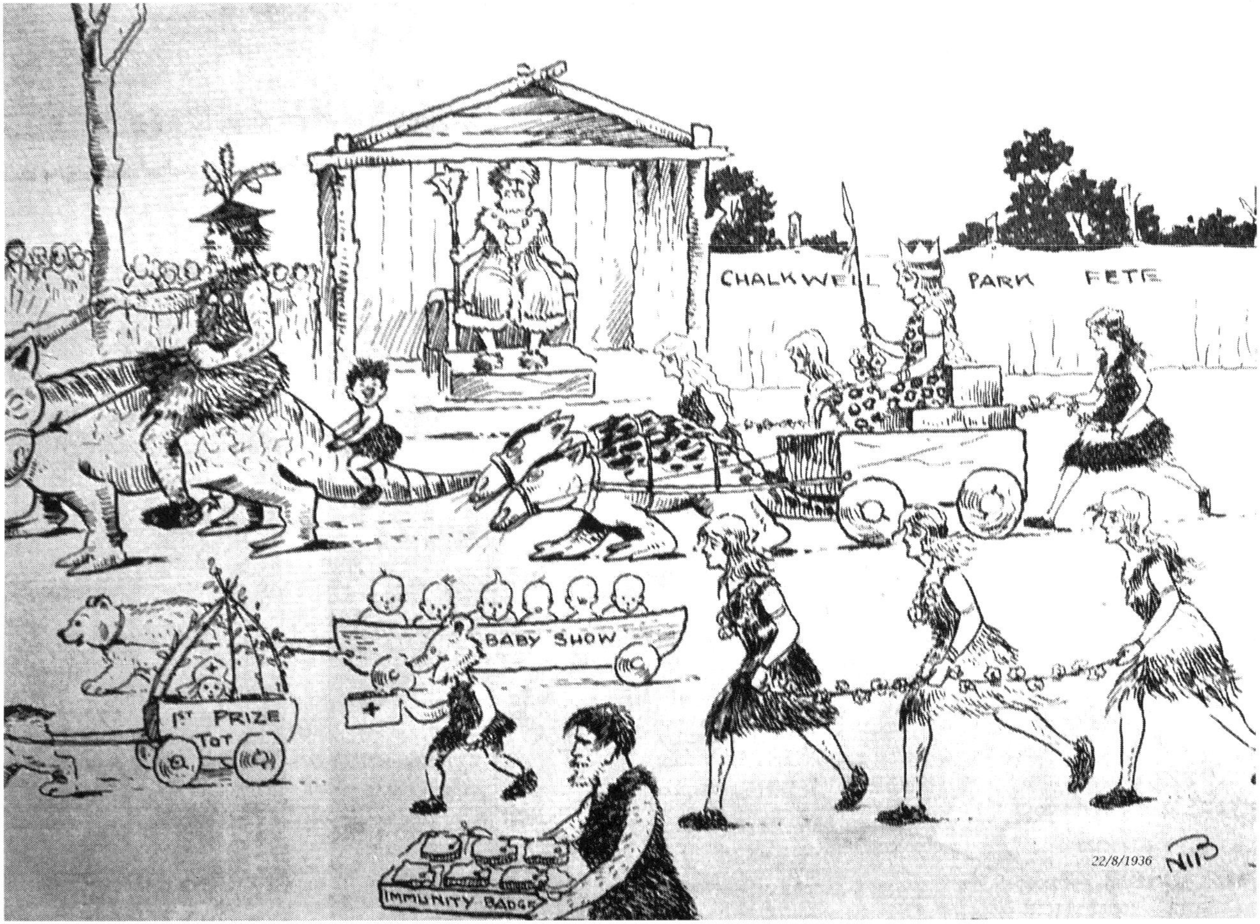
CHALKWELL PARK FETE
BABY SHOW
1ST PRIZE TOT
IMMUNITY BADGE
22/8/1936
NIB

Introduction

This book is dedicated to the fantastic creativity of Fred Naughten and Stan Harvey who were leading cartoonists for the Standard Newspaper group in the mid- 1930s.

One of the most popular staples of newspapers are the topical cartoons. The cartoonists' genius lies not just in drawing skills but in the ability to bring together contemporary and historical events in a single image. Such cartoons make us smile, sometimes laugh out loud or just reflect, no matter how grim the news of the day is. Fred's and Stan's work appeared weekly, first in the *Southend Pictorial Telegraph* and later in the *Southend-on-Sea & County Pictorial*.

F. T. (Fred) Naughten worked for the Southend Standard Group. He started as a junior in 1907 and worked his way up to be a correspondent. He was also well respected in yachting circles because of his weekly commentaries on sailing. However he is best remembered for his quirky cartoons, published once a fortnight in a series called *Southend and District Once Upon a Time*. All drawings carried his trademark pen name 'NIB' although to this day no one has been able to discern what NIB stood for.

Fred was perhaps exceptional in that he could draw on his widespread historical knowledge, although it must be said he often used a degree of creative licence.

We have no information about Stan Harvey's career or background other than that he worked with Fred at the *Standard* group. His cartoons carried his name and are largely self-explanatory. Stan's speciality was creating images conveying the lighter side of sport and public affairs. Although the personalities and circumstances have changed over the years, many of both Fred's and Stan's cartoons still carry relevance today.

In this book we show a selection of cartoons published over the four years from 1936 to 1939. For Fred's, the original captions are included although in some cases extra text has been added for clarity. The mid-thirties, despite high unemployment and dark clouds looming abroad, were optimistic times. The motor car was becoming ever more popular as were all types of consumer goods such as the 'must have' wireless for the home. It was the golden age of cinema and of course, for good or bad, there was no internet, e-mail or social media.

Andrew Summers

1936

1936 - Our journey begins

In the wider world away from Southend, the death of King George V in January was followed by an orderly succession with Edward VIII taking the helm. In April, Billy Butlin opened his first Butlin's holiday camp in Skegness, Lincolnshire. In May, the *Queen Mary* left Southampton on her maiden voyage and July saw the Post Office introduce the speaking clock. Fred Perry also won his third successive men's singles tennis title at Wimbledon. In the same month there was an attempted assassination of the King. In August, the summer Olympics opened in Berlin and on 3rd November, US President Franklin D. Roosevelt was re-elected for a second term. The Crystal Palace, which was originally located in Hyde Park and was the brainchild of Queen Victoria's husband Albert, burnt down in a spectacular fire at its new location in Penge, South London on 30th November.

Perhaps the most stunning news for the United Kingdom in 1936 was that, in December, the King, Edward VIII, who had only succeeded to the throne in January, abdicated in order to marry the American socialite Wallis Simpson.

KING EDWARD'S ABDICATION.

Bill Passed by Parliament.

A Happy New Year

In his first cartoon of the year Stan Harvey kick-started 1936 on an optimistic note. He looked forward to a splendid year. 1935 had ended wet and miserable. The New Year seemed to offer hope although there was great uncertainly in the wider world and high unemployment at home.

Stan looked forward to peace and prosperity, a glorious summer, fine weather for the sailing season and even a lowering of the rates!

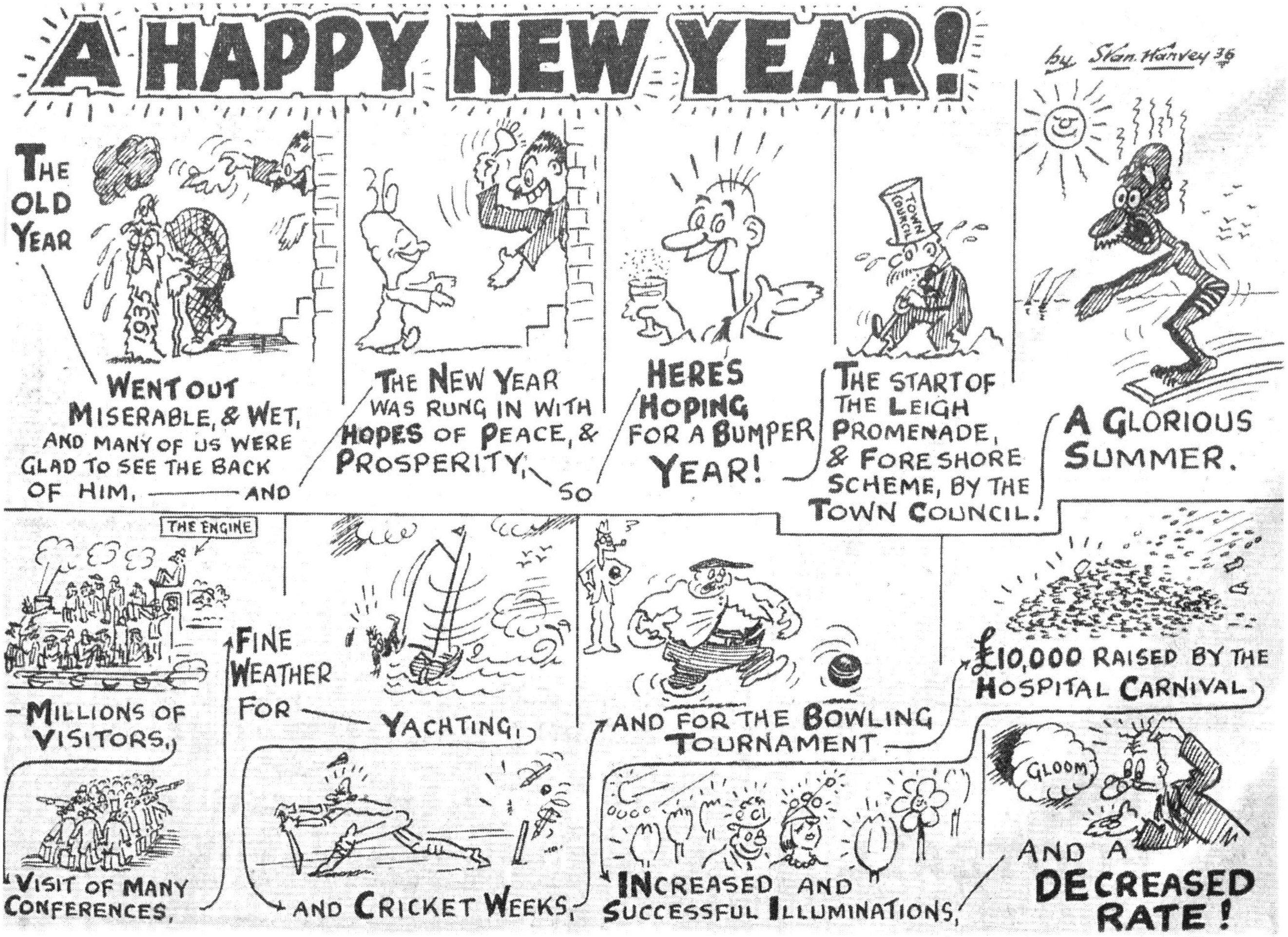
A HAPPY NEW YEAR!
by Stan. Harvey 36
THE OLD YEAR
1935
WENT OUT MISERABLE, & WET, AND MANY OF US WERE GLAD TO SEE THE BACK OF HIM, —— AND
36
THE NEW YEAR WAS RUNG IN WITH HOPES OF PEACE, & PROSPERITY, SO
HERE'S HOPING FOR A BUMPER YEAR!
TOWN COUNCIL
THE START OF THE LEIGH PROMENADE, & FORESHORE SCHEME, BY THE TOWN COUNCIL.
A GLORIOUS SUMMER.
THE ENGINE
- MILLIONS OF VISITORS,
FINE WEATHER FOR —— YACHTING,
AND FOR THE BOWLING TOURNAMENT
£10,000 RAISED BY THE HOSPITAL CARNIVAL
VISIT OF MANY CONFERENCES,
AND CRICKET WEEKS,
INCREASED AND SUCCESSFUL ILLUMINATIONS,
GLOOM
AND A DECREASED RATE!

Cowboy Builders?

January 11th 1936 saw the publication of Fred Naughten's first cartoon of the year. He delved back into history and chose one of his favourite subjects, Hadleigh Castle.

'Cowboy' builders seem to have been around for some time. Construction of Hadleigh Castle began shortly after the sealing of the Magna Carta, on land granted by King John to Hubert de Burgh, the Chief Justiciar of England. The castle was conceived as a defensive establishment against seaborne invaders and was built using Kentish rag stone. However, it never fulfilled this role. Due to poor construction and unstable ground, the castle walls needed continual shoring up and repair over the centuries, all at great expense. In 1551, King Edward VI, the son of Henry VIII, cut his losses and sold the castle and lands to a local man, Richard Riche, for £700.00. Riche promptly set about asset stripping and took as much of the stone as possible for use on his other properties. Hadleigh Castle has remained a ruin ever since.

Fred's caption simply read:- *The building of Hadleigh Castle 1217*

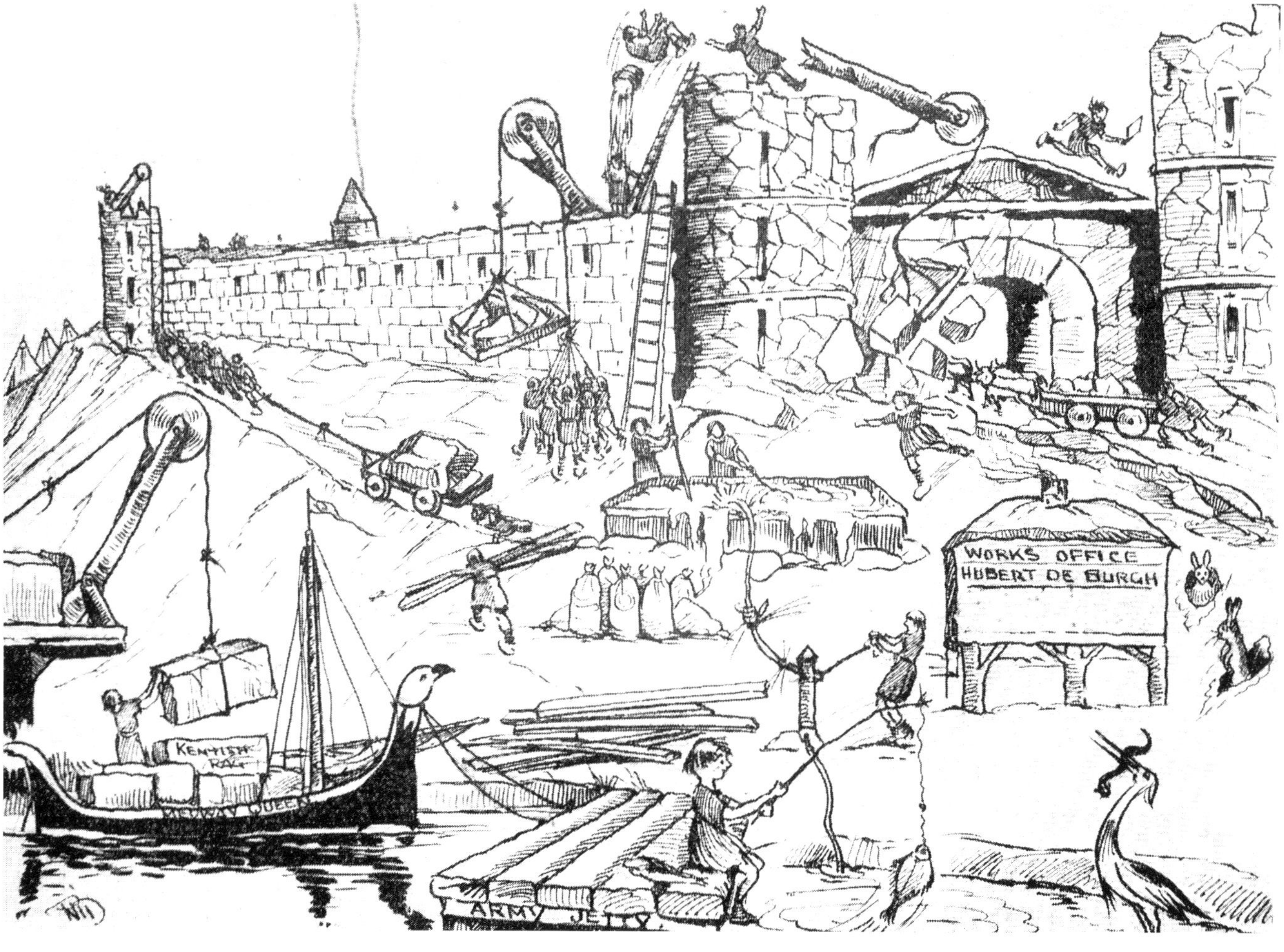
WORKS OFFICE
HUBERT DE BURGH
KENTISH RAG
MEDWAY QUEEN
ARMY JETTY

Golf, the new craze

By the mid-1930s golf was an increasingly popular pastime and no more so than on Belfairs golf course. The Belfairs course was developed on land that had been part of the Royal Forest for several hundred years. Royal Forest law gave exclusive rights to the King and his chosen nobles to hunt game in the forest. There were harsh penalties for commoners who transgressed.

Fred Naughten's cartoon shows medieval royalty making the transition from hunting to golf and perhaps enjoying the best of both worlds.

The caption read:-

When Hadleigh became a Royal Seat the King and his nobles hunted in the forest that lay between Thundersley and Prittlewell.

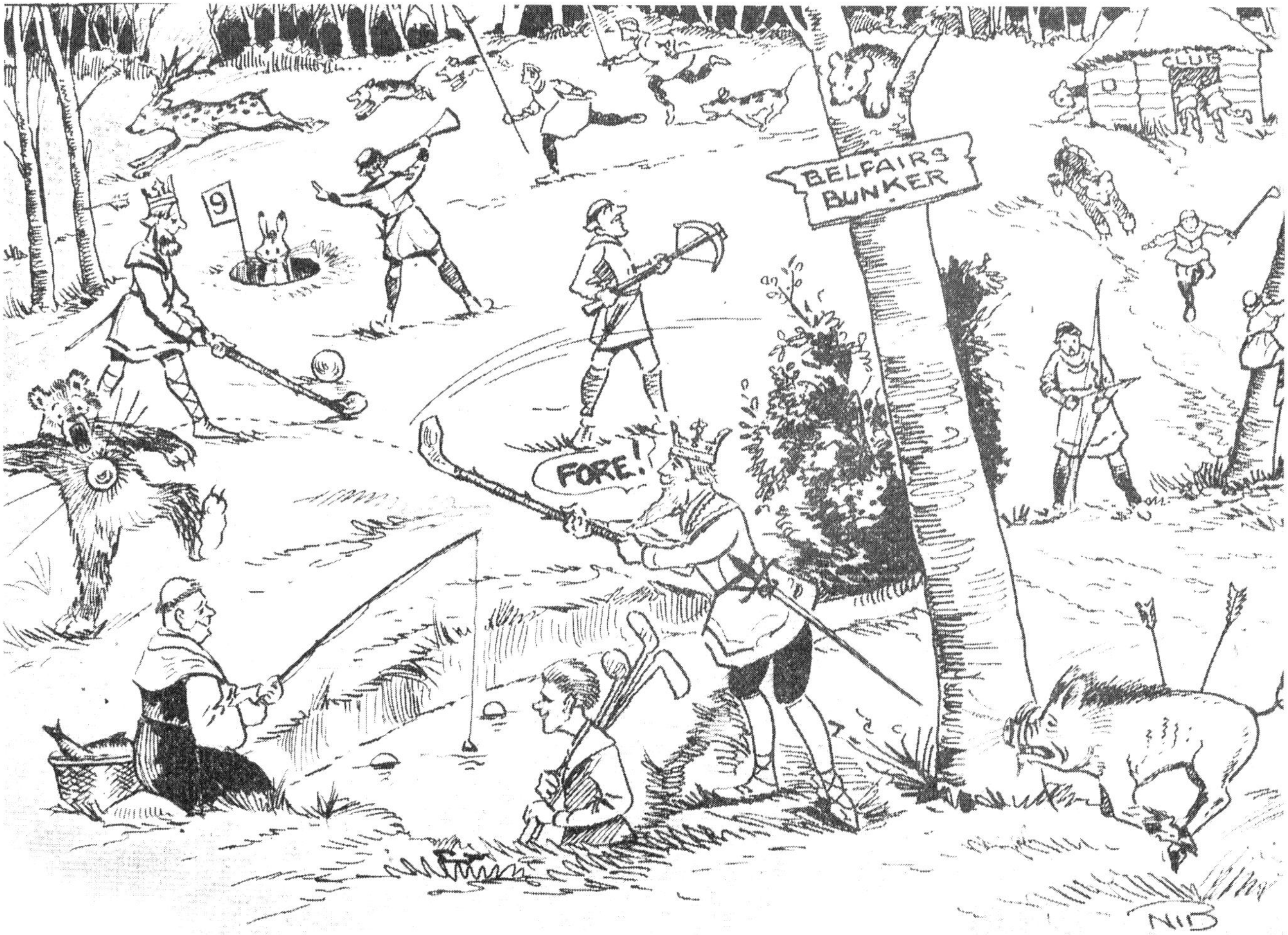
CLUB
BELFAIRS BUNKER
9
FORE!
NID

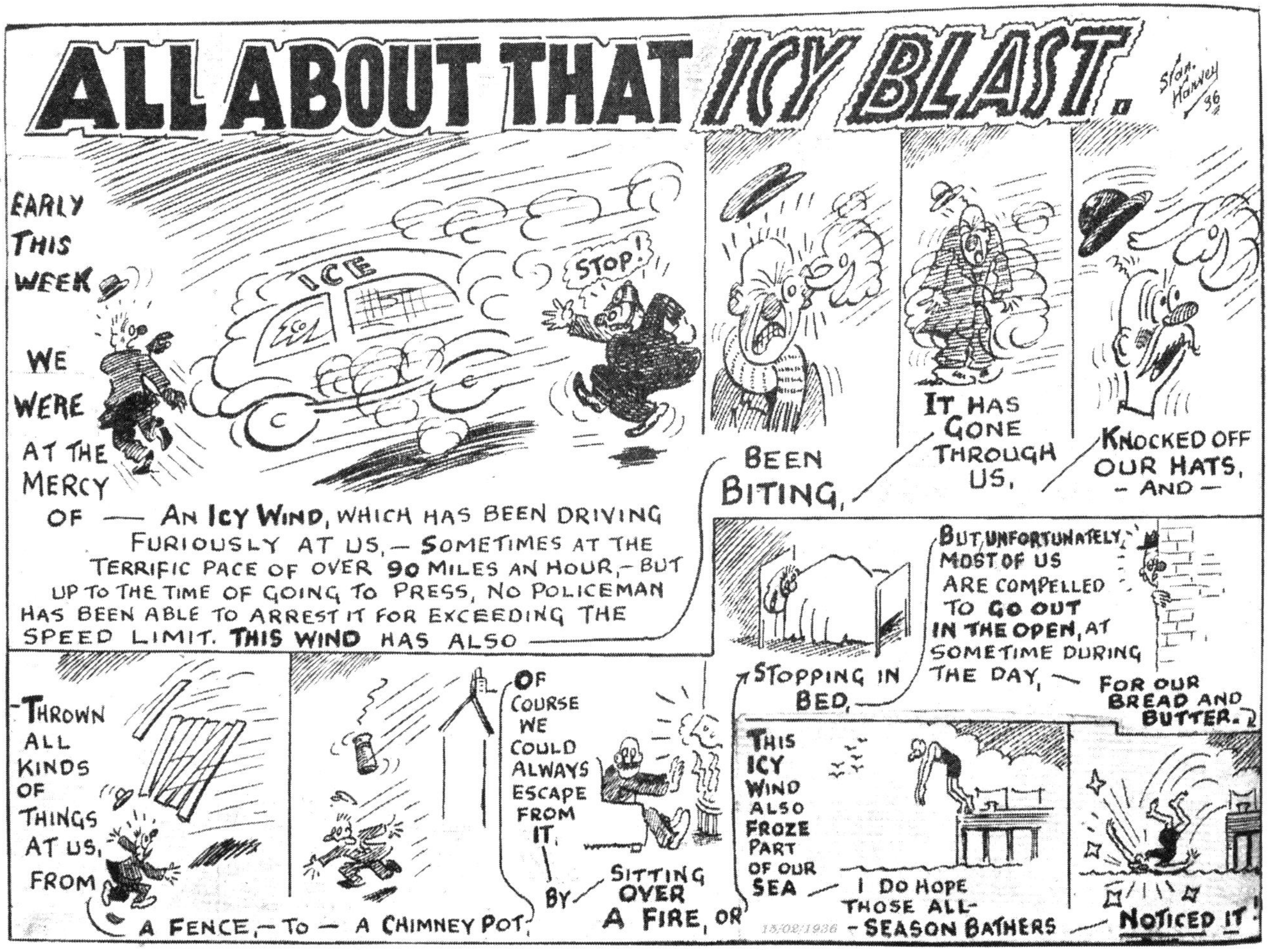
ALL ABOUT THAT ICY BLAST.
Stan. Harvey '36
EARLY THIS WEEK
WE WERE AT THE MERCY OF — AN ICY WIND, WHICH HAS BEEN DRIVING FURIOUSLY AT US, — SOMETIMES AT THE TERRIFIC PACE OF OVER 90 MILES AN HOUR, — BUT UP TO THE TIME OF GOING TO PRESS, NO POLICEMAN HAS BEEN ABLE TO ARREST IT FOR EXCEEDING THE SPEED LIMIT. THIS WIND HAS ALSO
ICE
STOP!
BEEN BITING,
IT HAS GONE THROUGH US,
KNOCKED OFF OUR HATS, — AND —
-THROWN ALL KINDS OF THINGS AT US, FROM
A FENCE, — TO — A CHIMNEY POT,
OF COURSE WE COULD ALWAYS ESCAPE FROM IT,
BY SITTING OVER A FIRE, OR
STOPPING IN BED,
BUT, UNFORTUNATELY, MOST OF US ARE COMPELLED TO GO OUT IN THE OPEN, AT SOMETIME DURING THE DAY, — FOR OUR BREAD AND BUTTER.
THIS ICY WIND ALSO FROZE PART OF OUR SEA
I DO HOPE THOSE ALL-SEASON BATHERS
NOTICED IT!
13/02/1936

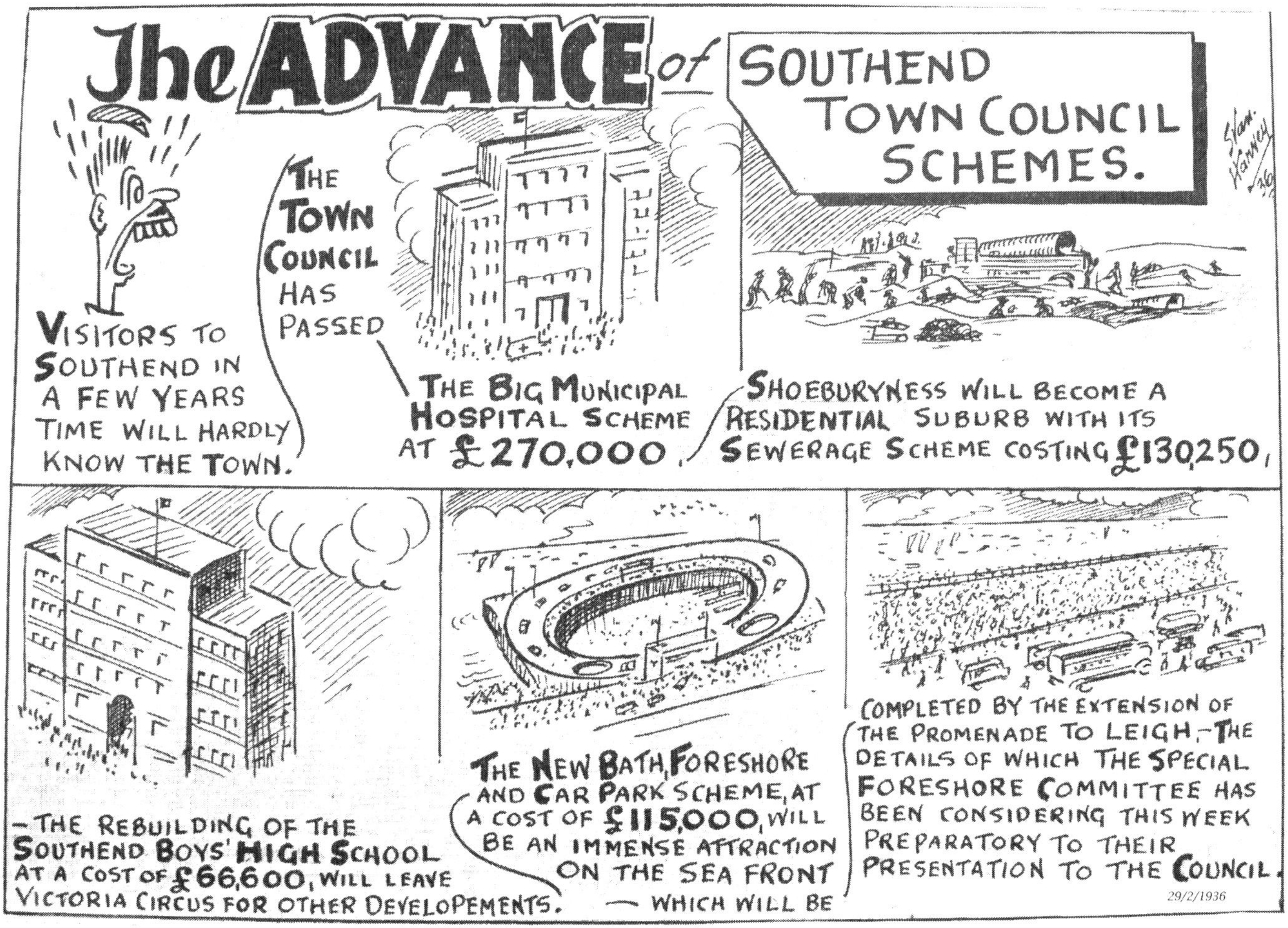
The ADVANCE of SOUTHEND TOWN COUNCIL SCHEMES.
Stan Hanney '36
VISITORS TO SOUTHEND IN A FEW YEARS TIME WILL HARDLY KNOW THE TOWN.
THE TOWN COUNCIL HAS PASSED
THE BIG MUNICIPAL HOSPITAL SCHEME AT £270,000,
SHOEBURYNESS WILL BECOME A RESIDENTIAL SUBURB WITH ITS SEWERAGE SCHEME COSTING £130,250,
– THE REBUILDING OF THE SOUTHEND BOYS' HIGH SCHOOL AT A COST OF £66,600, WILL LEAVE VICTORIA CIRCUS FOR OTHER DEVELOPEMENTS.
THE NEW BATH, FORESHORE AND CAR PARK SCHEME, AT A COST OF £115,000, WILL BE AN IMMENSE ATTRACTION ON THE SEA FRONT
— WHICH WILL BE
COMPLETED BY THE EXTENSION OF THE PROMENADE TO LEIGH, – THE DETAILS OF WHICH THE SPECIAL FORESHORE COMMITTEE HAS BEEN CONSIDERING THIS WEEK PREPARATORY TO THEIR PRESENTATION TO THE COUNCIL.

29/2/1936

The Dutch are Coming

This cartoon shows a dramatic scene from June 1667 when, during the Anglo-Dutch wars, Admiral De Ruyter, commanding a Dutch fleet, sailed into the River Thames. Sheerness Dockyard was destroyed and shortly afterwards Chatham Dockyard, the base of the English fleet, was attacked and several warships were burnt or captured. The Dutch also landed on Canvey Island. Locals were completely powerless to intervene. They lined the banks of the River Thames and watched with a mixture of horror and awe. The defensive establishments at Hadleigh Castle and Coalhouse and Tilbury Forts were collectively completely useless as a deterrent.

Fred's caption read:-

De Ruyter sailed up the Thames. He burnt Sheerness dockyard and destroyed several warships in the Medway. Landing at Canvey he fired several buildings and stole farm stock. The raid caused great alarm in Leigh.

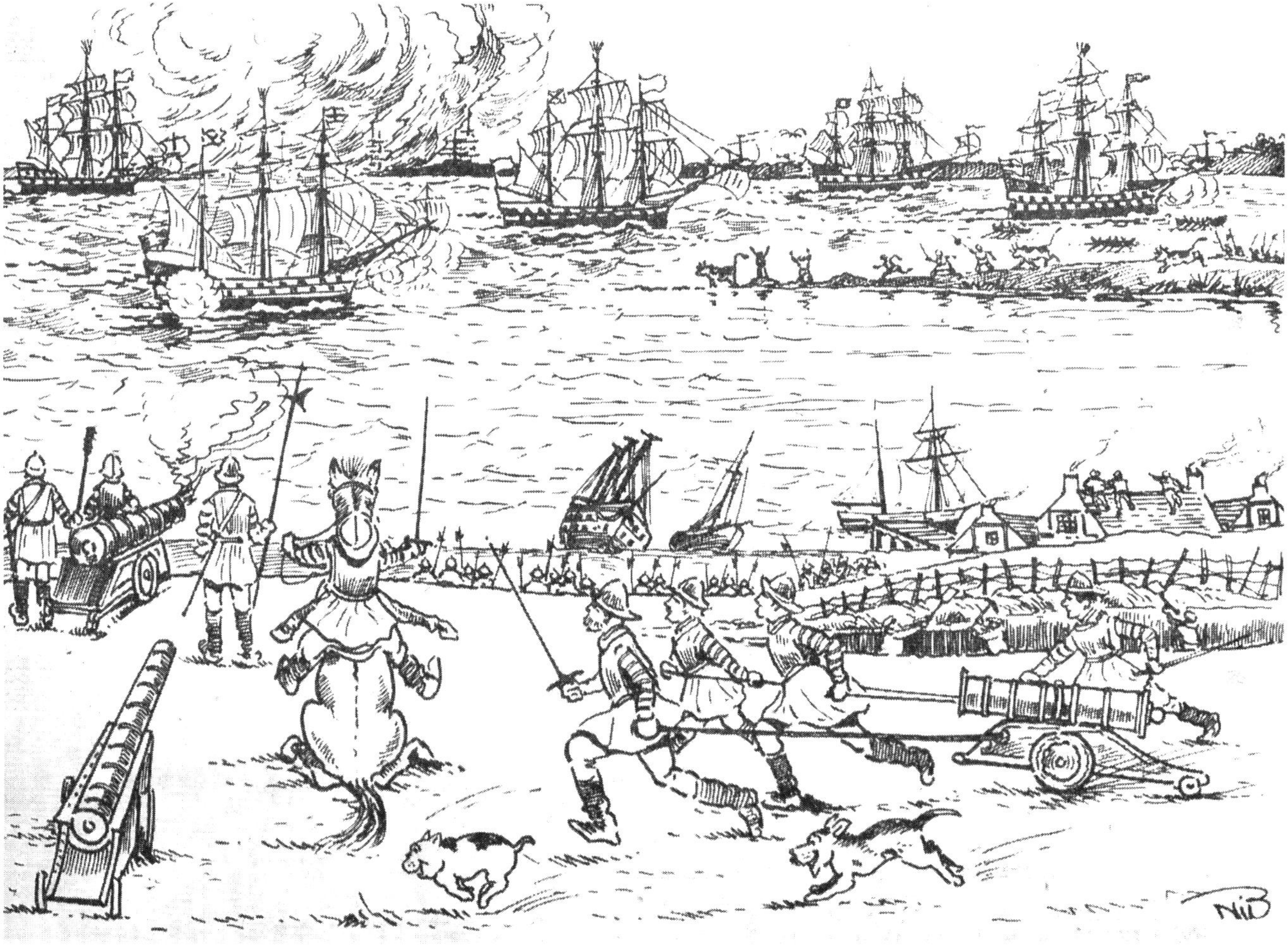

Smugglers

This shows revenue men chasing smugglers in Leigh-on-Sea in the 18th century as imagined by Fred Naughten.

The cartoonist wrote:-

Smuggling was rife throughout the district. Every creek from Benfleet to Battlesbridge offered shelter. Hadleigh castle and church belfries were used to hide liquor and other smuggled goods. At Leigh ten vessels from ten to fifteen tons were used in the illicit trade and the collector of customs made seizures every day.

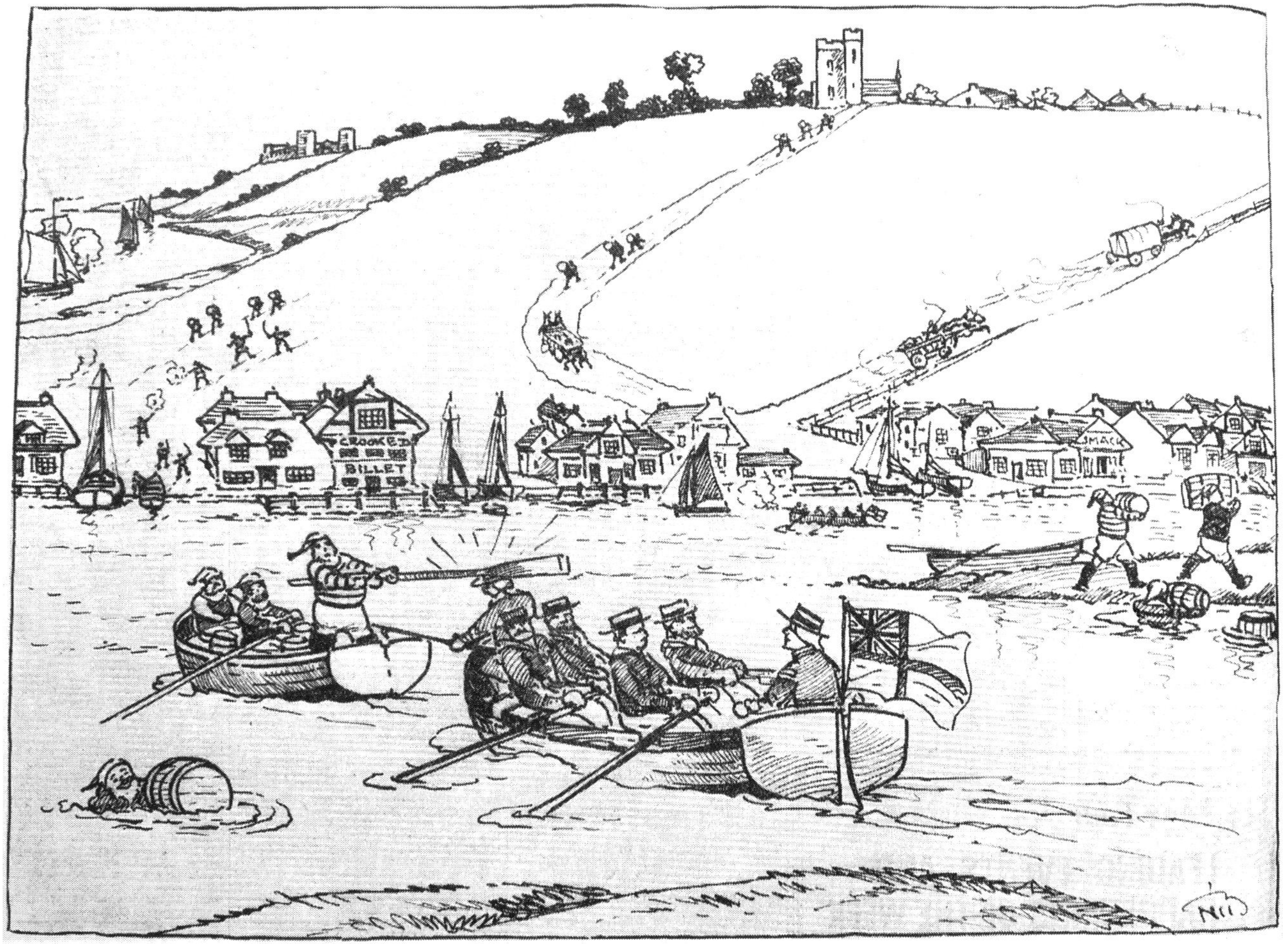
CROOKED
BILLET
SMACK

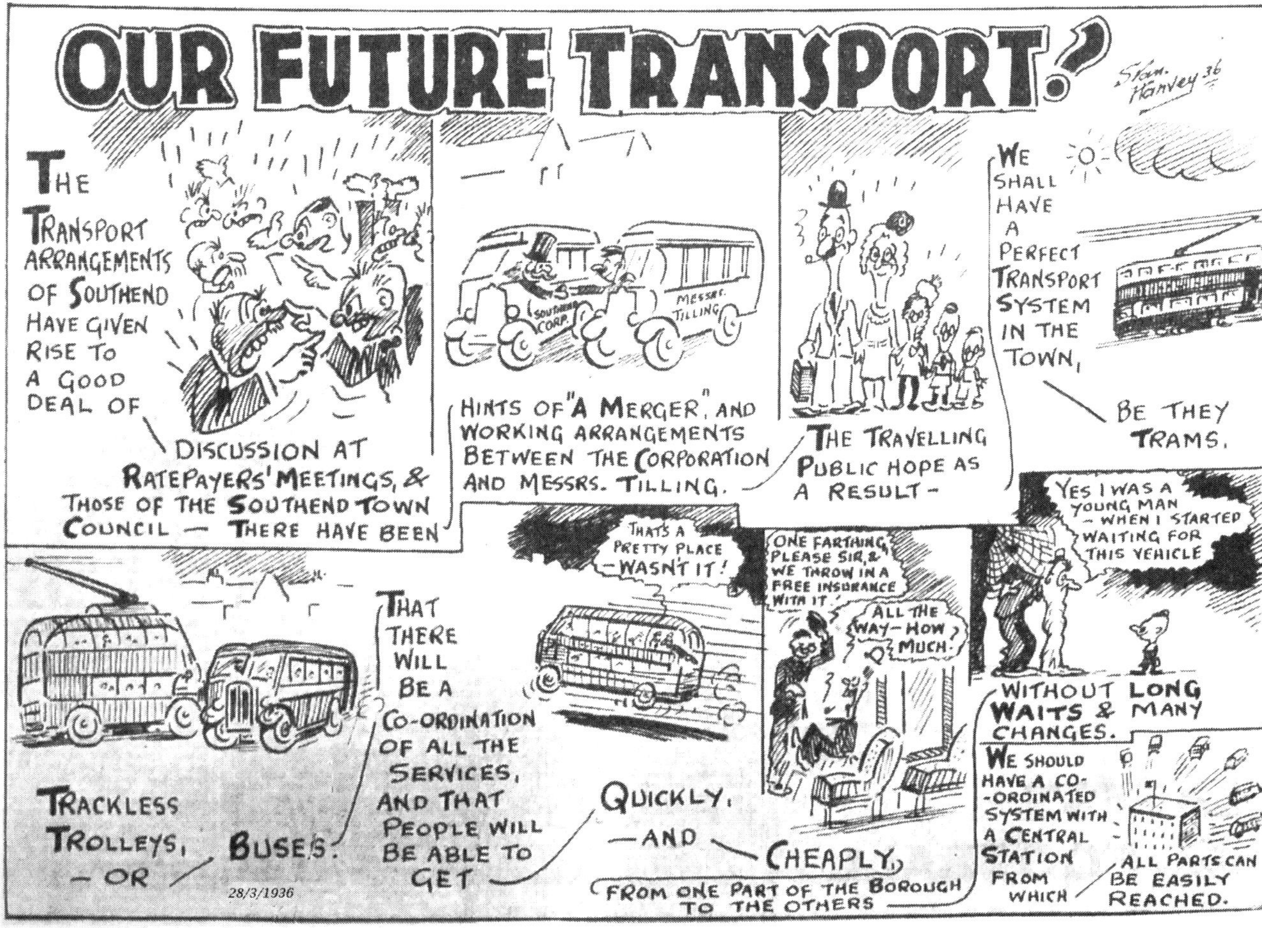

OUR FUTURE TRANSPORT.'
Stan. Harvey 36
THE TRANSPORT ARRANGEMENTS OF SOUTHEND HAVE GIVEN RISE TO A GOOD DEAL OF
DISCUSSION AT RATEPAYERS' MEETINGS, & THOSE OF THE SOUTHEND TOWN COUNCIL — THERE HAVE BEEN
SOUTHEND CORP.
MESSRS. TILLING
HINTS OF "A MERGER", AND WORKING ARRANGEMENTS BETWEEN THE CORPORATION AND MESSRS. TILLING.
THE TRAVELLING PUBLIC HOPE AS A RESULT -
WE SHALL HAVE A PERFECT TRANSPORT SYSTEM IN THE TOWN,
BE THEY TRAMS.
TRACKLESS TROLLEYS,
— OR
BUSES.
THAT THERE WILL BE A CO-ORDINATION OF ALL THE SERVICES, AND THAT PEOPLE WILL BE ABLE TO GET
THAT'S A PRETTY PLACE —WASN'T IT!
QUICKLY, —AND CHEAPLY,
FROM ONE PART OF THE BOROUGH TO THE OTHERS
ONE FARTHING, PLEASE SIR, & WE THROW IN A FREE INSURANCE WITH IT.
ALL THE WAY— HOW MUCH?
YES I WAS A YOUNG MAN — WHEN I STARTED WAITING FOR THIS VEHICLE
WITHOUT LONG WAITS & MANY CHANGES.
WE SHOULD HAVE A CO-ORDINATED SYSTEM WITH A CENTRAL STATION FROM WHICH
ALL PARTS CAN BE EASILY REACHED.

28/3/1936

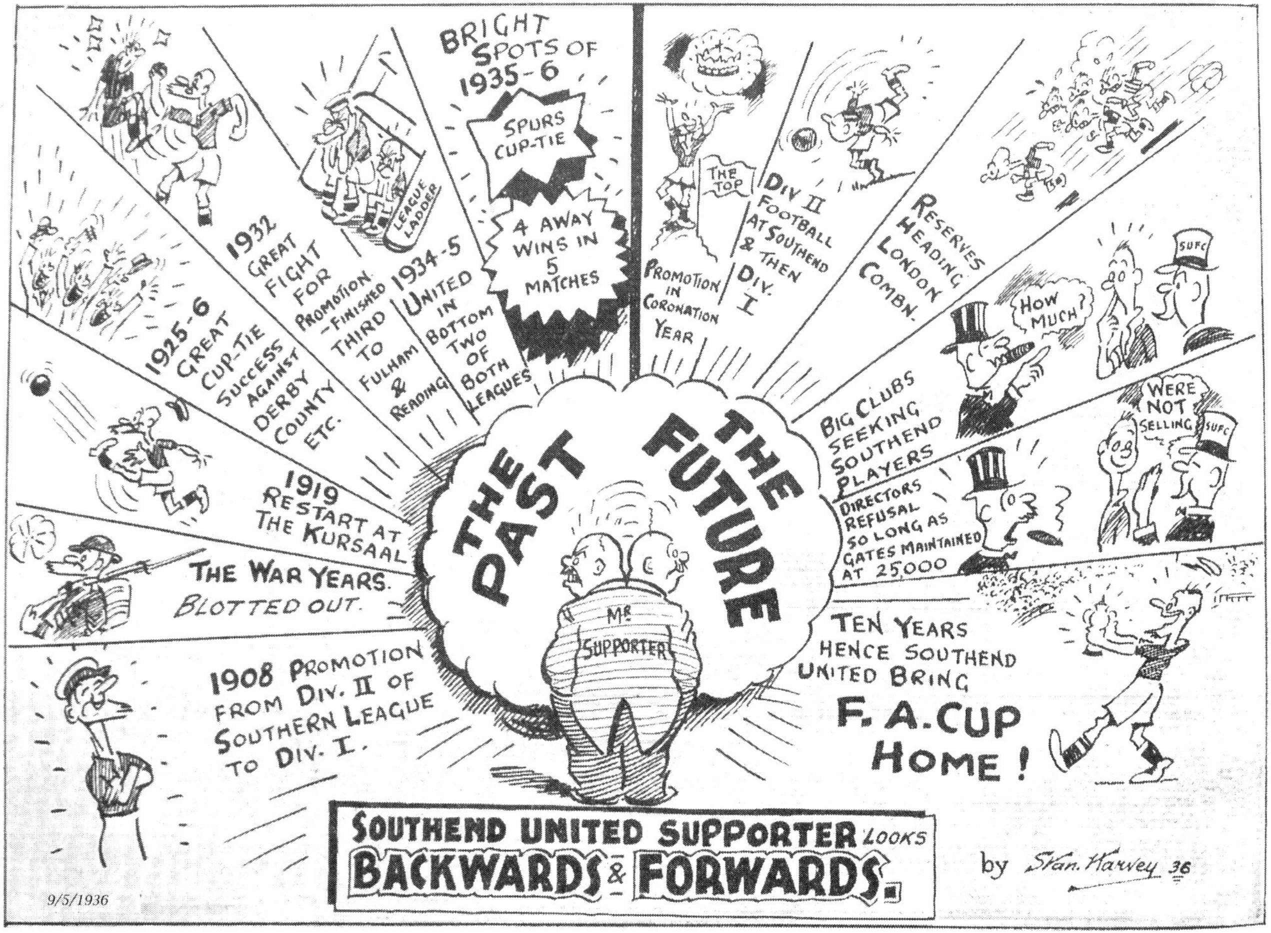

BRIGHT SPOTS OF 1935-6
SPURS CUP-TIE
4 AWAY WINS IN 5 MATCHES
THE TOP
PROMOTION IN CORONATION YEAR
DIV II FOOTBALL AT SOUTHEND & THEN DIV. I
RESERVES HEADING LONDON COMBN.
LEAGUE LADDER
1932 GREAT FIGHT FOR PROMOTION - FINISHED THIRD TO FULHAM & READING
1934-5 UNITED IN BOTTOM TWO OF BOTH LEAGUES
1925-6 GREAT CUP-TIE SUCCESS AGAINST DERBY COUNTY ETC.
1919 RESTART AT THE KURSAAL
THE WAR YEARS. BLOTTED OUT.
1908 PROMOTION FROM DIV. II OF SOUTHERN LEAGUE TO DIV. I.
THE PAST
THE FUTURE
MR SUPPORTER
SUFC
HOW MUCH?
BIG CLUBS SEEKING SOUTHEND PLAYERS
WE'RE NOT SELLING
DIRECTORS REFUSAL SO LONG AS GATES MAINTAINED AT 25,000
TEN YEARS HENCE SOUTHEND UNITED BRING F. A. CUP HOME!
SOUTHEND UNITED SUPPORTER LOOKS BACKWARDS & FORWARDS.
by Stan. Harvey 36
9/5/1936

A Harbour for Leigh on Sea or Canvey?

Grand plans for harbours and marinas along the Essex coast, from Shoeburyness stretching east, have come and gone over the years. Of course today there are large ports or docks at DP World and Tilbury and then smaller ones all the way up to the pool of London. The once thriving London docks are no more.

In May 1936 Southend Town Council had on its agenda discussion on a proposed local harbour in Leigh-on-Sea. This prompted the cartoon opposite and below was Fred Naughten's added caption:-

In the seventeenth century the Dutch drained 4,000 acres of Canvey Island. Would they have saved posterity much tribulation had they made the 4,000 a harbour instead of an island.

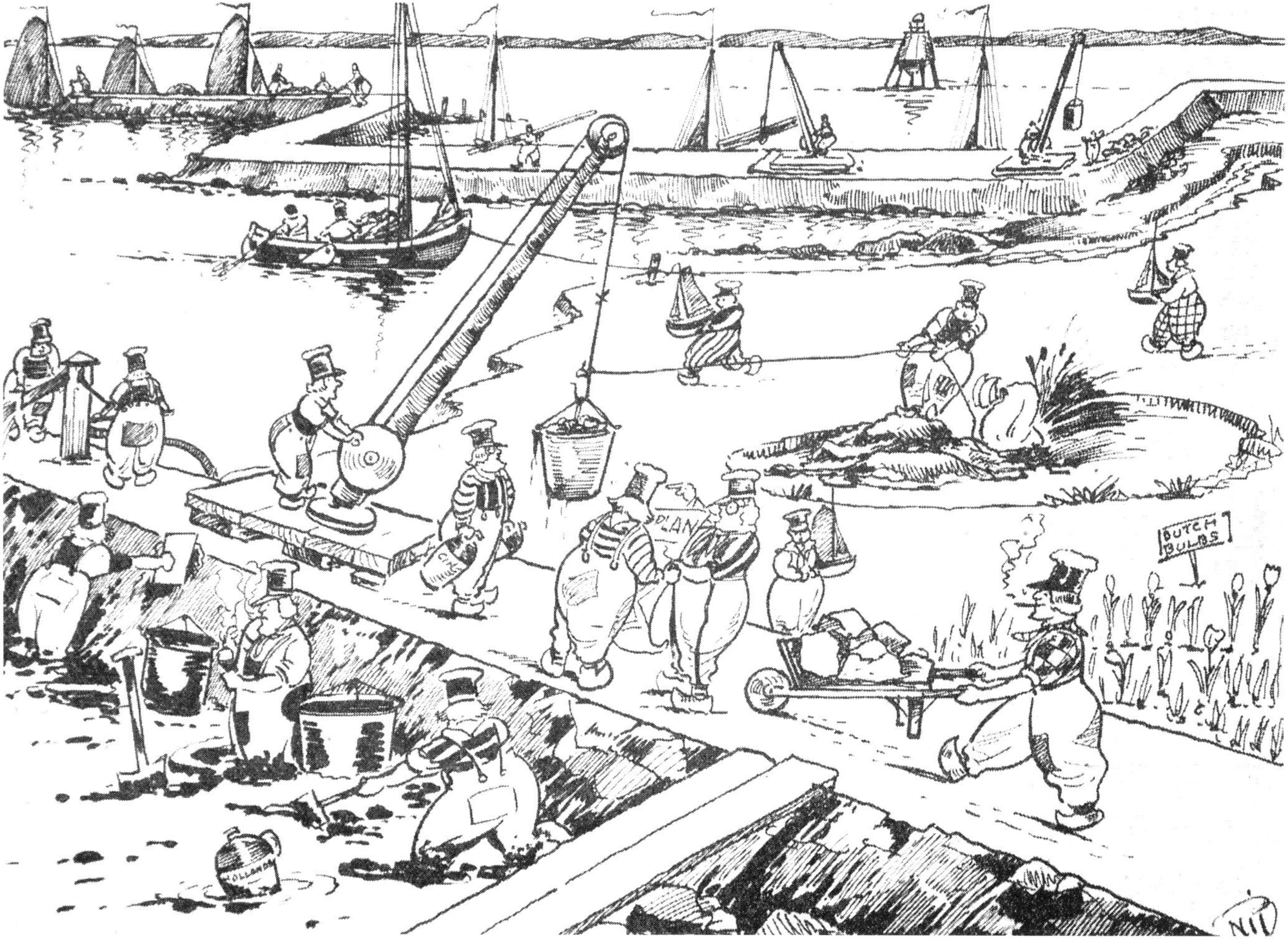
DUTCH BULBS
PLAN

Mutiny

In May Fred delved back into history and examined past events in the Thames estuary. The Nore (where the Thames Estuary meets the North Sea) was the name for the naval command area for eastern England and was much-used by the English fleet in 17th and 18th centuries. It was the scene of serious mutiny in 1797. Today the Nore refers to an anchorage area where ships wait to load or unload further up river.

His caption read:-

In 1797 due to a lack of food, poor pay and conditions aboard, sailors of the home fleet mutinied and seized several ships. The mutineers came ashore and raided farm houses in both Essex and Kent to get supplies. Richard Parker a former master's mate was elected as 'President of this floating republic'. He then presented a series of demands to Admiral Charles Buckner on behalf of the mutineers. The Navy rejected these and the mutiny was put down. Parker was convicted of treason and piracy and hanged from the yardarm of the ship he had seized, 'The Sandwich'.

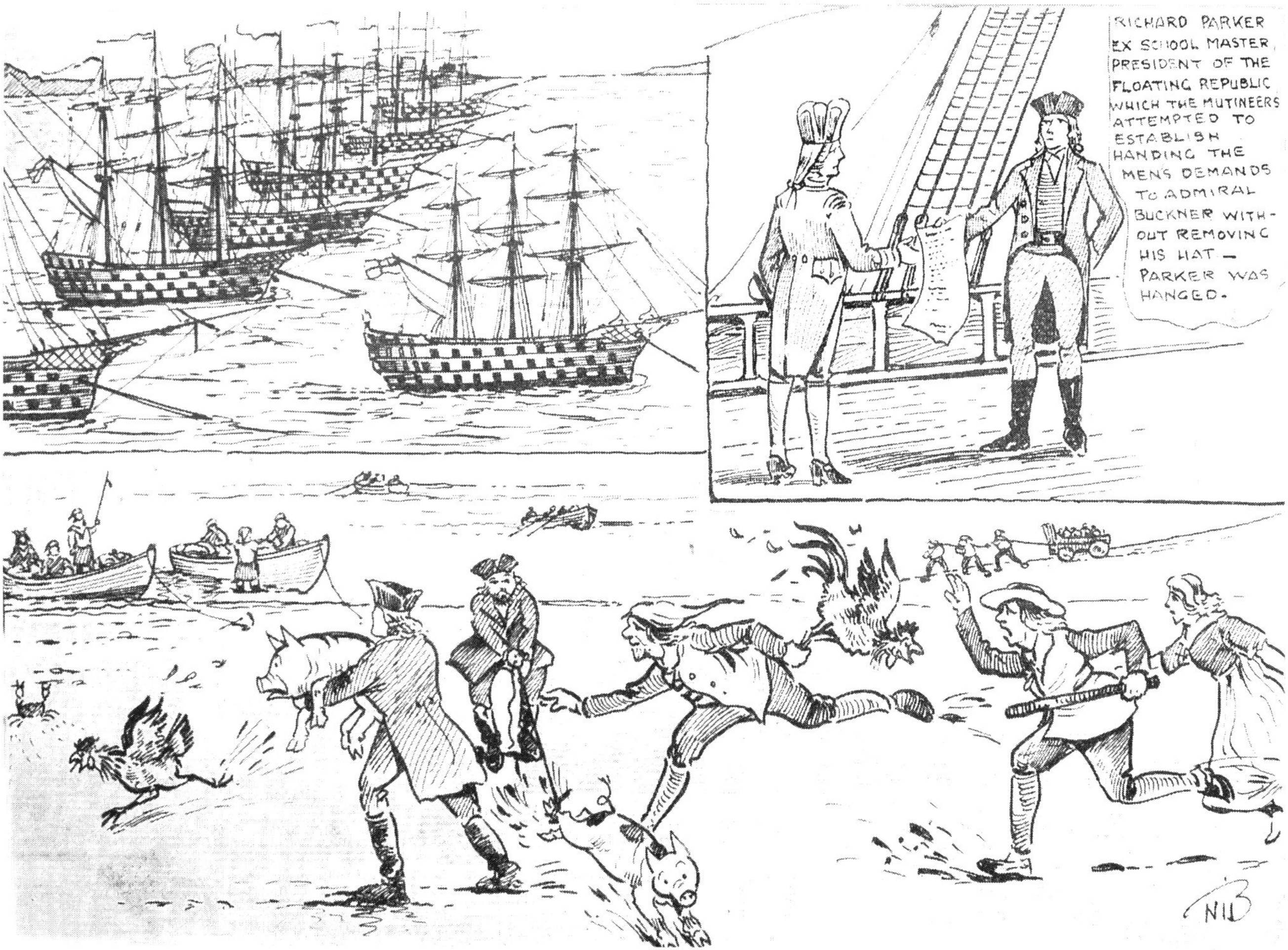
RICHARD PARKER
EX SCHOOL MASTER,
PRESIDENT OF THE
FLOATING REPUBLIC
WHICH THE MUTINEERS
ATTEMPTED TO
ESTABLISH
HANDING THE
MEN'S DEMANDS
TO ADMIRAL
BUCKNER WITH-
OUT REMOVING
HIS HAT —
PARKER WAS
HANGED.

The First Steamship Service

Fred Naughten imagined a scene on the Thames in 1815, the year of the Battle of Waterloo, before the railways came. In 1815 a small steamboat (possibly the *Duke of Argyll*) was used as the first regular passenger service between London and Margate along the River Thames.

Fast forwarding to 1936, when the cartoon opposite was published, passenger ships such as the Royal Eagle were in regular service and they were very popular. They carried thousands of passengers on day or weekend trips from London, Gravesend and Tilbury. After calling at Southend Pier they sailed on around the coast to Clacton and often to France and Belgium.

Back in 1815 Southend Pier had yet to be built, so the *Duke of Argyll* didn't call. However, this didn't stop enterprising locals offering trips out to see the new steamer passing. Fred's caption read:-

Not the Royal Eagle. In 1815 a small steamer ran the first passenger service between London and Margate.

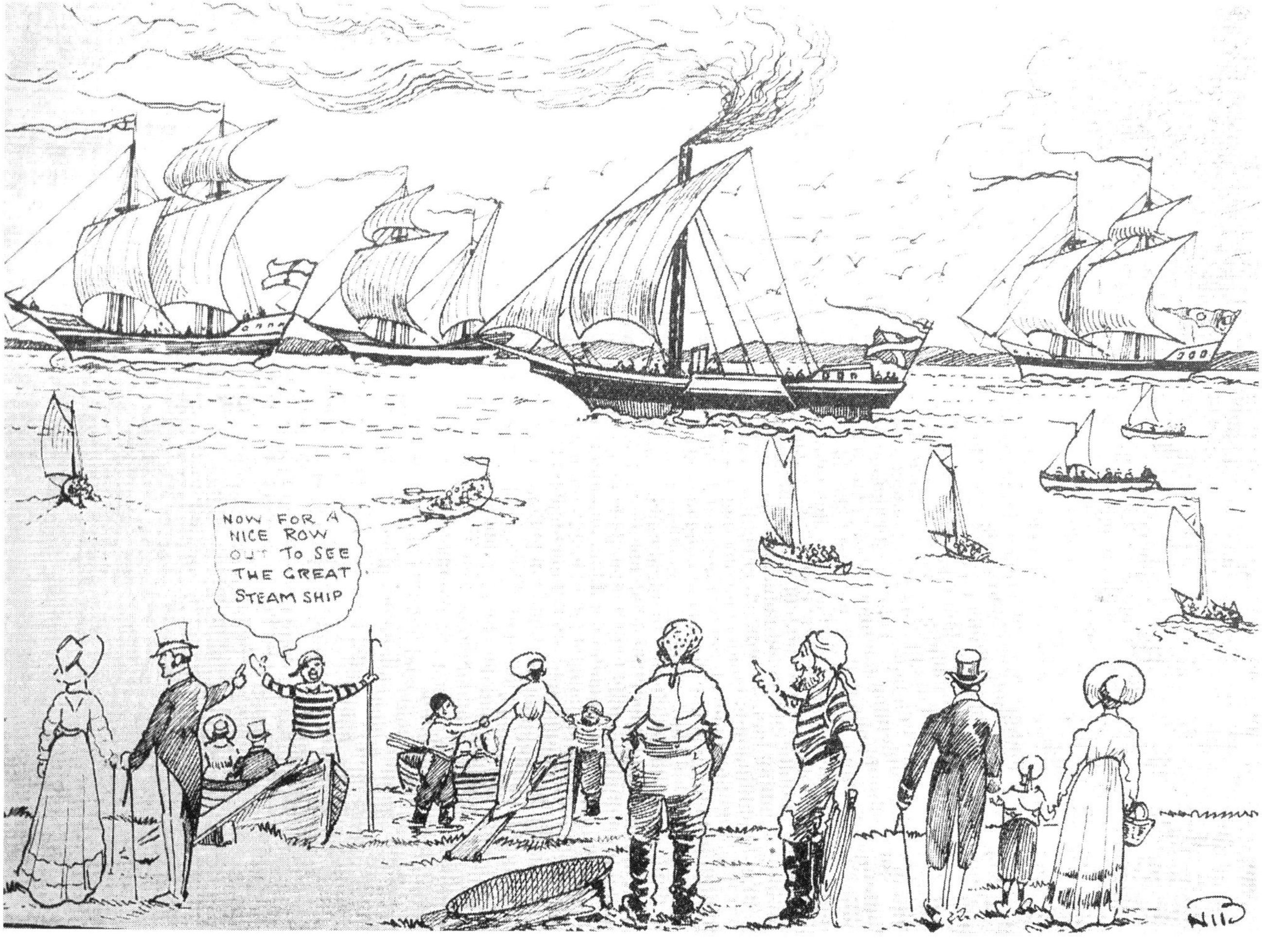
NOW FOR A NICE ROW OUT TO SEE THE GREAT STEAM SHIP

The King Has A Temper

Rochford Hall, which is now occupied by the Rochford Hundred Golf Club, was once home to the Boleyn family. Anne Boleyn was the second wife of Henry VIII. Much married Henry was known to have an eye for the ladies and was famously bad tempered, the more so as he grew older. It is said that Henry courted Anne at Rochford as well as her sister Mary.

Fred used historic licence and produced the cartoon opposite which appeared almost 400 years to the day after the event in the cartoon supposedly took place.

The caption read:-

Henry flew into a rage after losing a game of golf and broke his clubs before the hunt ball in 1536. All around fled in terror, especially the ladies.

Whilst it was known that Henry hunted in the Essex forests, despite all the legends and rumours, there is no documentary evidence of Henry VIII visiting Rochford Hall or even of Ann Boleyn ever having lived there.

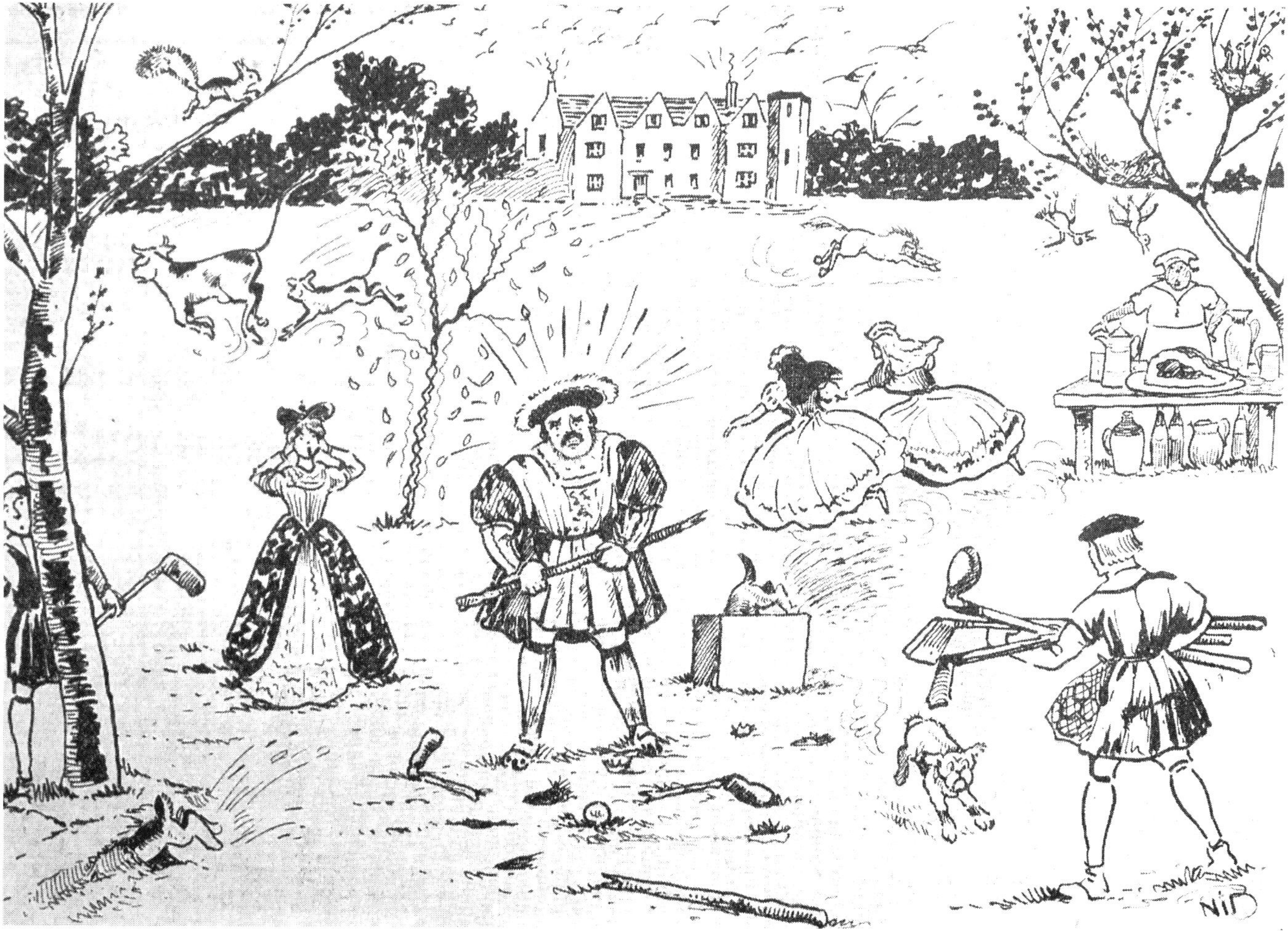

Never, Never Land

Fred Naughten created this cartoon with a simple caption that read:-

The earliest record of illuminations in the Borough.

It showed admission to *Never, Never Land* as being '3 Tiger's teeth'. The *Never, Never Land* on Westcliff Esplanade was originally opened during Fred's time at the *Southend Pictorial Telegraph* in 1935. However its heyday came 20 years later during the mid-1950s. Trippers would queue for hours to visit the park, to see its magical illuminated waterfalls, enchanted castle, models and miniature railway. The park closed at the end of the 1972 season but was refurbished and revived in 1987 with new attractions, although it never attracted the same number of visitors as in the 1950s. Due to falling visitor numbers and increased running costs *Never, Never Land* closed its doors for the final time in January 2001. Originally *Never, Never Land* - an imaginary place where everything happens exactly as you would like it to happen - was where Peter Pan went to avoid growing up. So perhaps in this context today, we should never say never to a return to Southend!

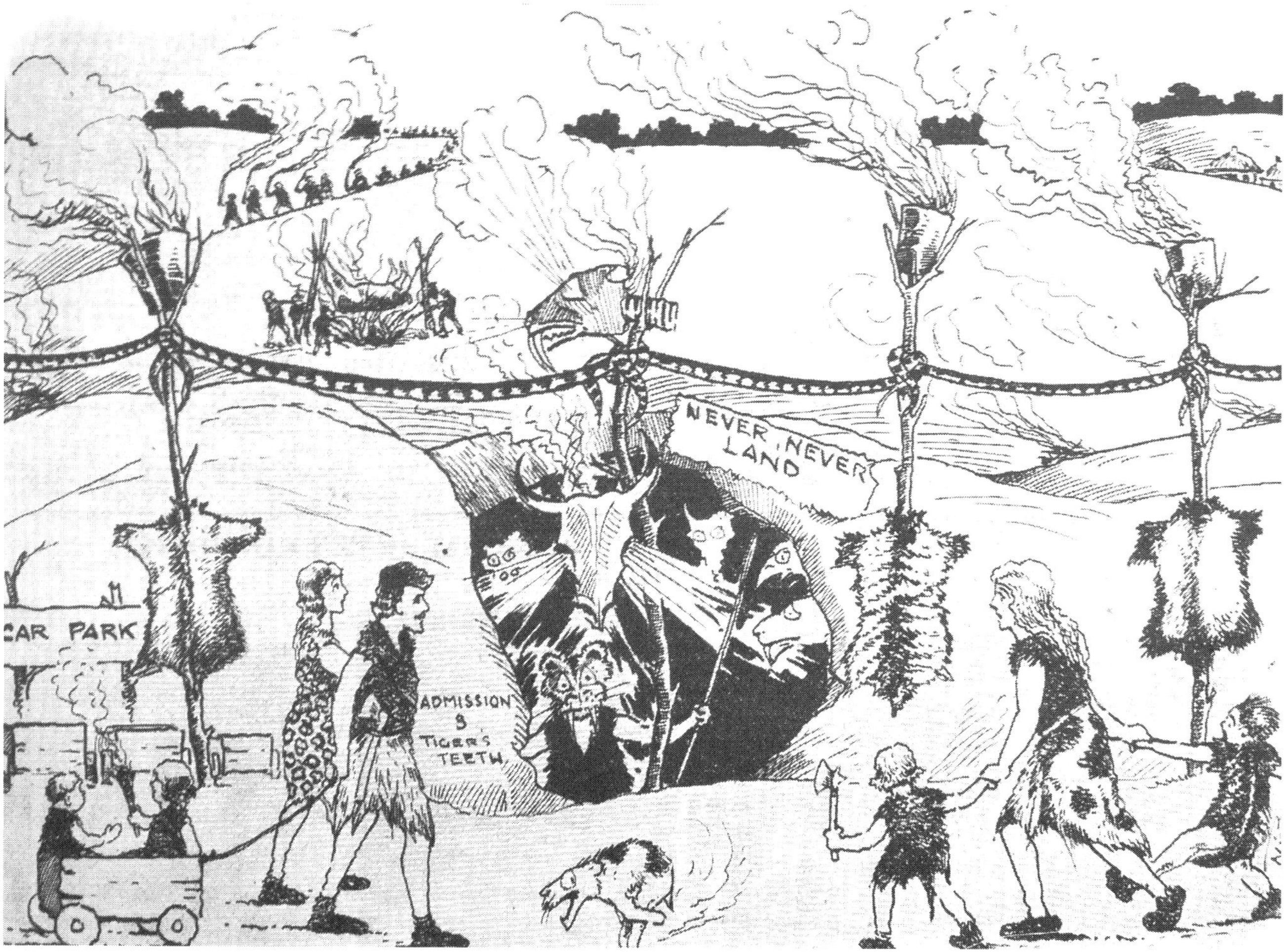
CAR PARK
ADMISSION 3 TIGERS TEETH.
NEVER NEVER LAND

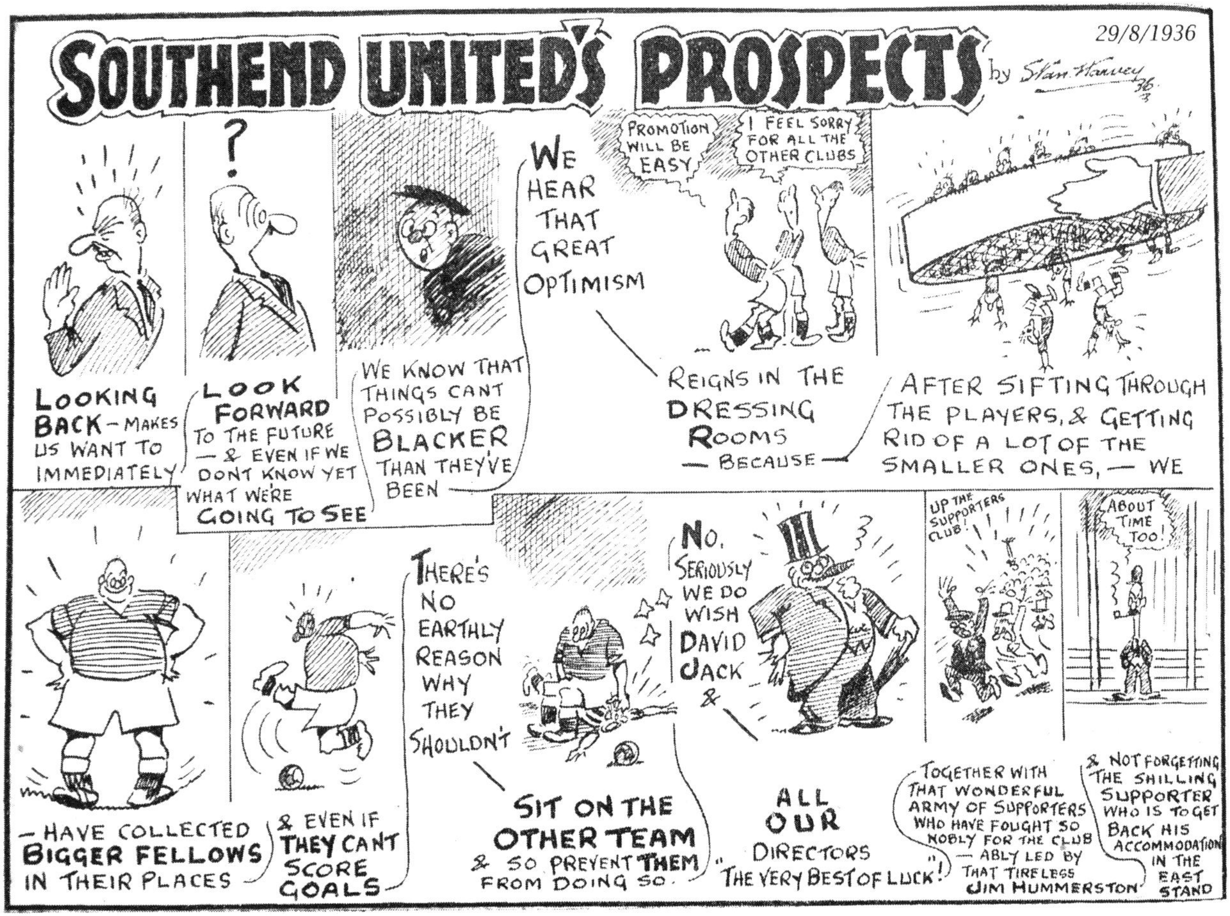
SOUTHEND UNITED'S PROSPECTS
by Stan Harvey 36
29/8/1936
LOOKING BACK — MAKES US WANT TO IMMEDIATELY
LOOK FORWARD TO THE FUTURE — & EVEN IF WE DONT KNOW YET WHAT WE'RE GOING TO SEE
WE KNOW THAT THINGS CANT POSSIBLY BE BLACKER THAN THEY'VE BEEN
WE HEAR THAT GREAT OPTIMISM
PROMOTION WILL BE EASY
I FEEL SORRY FOR ALL THE OTHER CLUBS
REIGNS IN THE DRESSING ROOMS — BECAUSE —
AFTER SIFTING THROUGH THE PLAYERS, & GETTING RID OF A LOT OF THE SMALLER ONES, — WE
— HAVE COLLECTED BIGGER FELLOWS IN THEIR PLACES —
& EVEN IF THEY CANT SCORE GOALS —
THERE'S NO EARTHLY REASON WHY THEY SHOULDN'T
SIT ON THE OTHER TEAM & SO PREVENT THEM FROM DOING SO.
NO, SERIOUSLY WE DO WISH DAVID JACK &
ALL OUR DIRECTORS "THE VERY BEST OF LUCK!"
UP THE SUPPORTERS CLUB!
TOGETHER WITH THAT WONDERFUL ARMY OF SUPPORTERS WHO HAVE FOUGHT SO NOBLY FOR THE CLUB — ABLY LED BY THAT TIRELESS JIM HUMMERSTON
ABOUT TIME TOO!
& NOT FORGETTING THE SHILLING SUPPORTER WHO IS TO GET BACK HIS ACCOMMODATION IN THE EAST STAND

With the opening of the football season Fred showed the game in Roman times

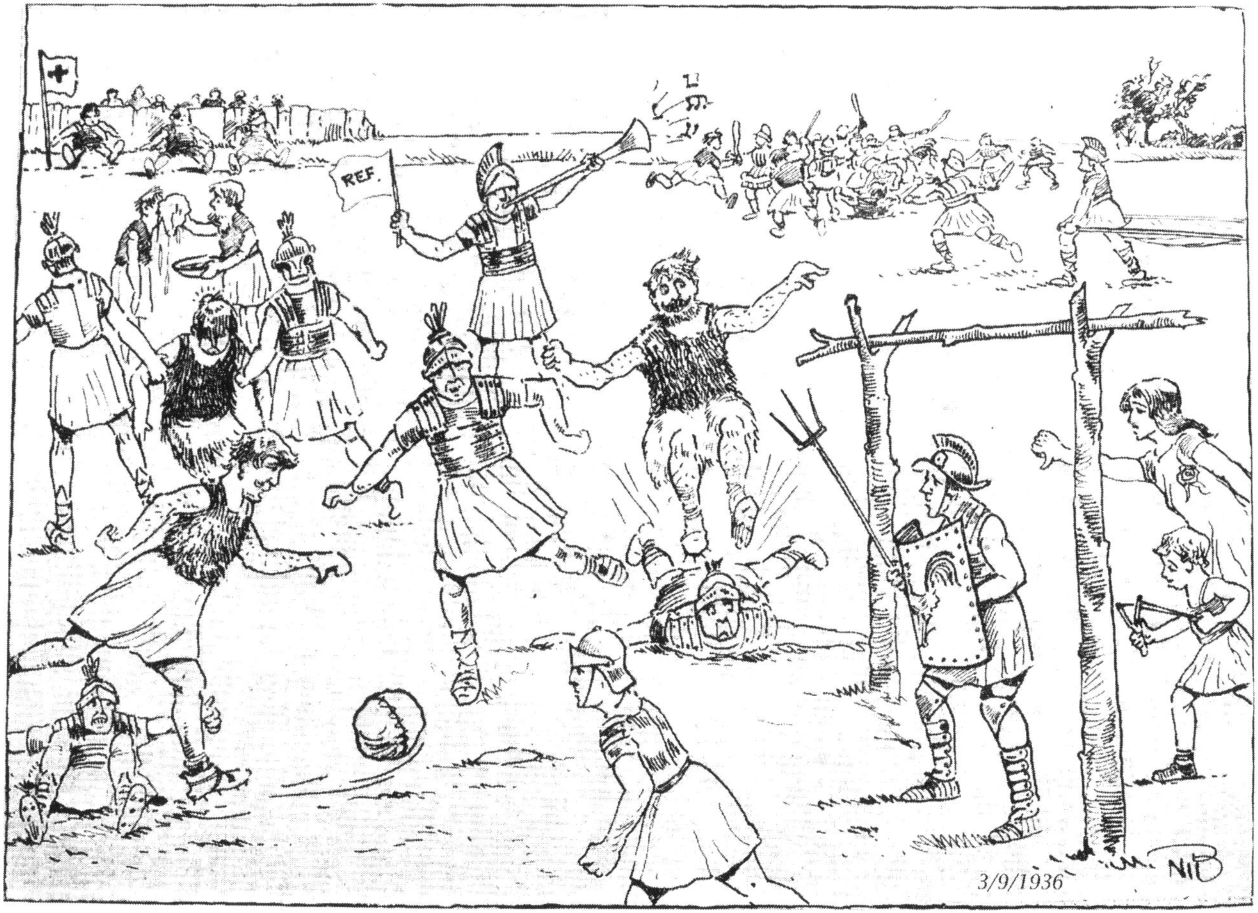
REF.
3/9/1936
NIB

Road Mayhem

With the new motor age gaining pace and the Arterial Road to Southend having been opened for a few years, Fred covered one of his favourite topics in the cartoon opposite, published on October 3rd 1936. The topic was transport between London and Southend-on-Sea and with motor accidents featuring weekly in the newspaper he took up the theme of dangerous roads. Fred looked back and imagined the scene in 1736.

The caption read:-

Dangerous Driving and the Southend Arterial Road, 1736. A hold-up at Gallows Corner.
In the eighteenth century the patrons of Southend mainly belonged to the leisure classes travelling by coach. The roads were unsafe owing to the presence of highwaymen and footpads.

Fred returned to the subject many times over the years.

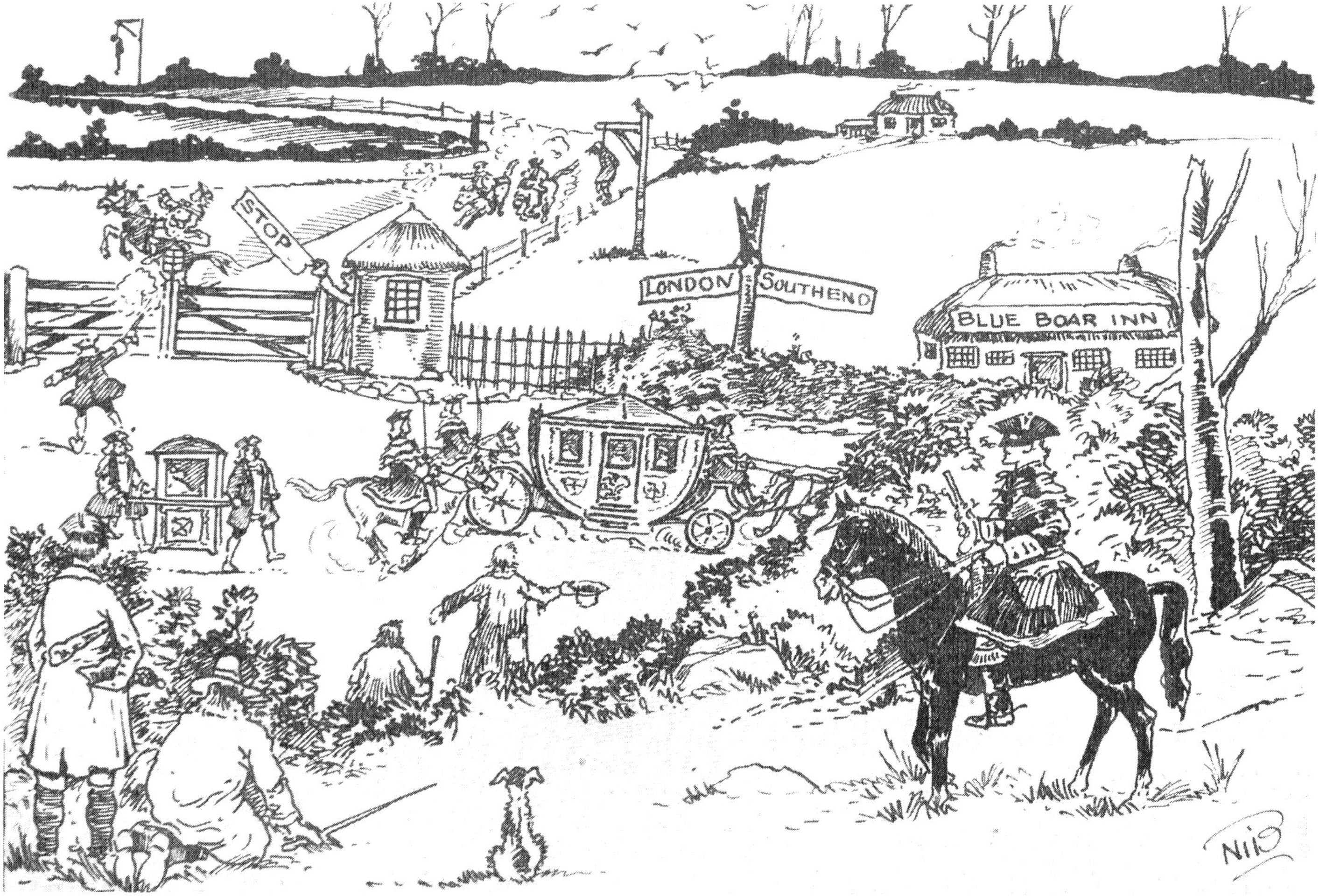
STOP
LONDON
SOUTHEND
BLUE BOAR INN
NIB

Smuggling II

With smuggling the topic again, this time the scene shifted from Leigh-on-Sea to around the Rivers Roach and Crouch.

The caption read:-

In days gone by smuggling was rife in the district. Paglesham was a stronghold of smugglers and a cutter was fitted out with six brass guns to fight the Revenue ships. Apparently in one year no fewer than 13,476 gallons of liquor were landed.

Paglesham later became the last mooring place of Charles Darwin's former ship, *HMS Beagle*. After her round the world voyages, the *Beagle* was refitted, transferred to Customs and Excise and towed to the River Roach. The ship, now a hulk, was renamed *Southend Watch Vessel No 7*. For over 20 years the crew of *Watch Vessel No 7* remained on station at Pagelsham on the lookout for contrabandistas. The last known record of the hulk was in 1870 when it was sold for scrap. Over the years there have been searches in the mud for the remains of the famous ship but to date nothing substantial has been uncovered.

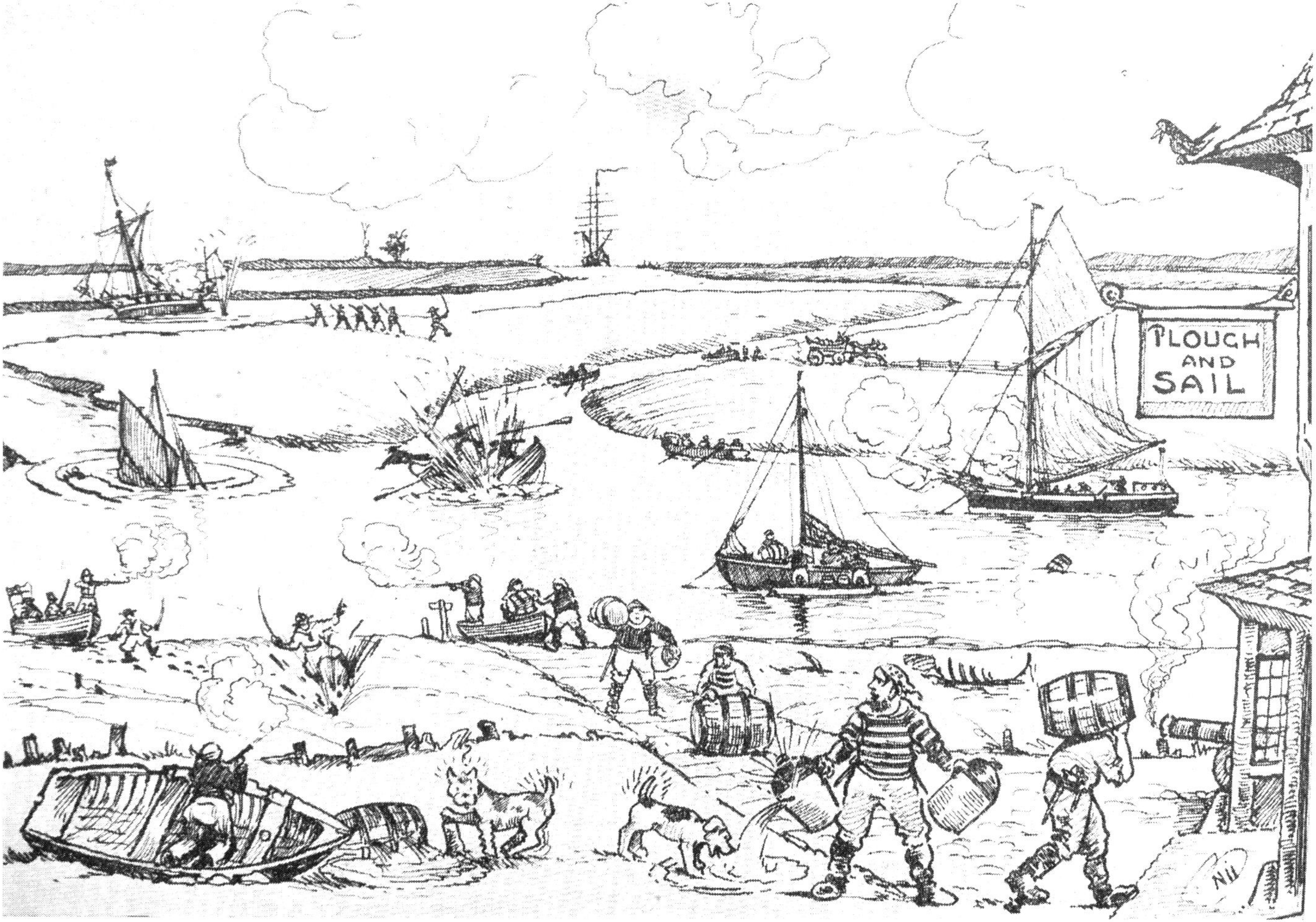
PLOUGH
AND
SAIL

A century ago the electors could not be charged with the same apathy as they are today

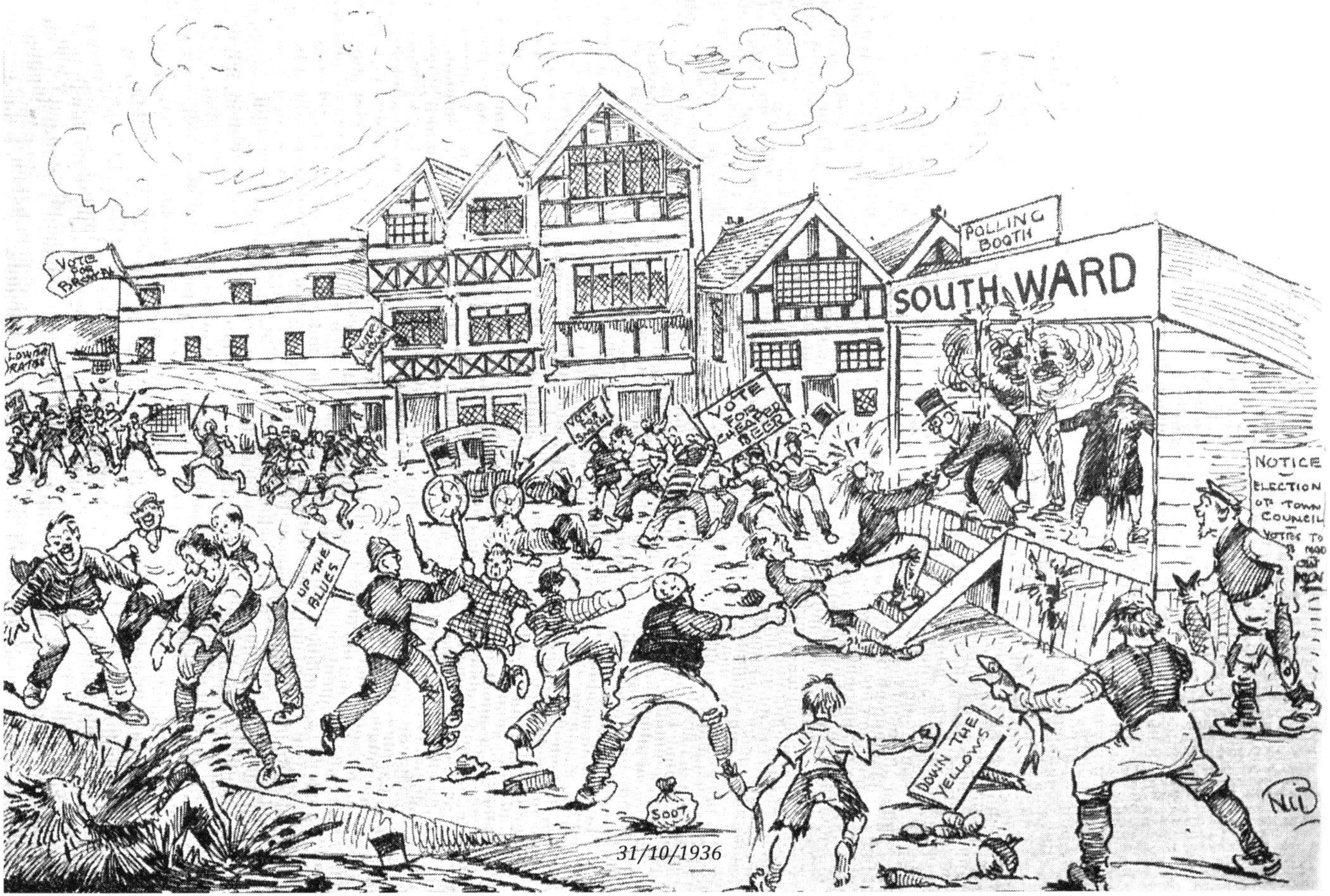
POLLING BOOTH
SOUTH WARD
VOTE FOR CHEAPER BEER
NOTICE
ELECTION
COUNCIL
UP THE BLUES
DOWN THE YELLOWS
SOOT
31/10/1936

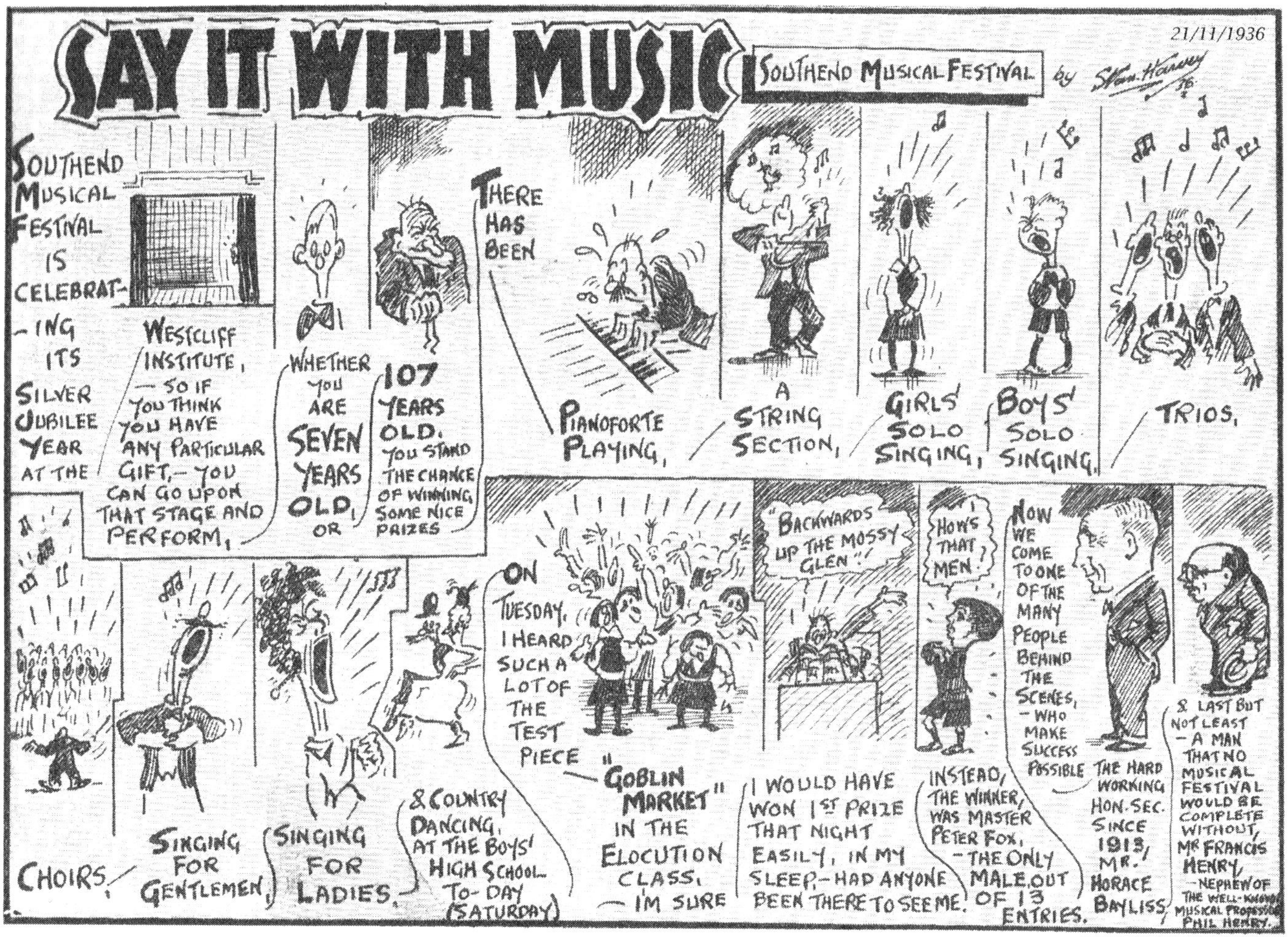
SAY IT WITH MUSIC
21/11/1936
SOUTHEND MUSICAL FESTIVAL
by
SOUTHEND MUSICAL FESTIVAL IS CELEBRAT-ING ITS SILVER JUBILEE YEAR AT THE
WESTCLIFF INSTITUTE, — SO IF YOU THINK YOU HAVE ANY PARTICULAR GIFT, — YOU CAN GO UPON THAT STAGE AND PERFORM,
WHETHER YOU ARE SEVEN YEARS OLD, OR
107 YEARS OLD. YOU STAND THE CHANCE OF WINNING SOME NICE PRIZES
THERE HAS BEEN
PIANOFORTE PLAYING,
A STRING SECTION,
GIRLS' SOLO SINGING,
BOYS' SOLO SINGING,
TRIOS,
CHOIRS,
SINGING FOR GENTLEMEN,
SINGING FOR LADIES,
& COUNTRY DANCING, AT THE BOYS' HIGH SCHOOL TO-DAY (SATURDAY)
ON TUESDAY, I HEARD SUCH A LOT OF THE TEST PIECE "GOBLIN MARKET" IN THE ELOCUTION CLASS, — I'M SURE
"BACKWARDS UP THE MOSSY GLEN"
I WOULD HAVE WON 1ST PRIZE THAT NIGHT EASILY, IN MY SLEEP, — HAD ANYONE BEEN THERE TO SEE ME.
HOW'S THAT MEN?
INSTEAD, THE WINNER, WAS MASTER PETER FOX, — THE ONLY MALE OUT OF 13 ENTRIES.
NOW WE COME TO ONE OF THE MANY PEOPLE BEHIND THE SCENES, — WHO MAKE SUCCESS POSSIBLE
THE HARD WORKING HON. SEC. SINCE 1913, MR. HORACE BAYLISS,
& LAST BUT NOT LEAST — A MAN THAT NO MUSICAL FESTIVAL WOULD BE COMPLETE WITHOUT, MR FRANCIS HENRY, — NEPHEW OF THE WELL-KNOWN MUSICAL PROFESSOR PHIL HENRY.

The Crowstone at Chalkwell

The Crowstone has always sparked much interest.

Fred Naughten wrote in respect of the image opposite:-

The Crowstone at Chalkwell formerly marked the end of the jurisdiction on the Essex side of the City of London and later the Thames Conservancy. The Lord Mayor of London came to Southend once every seven years on a tour of inspection. This was celebrated with much festivity and furthermore, the Lord Mayor's name and his senior officials were engraved on the stone to mark the visit. The earliest date deciphered was 1771 and the last entry was 1858.

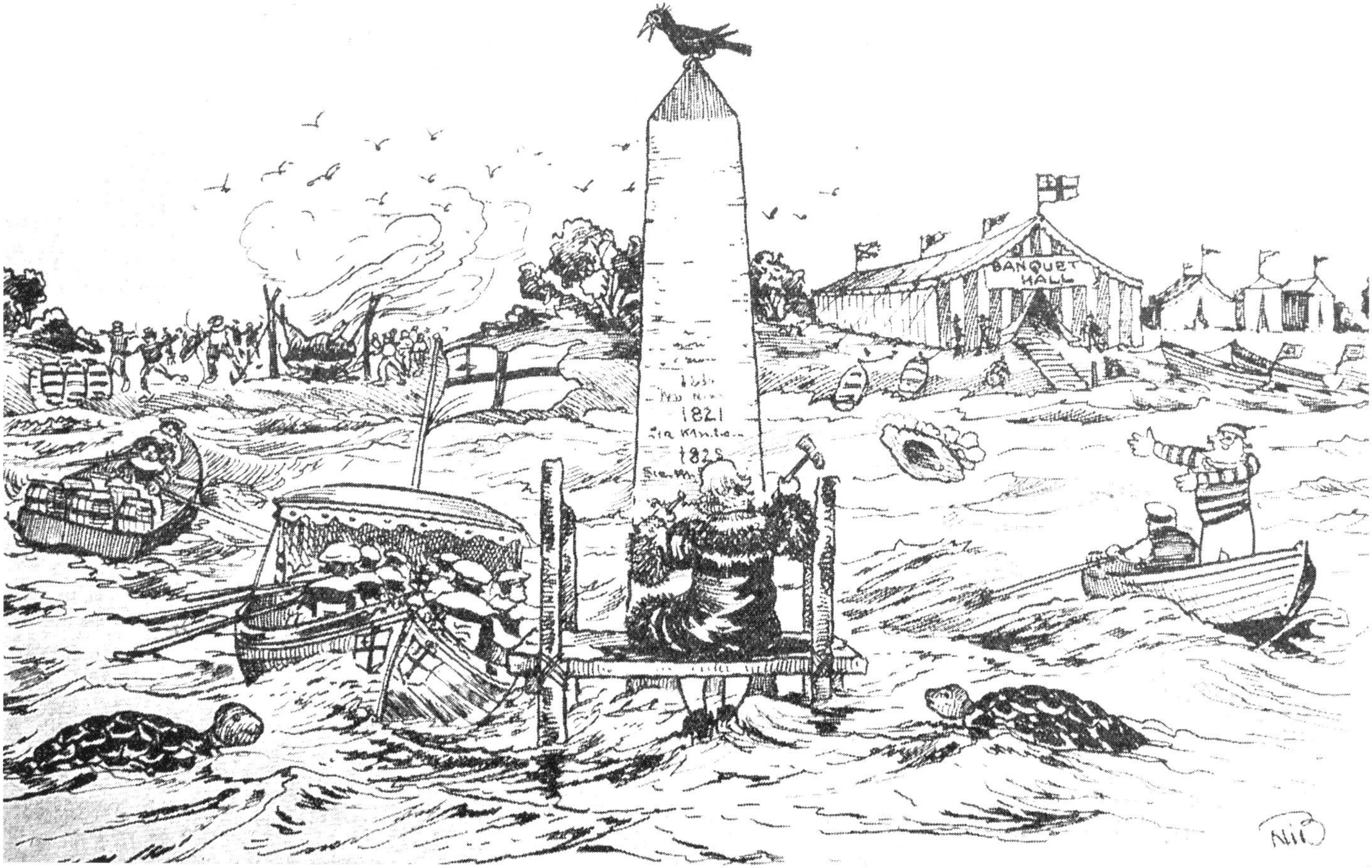
BANQUET HALL
1821
1825

In 1644 the Puritans put a ban on feasts and celebration and Christmas day was made a day of fasting. There was little cheer in Southend that year.

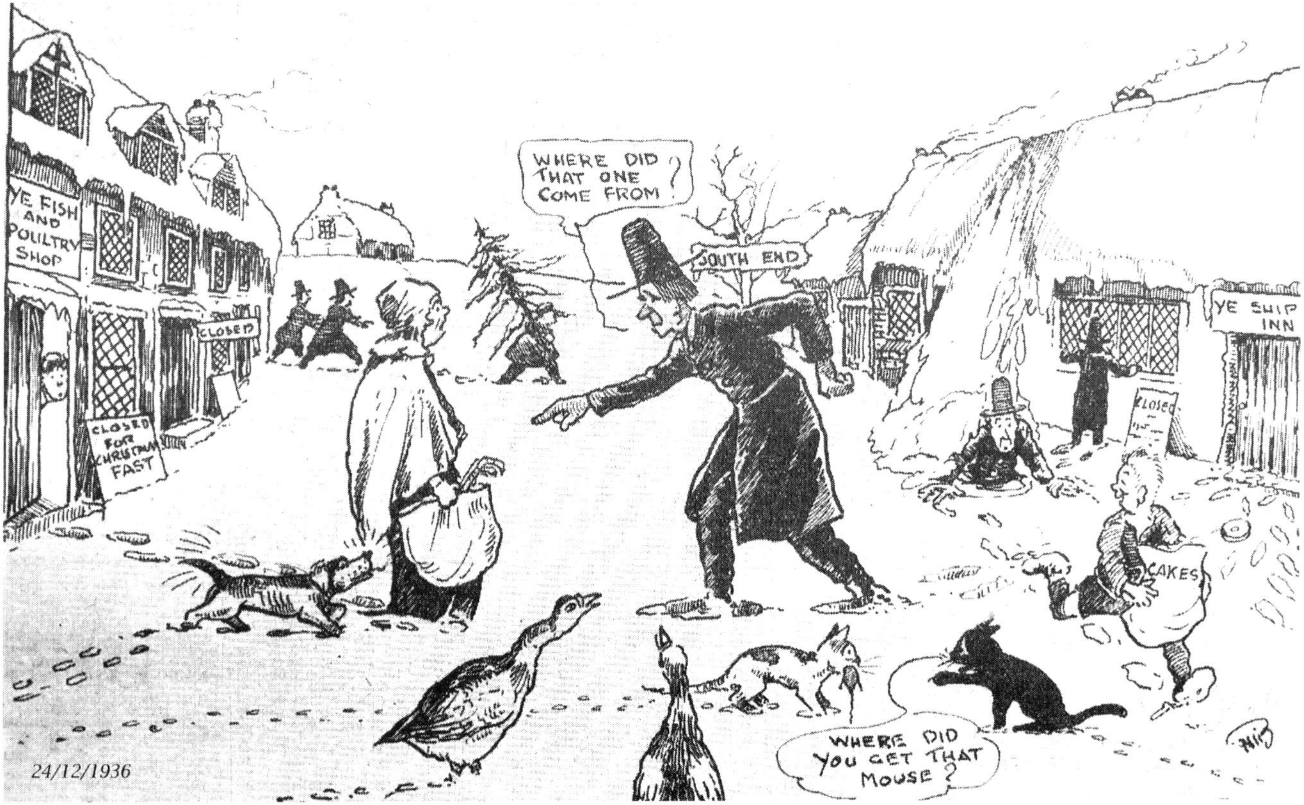
YE FISH AND POULTRY SHOP
CLOSED
CLOSED FOR CHRISTMAS FAST
WHERE DID THAT ONE COME FROM?
SOUTH END
YE SHIP INN
CLOSED
CAKES
WHERE DID YOU GET THAT MOUSE?
24/12/1936

1937

1937

1937 witnessed ominous developments in the heart of Europe with a savage civil war raging in Spain, which resulted in 4,000 child refugees from the Basque country coming to Southampton. On May 6th 1937, the airship *Hindenburg* exploded in flames at Lakehurst, New Jersey, USA, killing 35 of the 97 on board. The disaster effectively ended airships being used as a means of passenger travel. In 1937 there was also an assassination attempt on King George in Belfast and later in the year 43 people died as the result of a typhoid outbreak in Croydon.

Nevertheless, as the year started the country did its best to look on the bright side which was neatly summed up by Stan Harvey's cartoon shown opposite.

The news of the Coronation of George VI at Westminster Abbey was warmly welcomed and on 28th May Britain had a new Prime Minister, Neville Chamberlain, after Stanley Baldwin retired. In Essex, in June, *Warners* Dovercourt Bay Holiday Camp and Lido opened and a month later the 999 emergency telephone number was introduced. Last but not least December 1937 saw the first issue of *The Dandy*, the children's comic featuring the heroic *Desperate Dan*. The comic survived for 75 years only ceasing publication in 2012.

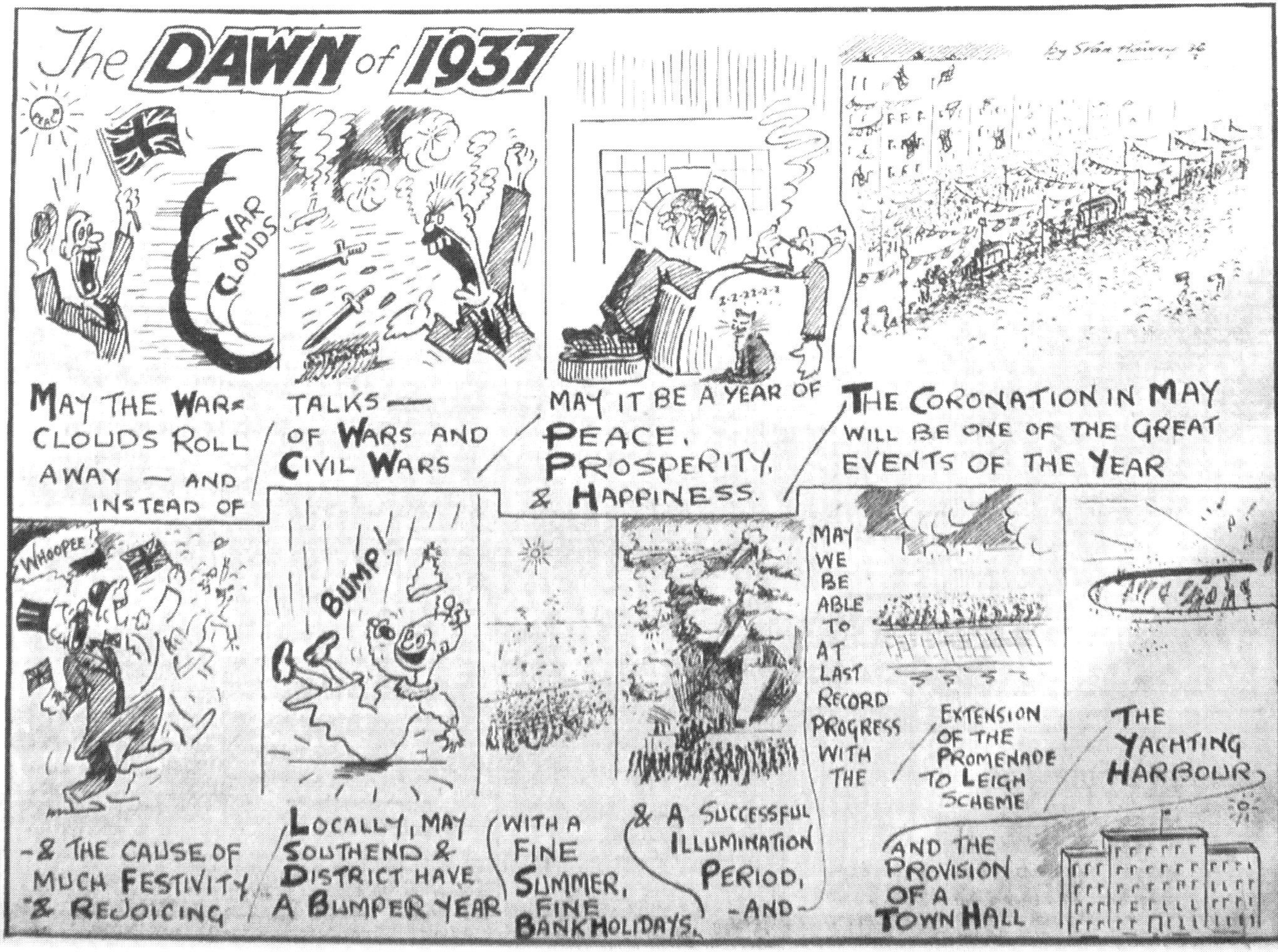
The DAWN of 1937
PEACE
WAR CLOUDS
MAY THE WAR-CLOUDS ROLL AWAY — AND INSTEAD OF
TALKS — OF WARS AND CIVIL WARS
MAY IT BE A YEAR OF PEACE, PROSPERITY, & HAPPINESS.
THE CORONATION IN MAY WILL BE ONE OF THE GREAT EVENTS OF THE YEAR
WHOOPEE!
-& THE CAUSE OF MUCH FESTIVITY & REJOICING
BUMP!
LOCALLY, MAY SOUTHEND & DISTRICT HAVE A BUMPER YEAR
WITH A FINE SUMMER, FINE BANK HOLIDAYS,
& A SUCCESSFUL ILLUMINATION PERIOD, -AND-
MAY WE BE ABLE TO AT LAST RECORD PROGRESS WITH THE
EXTENSION OF THE PROMENADE TO LEIGH SCHEME
THE YACHTING HARBOUR
AND THE PROVISION OF A TOWN HALL

The First Trains

For his first cartoon of the year Fred Naughten turned his attention to the railways. Fred explained that the steaming monsters caused both alarm and celebration. People and goods could now travel back and forth from the capital quickly, in relative comfort, and the railways created a boom in housebuilding and leisure opportunities in Southend.

On the other hand, Thames Barge owners and horse and coach drivers were more apprehensive as this new form of transport would damage their livelihoods. Farmers too feared for their livestock and the deadly consequences of their animals straying onto the railway lines. The caption read:-

Southend's rapid rise to popularity dated back to 1854 when the first train run by the old London, Tilbury and Southend Railway Company arrived and created a sensation in the district.

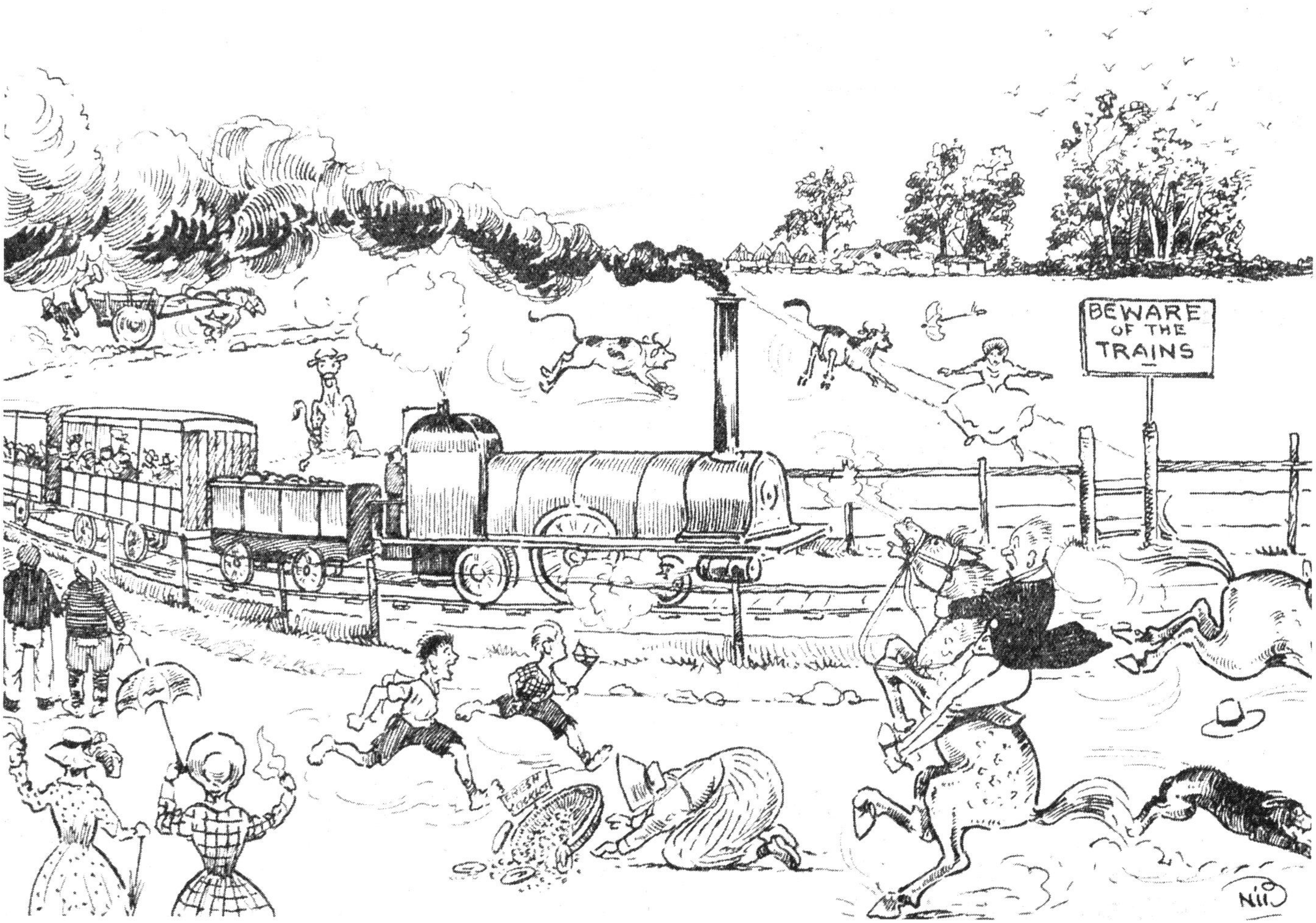
BEWARE
OF THE
TRAINS

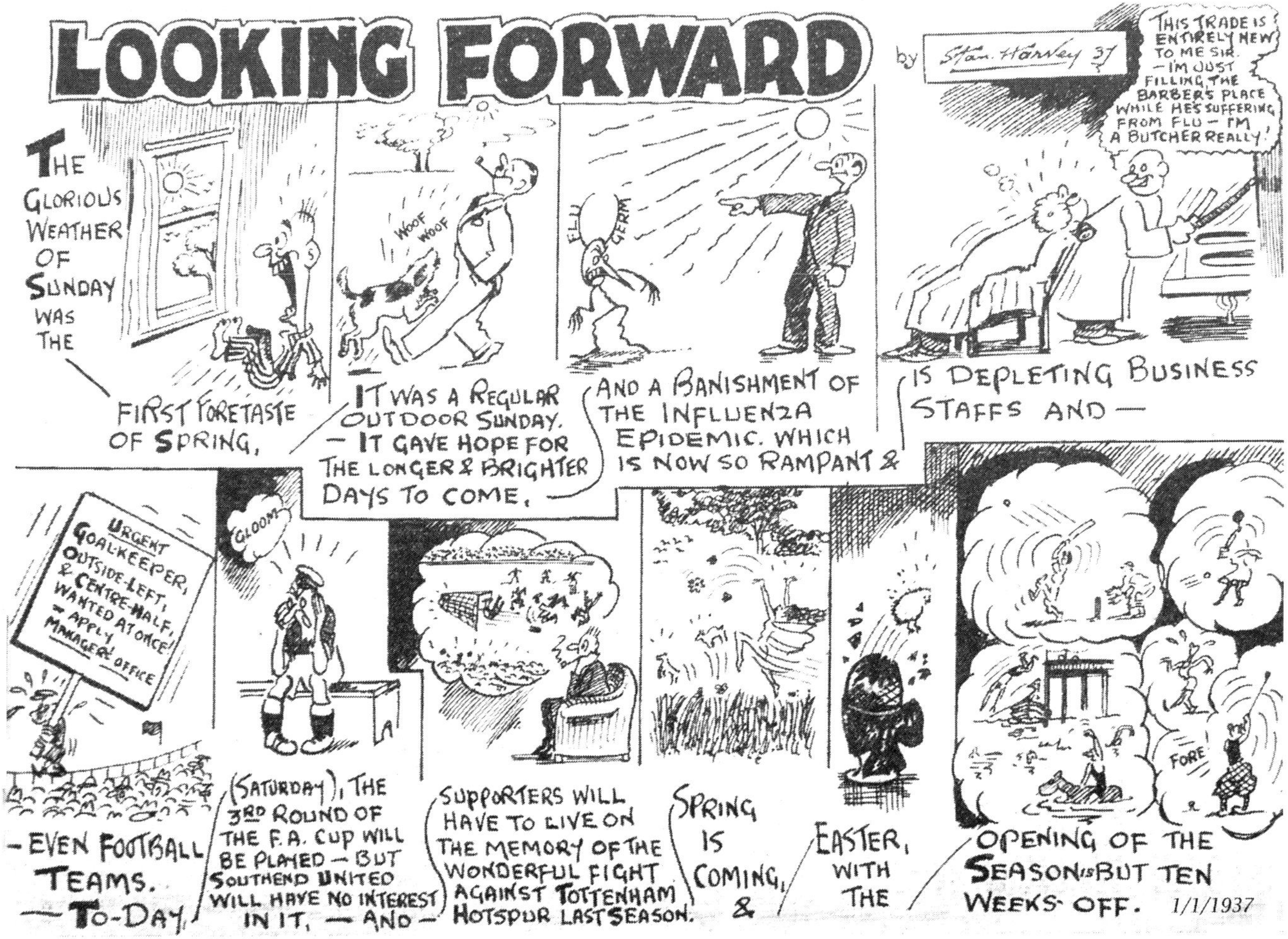
LOOKING FORWARD
by Stan. Harvey 37
THIS TRADE IS ENTIRELY NEW TO ME SIR. — I'M JUST FILLING THE BARBER'S PLACE WHILE HE'S SUFFERING FROM FLU — I'M A BUTCHER REALLY!
THE GLORIOUS WEATHER OF SUNDAY WAS THE
FIRST FORETASTE OF SPRING,
WOOF WOOF
IT WAS A REGULAR OUTDOOR SUNDAY. — IT GAVE HOPE FOR THE LONGER & BRIGHTER DAYS TO COME,
FLU GERM
AND A BANISHMENT OF THE INFLUENZA EPIDEMIC. WHICH IS NOW SO RAMPANT &
IS DEPLETING BUSINESS STAFFS AND —
URGENT GOAL-KEEPER, OUTSIDE-LEFT, & CENTRE-HALF, WANTED AT ONCE! — APPLY MANAGER'S OFFICE
— EVEN FOOTBALL TEAMS. — TO-DAY,
GLOOM
(SATURDAY), THE 3RD ROUND OF THE F.A. CUP WILL BE PLAYED — BUT SOUTHEND UNITED WILL HAVE NO INTEREST IN IT, — AND —
SUPPORTERS WILL HAVE TO LIVE ON THE MEMORY OF THE WONDERFUL FIGHT AGAINST TOTTENHAM HOTSPUR LAST SEASON.
SPRING IS COMING, &
EASTER, WITH THE
FORE
OPENING OF THE SEASON IS BUT TEN WEEKS OFF.
1/1/1937

A busy day in the early 'nineties' (1890s).
Mixed traffic on the London –Southend Road.

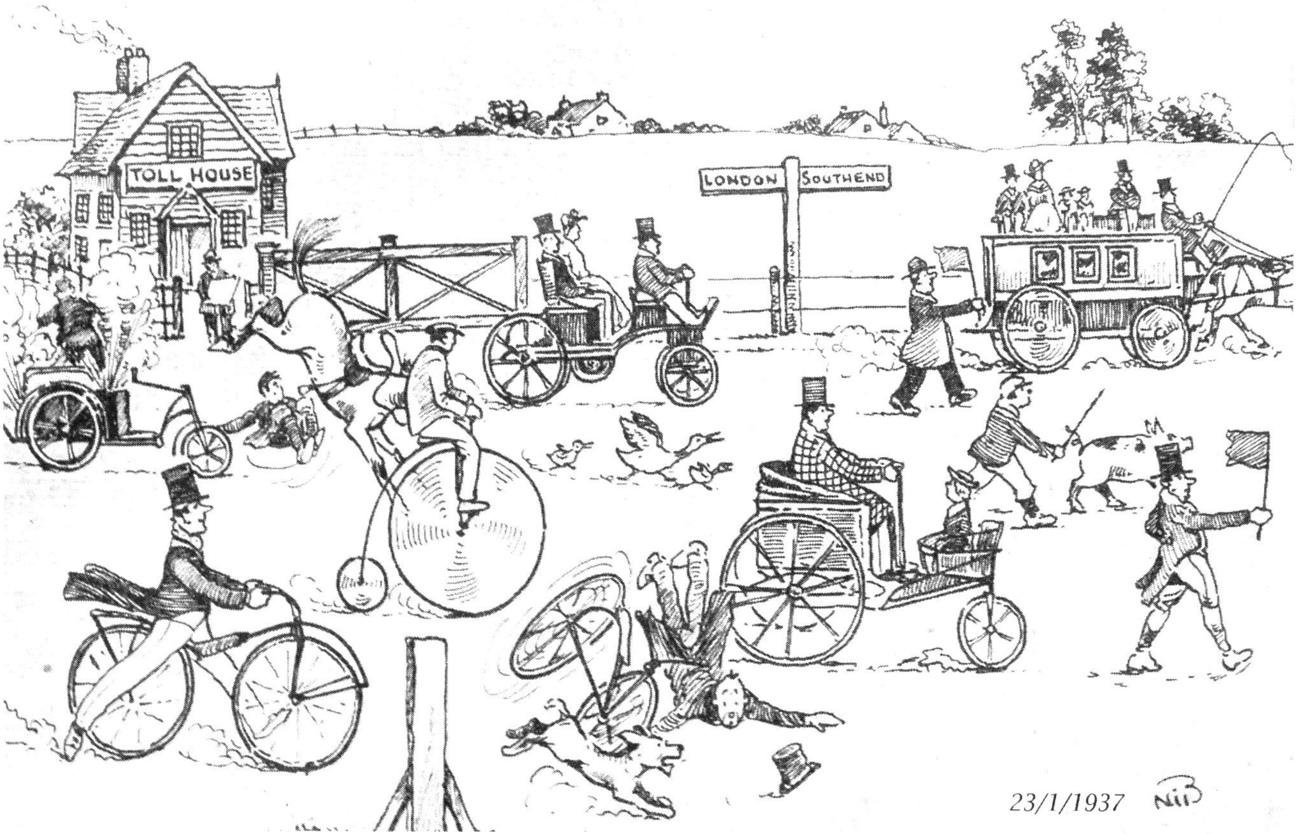
TOLL HOUSE
LONDON
SOUTHEND
23/1/1937

From Ducking Pools to Swimming Pools

Although 'public bathing' has been around since Roman times, one hundred years before this cartoon was published there were no public swimming pools in Southend. By 1937 the picture was completely different. We don't have a record of when the first public pool in Southend was built but in 1915 the Westcliff Pool opened and was for many years the main attraction along the Western Esplanade.

Fred Naughten, referring back to the 1830s, suggested that although there were no public pools, ducking pools were still fashionable and used especially as a means of deciding arguments between husband and wife. Fred Naughten's caption for the cartoon opposite read:-

There was no talk of a swimming bath in Southend a century ago, but when a wife had too much to say she was 'referred back' to the duck pond to stop an argument.

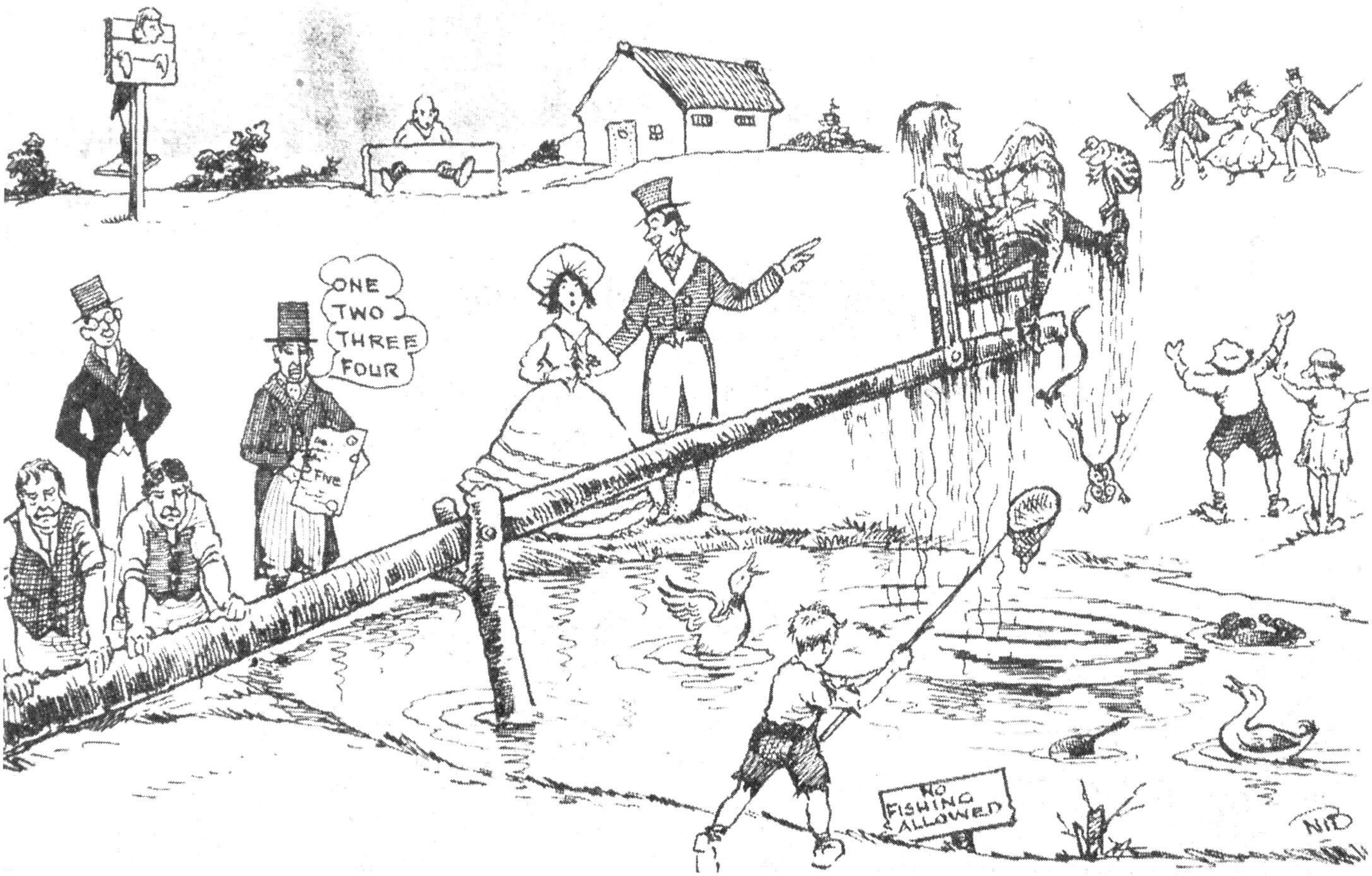
ONE
TWO
THREE
FOUR
FIVE
NO FISHING ALLOWED
NID

Raising Local Taxes

Local council tax rises are never popular. Efforts by Southend Council to raise funds to build a harbour in Leigh-on-Sea, allegedly as part of new sea defences, drew widespread opposition from ratepayers and local fisherman alike. Naughten made a clever comparison by loosely comparing Southend Council's somewhat heavy handed efforts to raise money for the harbour with that of the Vikings' demands for 'Danegeld'. Eleven hundred years ago the Vikings ruled this part of Essex and the Saxon King, Alfred, (he's the one who burnt the cakes) had to pay them in 'Dangeld' much to the disgust of many of his subjects.

This was money, raised in taxes, then handed over to the Vikings, in gold or silver, in order to hopefully stop them raiding Saxon lands. Fred's caption read: -

When money was needed for defence against the Danes a tax was raised which amounts to four groats per swineherd. A harbour for Leigh was not popular.

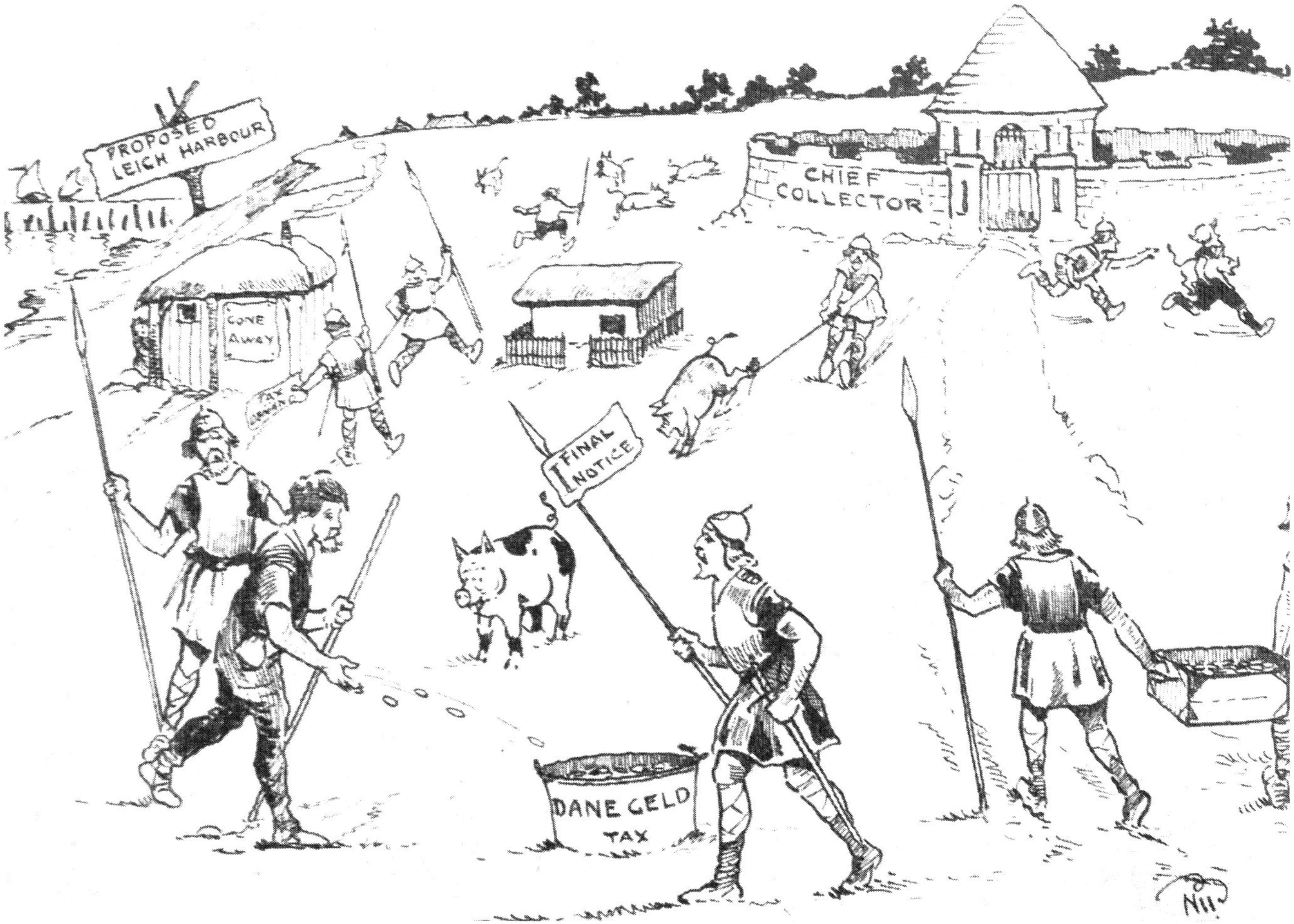
PROPOSED LEIGH HARBOUR
CHIEF COLLECTOR
GONE AWAY
FINAL NOTICE
DANE GELD
TAX

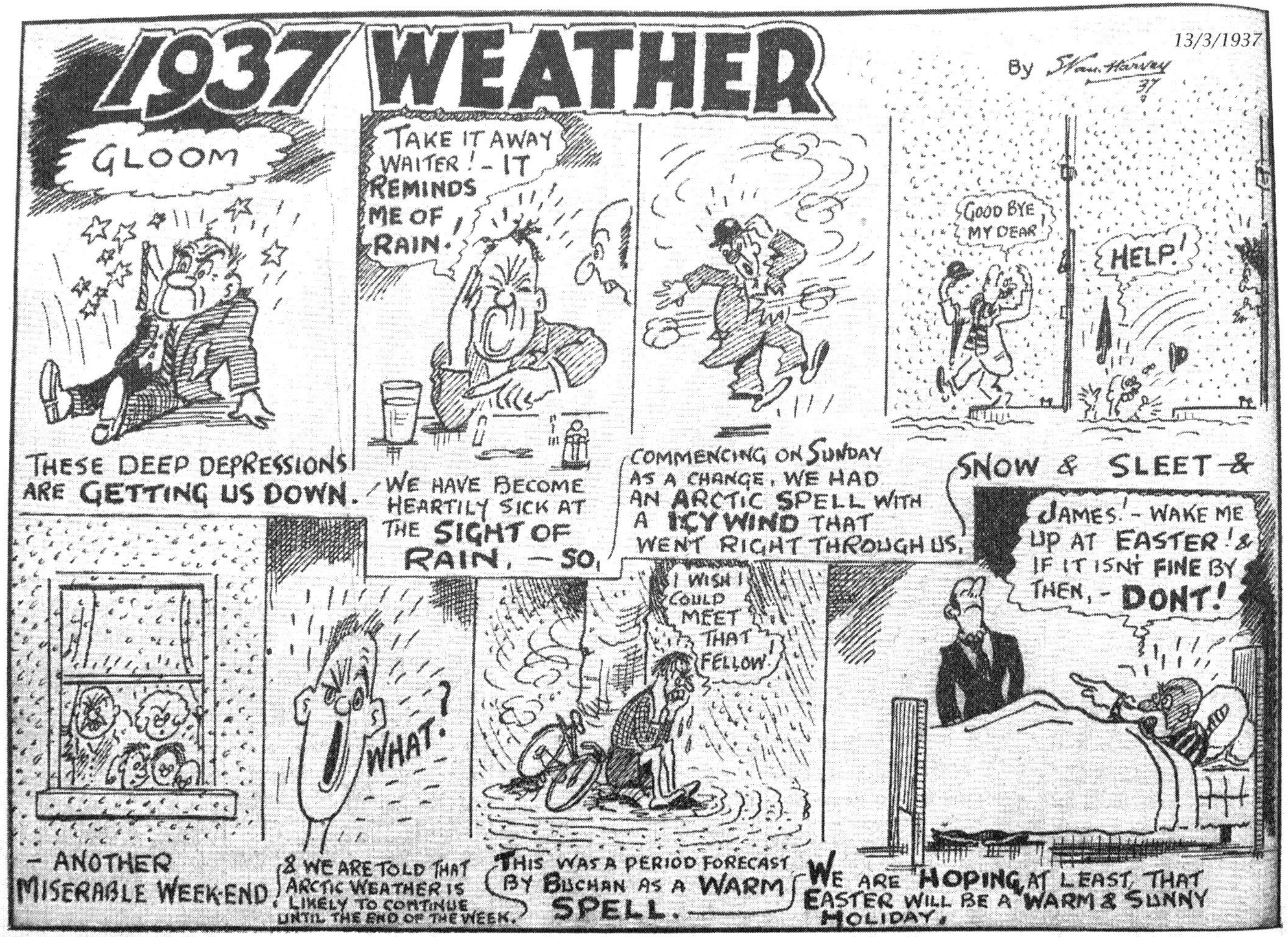
1937 WEATHER
13/3/1937
By Stan. Harvey 37
GLOOM
THESE DEEP DEPRESSIONS ARE GETTING US DOWN.
TAKE IT AWAY WAITER! - IT REMINDS ME OF RAIN.
WE HAVE BECOME HEARTILY SICK AT THE SIGHT OF RAIN, - SO,
COMMENCING ON SUNDAY AS A CHANGE, WE HAD AN ARCTIC SPELL WITH A ICY WIND THAT WENT RIGHT THROUGH US.
GOOD BYE MY DEAR
HELP!
SNOW & SLEET &
- ANOTHER MISERABLE WEEK-END.
WHAT?
& WE ARE TOLD THAT ARCTIC WEATHER IS LIKELY TO CONTINUE UNTIL THE END OF THE WEEK.
I WISH I COULD MEET THAT FELLOW
THIS WAS A PERIOD FORECAST BY BUCHAN AS A WARM SPELL.
JAMES! - WAKE ME UP AT EASTER! & IF IT ISN'T FINE BY THEN, - DONT!
WE ARE HOPING, AT LEAST, THAT EASTER WILL BE A WARM & SUNNY HOLIDAY.

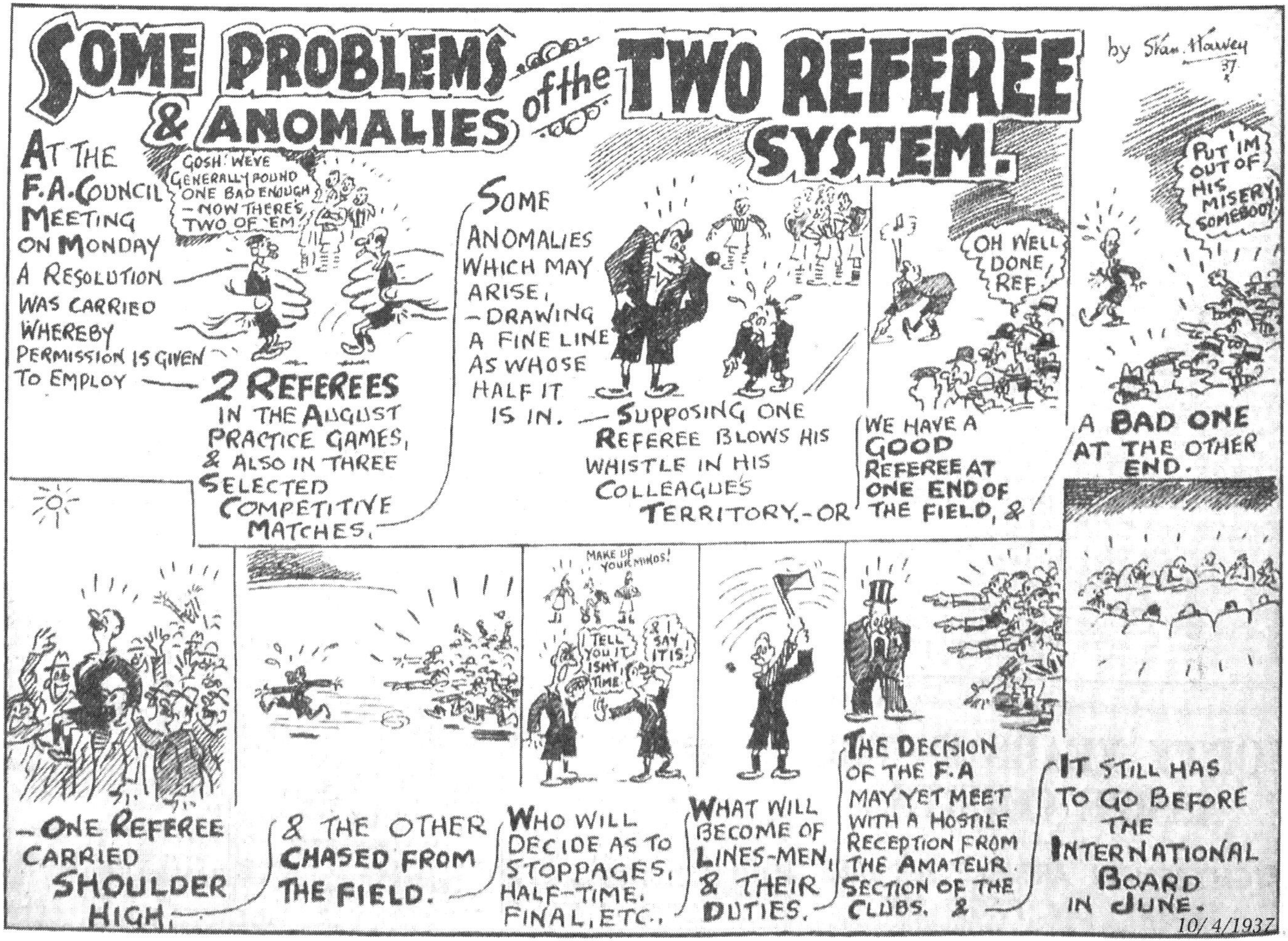
SOME PROBLEMS & ANOMALIES of the TWO REFEREE SYSTEM.
by Stan Harvey 37
AT THE F.A. COUNCIL MEETING ON MONDAY A RESOLUTION WAS CARRIED WHEREBY PERMISSION IS GIVEN TO EMPLOY
GOSH! WE'VE GENERALLY FOUND ONE BAD ENOUGH — NOW THERE'S TWO OF 'EM!
2 REFEREES IN THE AUGUST PRACTICE GAMES, & ALSO IN THREE SELECTED COMPETITIVE MATCHES.
SOME ANOMALIES WHICH MAY ARISE, — DRAWING A FINE LINE AS WHOSE HALF IT IS IN.
— SUPPOSING ONE REFEREE BLOWS HIS WHISTLE IN HIS COLLEAGUE'S TERRITORY. - OR
OH WELL DONE REF!
WE HAVE A GOOD REFEREE AT ONE END OF THE FIELD, &
PUT 'IM OUT OF HIS MISERY, SOMEBODY!
A BAD ONE AT THE OTHER END.
— ONE REFEREE CARRIED SHOULDER HIGH,
& THE OTHER CHASED FROM THE FIELD.
MAKE UP YOUR MINDS!
I TELL YOU IT ISN'T TIME
& I SAY IT IS!
WHO WILL DECIDE AS TO STOPPAGES, HALF-TIME, FINAL, ETC.,
WHAT WILL BECOME OF LINES-MEN, & THEIR DUTIES.
THE DECISION OF THE F.A MAY YET MEET WITH A HOSTILE RECEPTION FROM THE AMATEUR SECTION OF THE CLUBS. &
IT STILL HAS TO GO BEFORE THE INTERNATIONAL BOARD IN JUNE.
10/4/1937

Notice to Quit - The Houseboat Colony of Leigh-on-Sea

In the mid 1930s, due to the housing shortage, a houseboat colony took hold near the sea wall at Leigh-on-Sea, much to the annoyance of Southend Council. Many of the houseboats were in a poor state of repair, without running water or basic facilities, and were considered to be a health hazard. Despite the council's best efforts the houseboat owners refused to budge. Fred Naughten suggested the corporation take a leaf out of King Alfred's book and employ his special Saxon style 'notice to quit' methods to remove the unwelcome residents. Just over one thousand years ago Alfred had successfully driven the Vikings out of their Benfleet creek encampment during what was called the 'The Battle of Benfleet'. Southend Council chose not to copy Alfred and instead through legal process purchased the foreshore. By the end of 1948 most of the houseboat residents had been evicted. Some of the boats, still in good condition, were towed to Benfleet. The rest were abandoned and left to rot. Fred wrote:-

An early attempt to form a house boat colony was made at Leigh and Benfleet when the Danes came over in the latter part of the eighth century. King Alfred gave them them notice to quit and his methods proved effective.

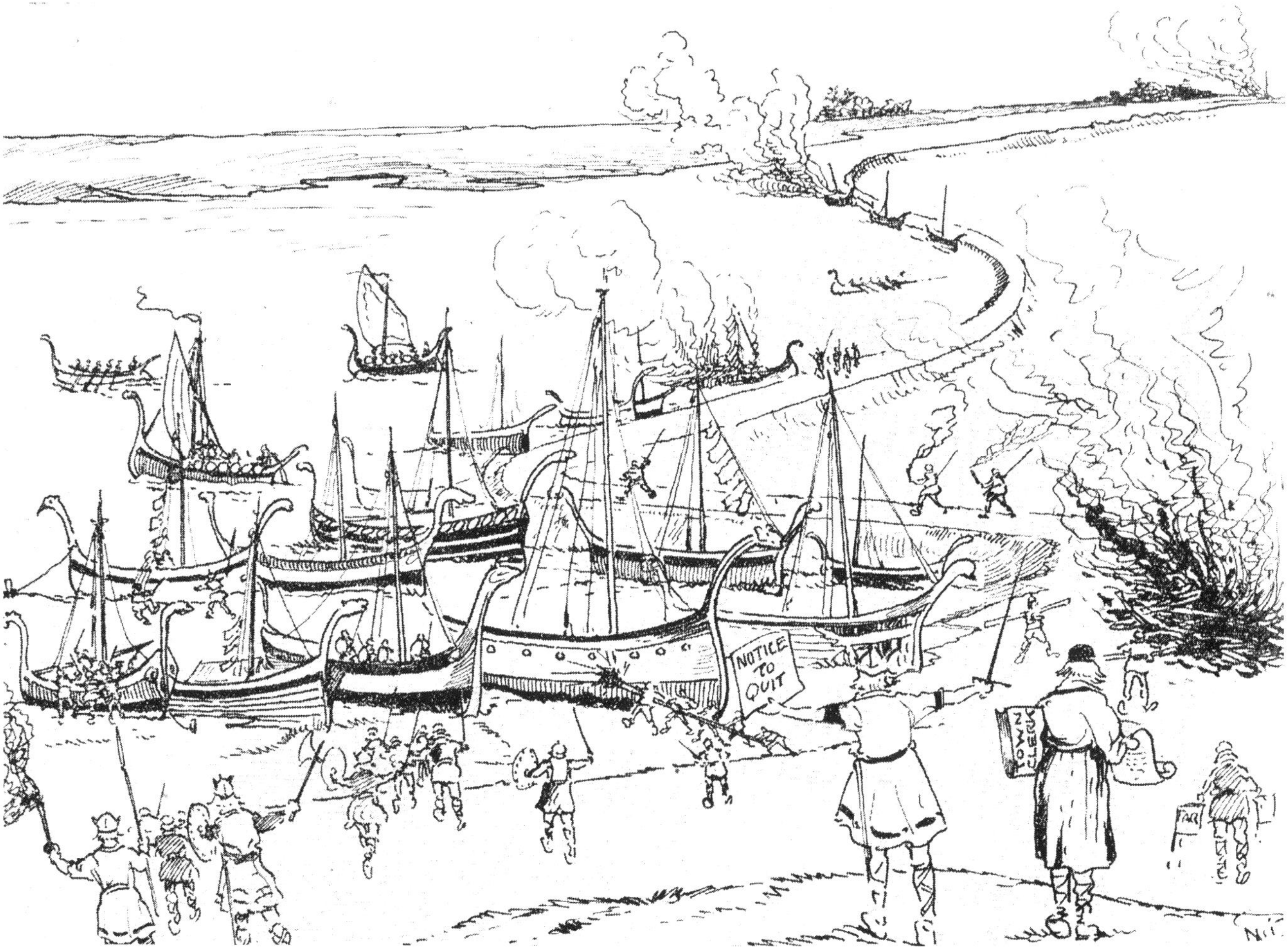
NOTICE TO QUIT

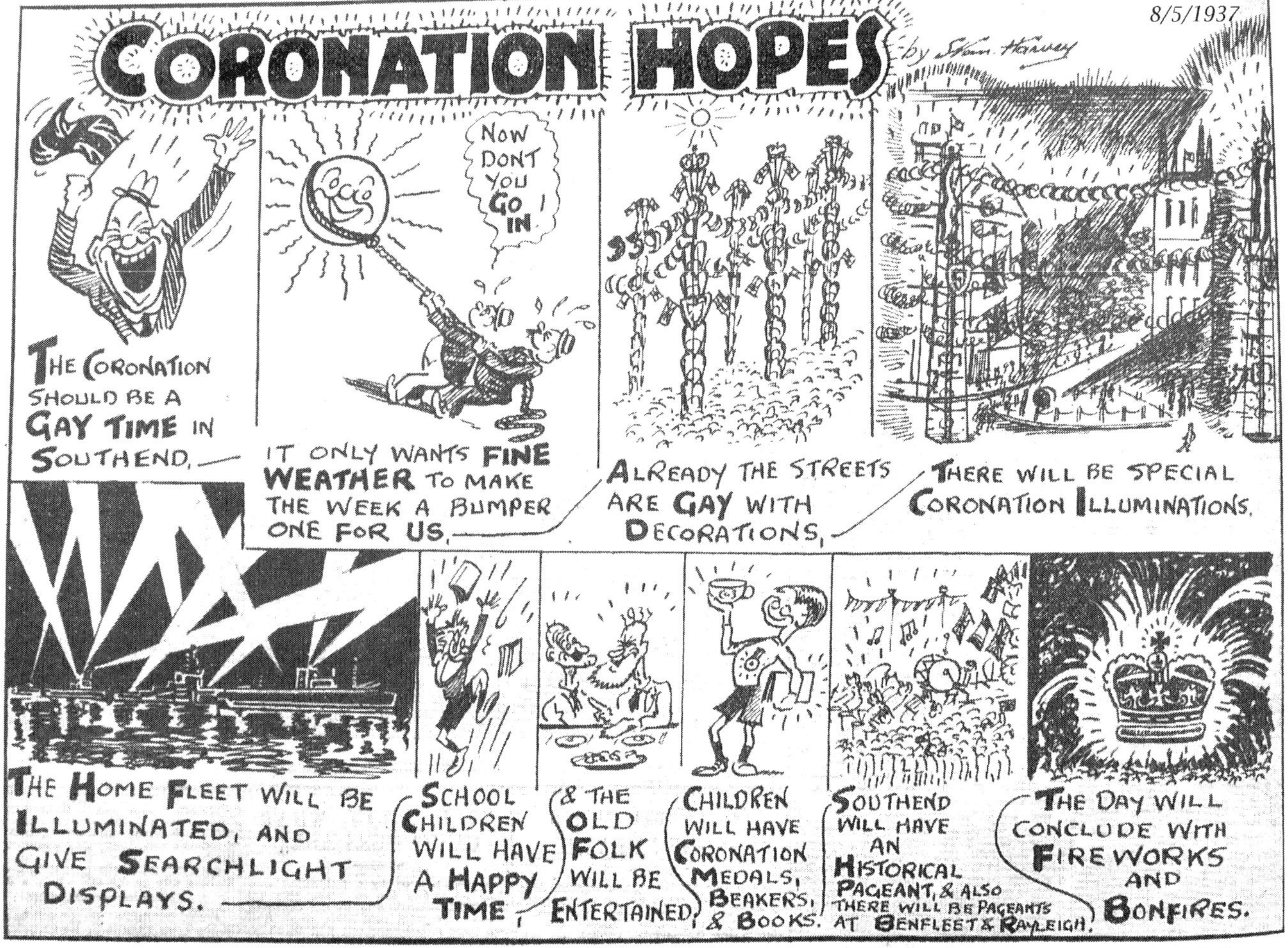
8/5/1937
CORONATION HOPES
by Stan Harvey
NOW DONT YOU GO IN
THE CORONATION SHOULD BE A GAY TIME IN SOUTHEND,
IT ONLY WANTS FINE WEATHER TO MAKE THE WEEK A BUMPER ONE FOR US,
ALREADY THE STREETS ARE GAY WITH DECORATIONS,
THERE WILL BE SPECIAL CORONATION ILLUMINATIONS,
THE HOME FLEET WILL BE ILLUMINATED, AND GIVE SEARCHLIGHT DISPLAYS.
SCHOOL CHILDREN WILL HAVE A HAPPY TIME,
& THE OLD FOLK WILL BE ENTERTAINED,
CHILDREN WILL HAVE CORONATION MEDALS, BEAKERS, & BOOKS.
SOUTHEND WILL HAVE AN HISTORICAL PAGEANT, & ALSO THERE WILL BE PAGEANTS AT BENFLEET & RAYLEIGH,
THE DAY WILL CONCLUDE WITH FIREWORKS AND BONFIRES.

SAILORS DON'T CARE! – *The only outdoor celebration carried out on Coronation afternoon was the Spot Cruise. Despite the rain and lack of wind over sixty boats turned out and continued until 3.30.*

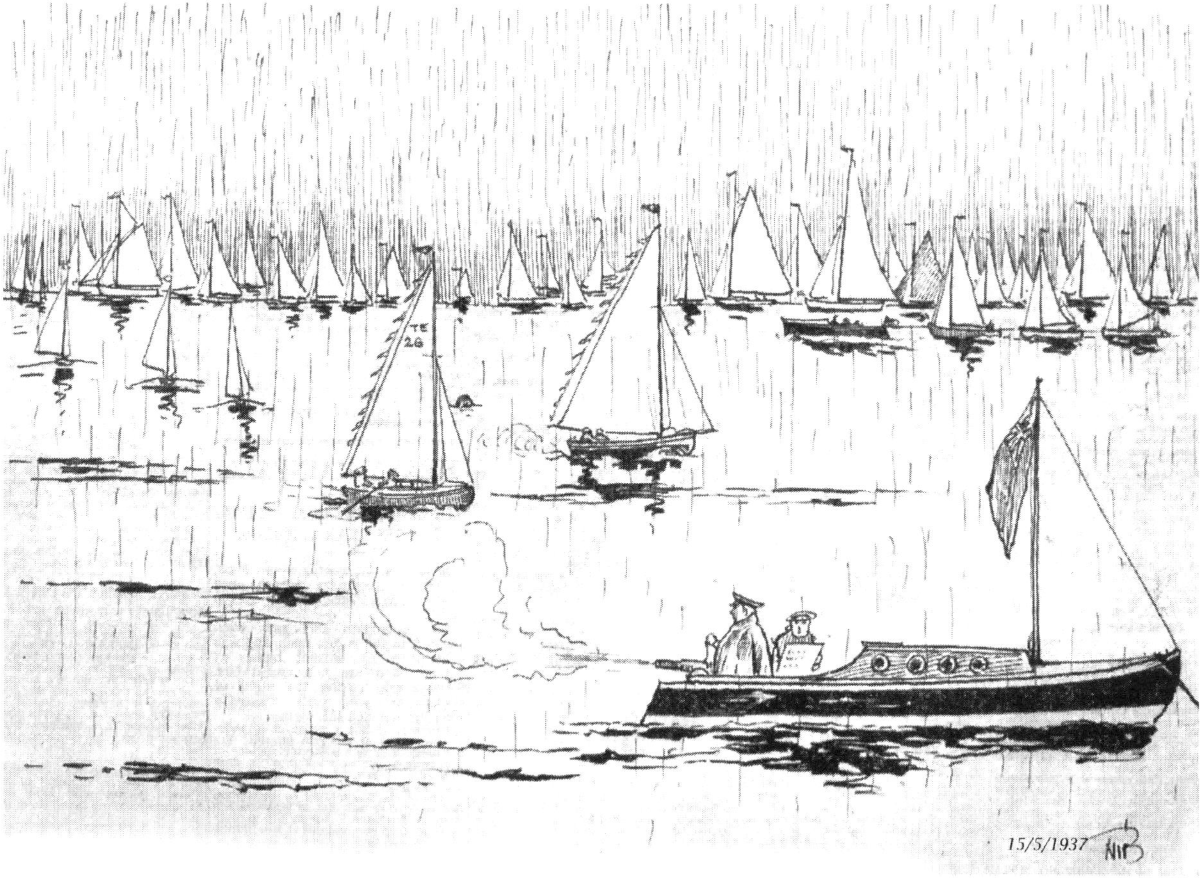
TE
26
15/5/1937

Porters - a writer's retreat?

Fred Naughten reported that Benjamin Disraeli, later the Earl of Beaconsfield and future British Prime Minister, stayed at Porters, the Civic House & Mayor's Parlour, in Southend, between 1833 and 1834.

During his residence Disraeli enjoyed bathing, bracing sea walks, bowling, sailing and the night-time illuminations. Disraeli was also a successful author. He spent much of his time at Porters writing his ninth novel *Henrietta Temple*. At the same time he was having an affair with Lady Henrietta Sykes, the wife of Sir Francis Sykes, with Henrietta being the inspiration for the novel. One hundred years later, in May 1937, the then Prime Minister Stanley Baldwin resigned, and Fred wondered if he too would come to Porters to write his memoirs and enjoy the pleasures that Southend-on-Sea could offer. Fred Naughten's caption read:-

Mr Benjamin Disraeli (The Earl of Beaconsfield) stayed at Porters 1833-4.
Will Mr Stanley Baldwin repeat history and come to Southend to write his memoirs?

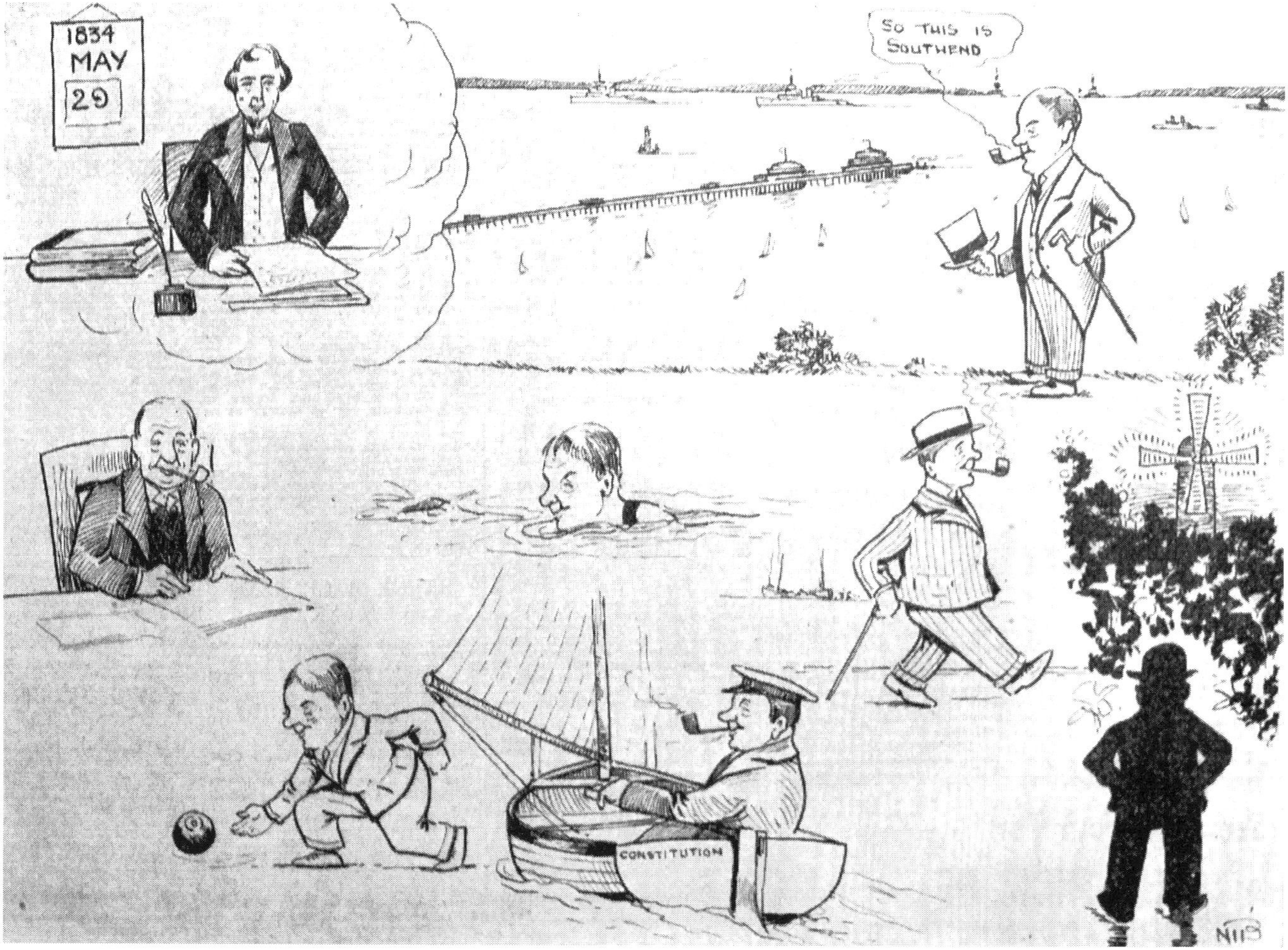
1834
MAY
29
SO THIS IS
SOUTHEND
CONSTITUTION
NIB

Royal Terrace
Southend-on-Sea

At the beginning of the nineteenth century Southend was a fashionable seaside resort and patronized by royalty. In 1801, Princess Charlotte of Wales, at the age of five years, was ordered to take sea-bathing at Southend for the benefit of her health. In 1805, Princess Caroline of Wales stayed for three months at Royal Terrace.

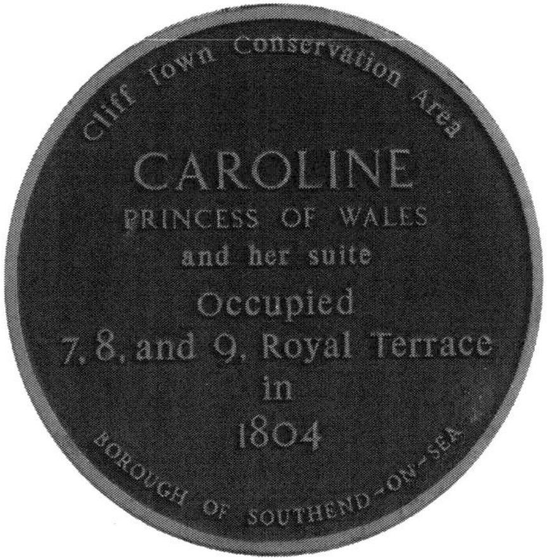
Cliff Town Conservation Area
CAROLINE
PRINCESS OF WALES
and her suite
Occupied
7, 8, and 9, Royal Terrace
in
1804
BOROUGH OF SOUTHEND-ON-SEA

Little did Fred know, back in 1937, that a heritage plaque would later be put up on Royal Terrace to mark the spot where Princess Caroline stayed.

In November 1817, Princess Charlotte died after giving birth to her only child, a stillborn son. This tragic event changed the course of the British Monarchy. Fred's caption was:-

At the time the Southend season then lasted from July to the end of September.

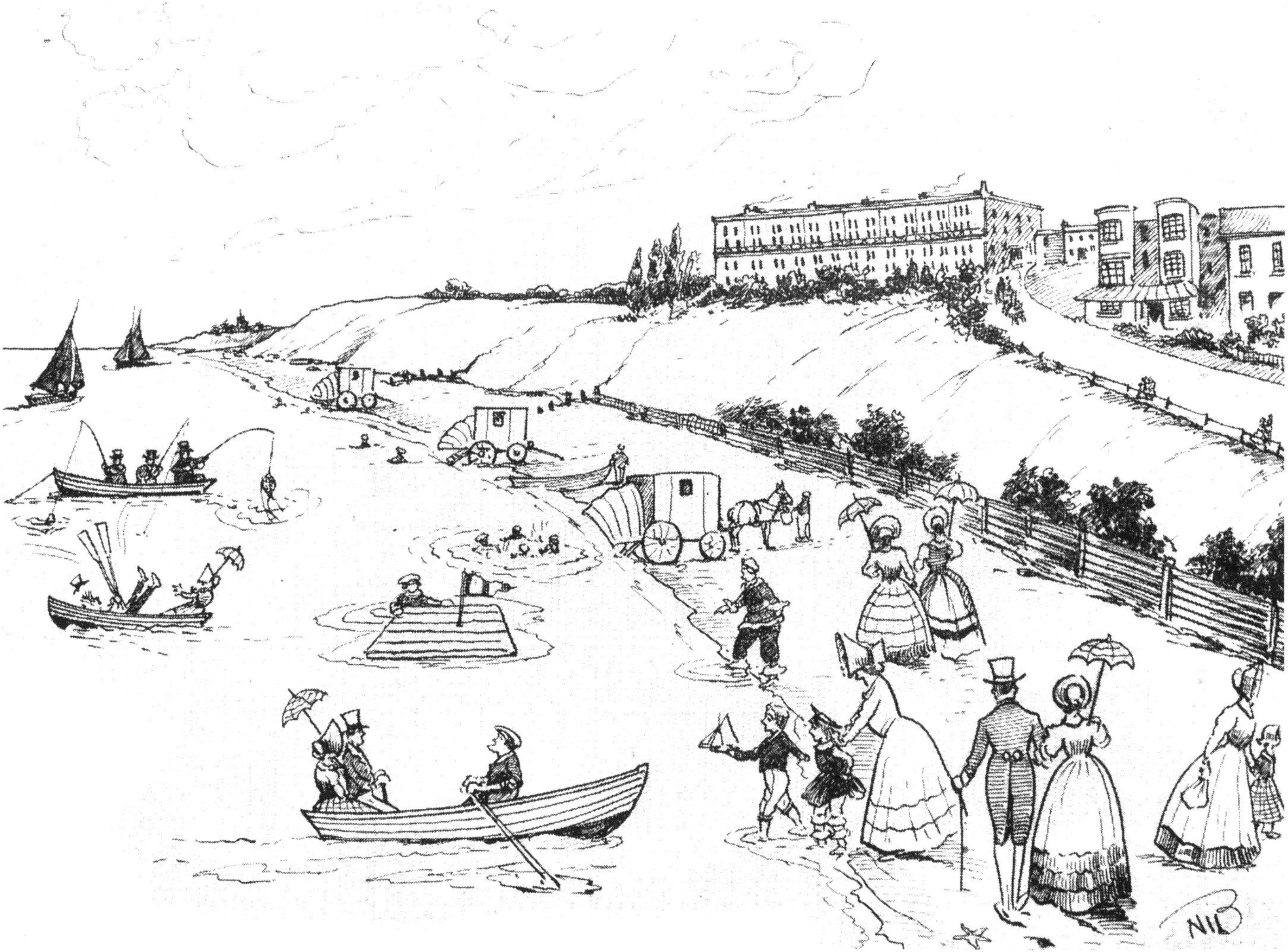

Cricket Week 1344

It's not quite cricket as we know it, but according to Fred Naughten,

A Bodleian Library manuscript dated April 1344 recorded 'that cricket was played by monks'.

Naughten used this revelation to create the image opposite and suggested that if this were the case, the monks from the 12th century Cluniac Monastery would have played cricket in Priory Park. Naturally the press would be in attendance. Unfortunately, we can't find any evidence of a 1344 manuscript about cricket, but in 2008 the Bodleian Library did publish a book called 'The Original Laws of Cricket', which refers to cricket rules made in 1744. However, by then, the Prittlewell monks were long gone.

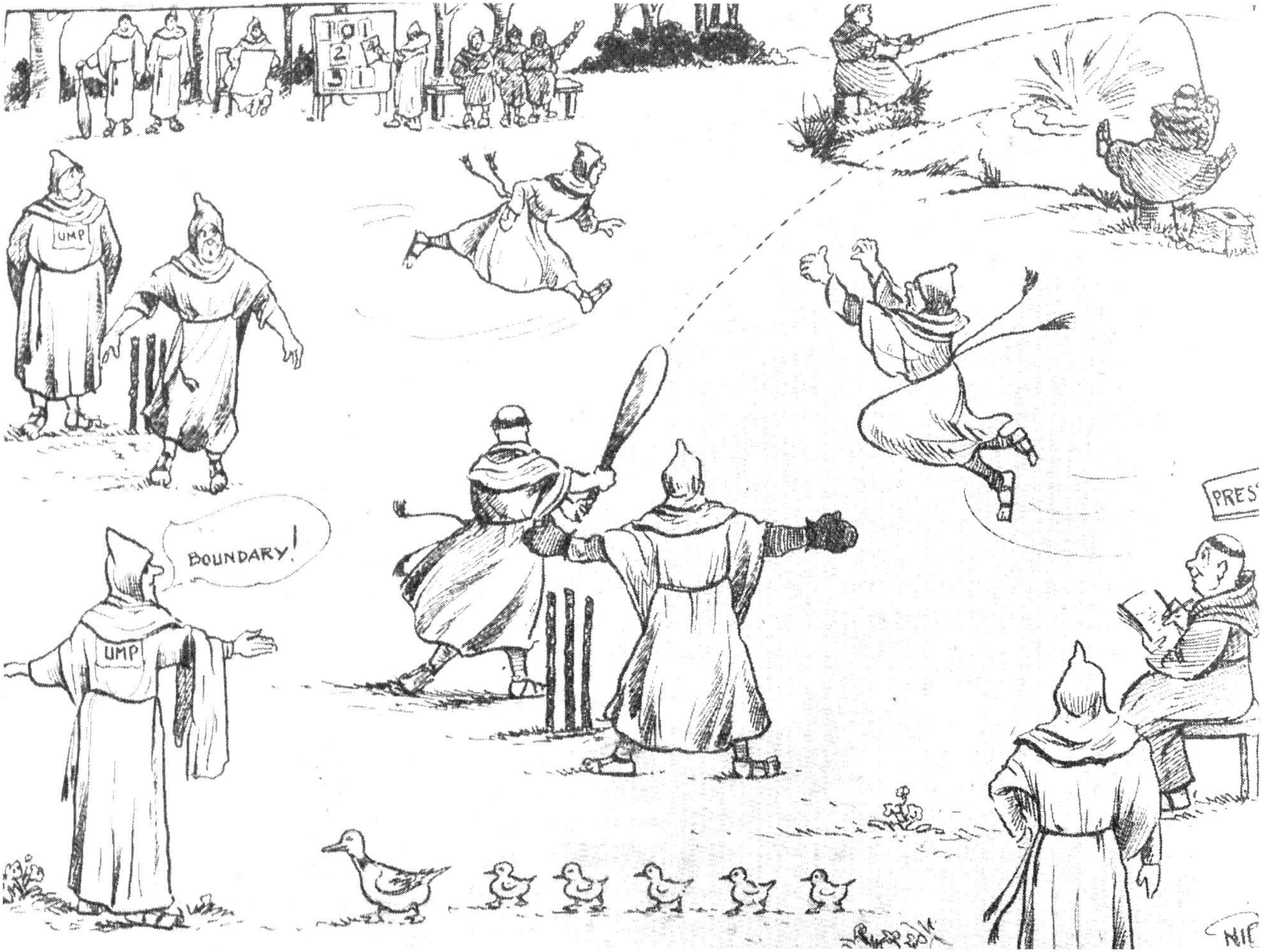
UMP
BOUNDARY!
UMP
PRES

The Bowling Tournament

According to Fred Naughten's caption:-

In the year 1541 anyone playing bowls outside his garden or orchard was liable to a fine of 6s. 8d, but those possessed of lands of the yearly value of £100 might obtain licences to play on their own greens.

It is said King Charles I (1625-1649) featured in the image, was an enthusiastic bowler and played for high stakes. It is recorded that after one contest, his losses were £1,000.

Halidom: Something held sacred

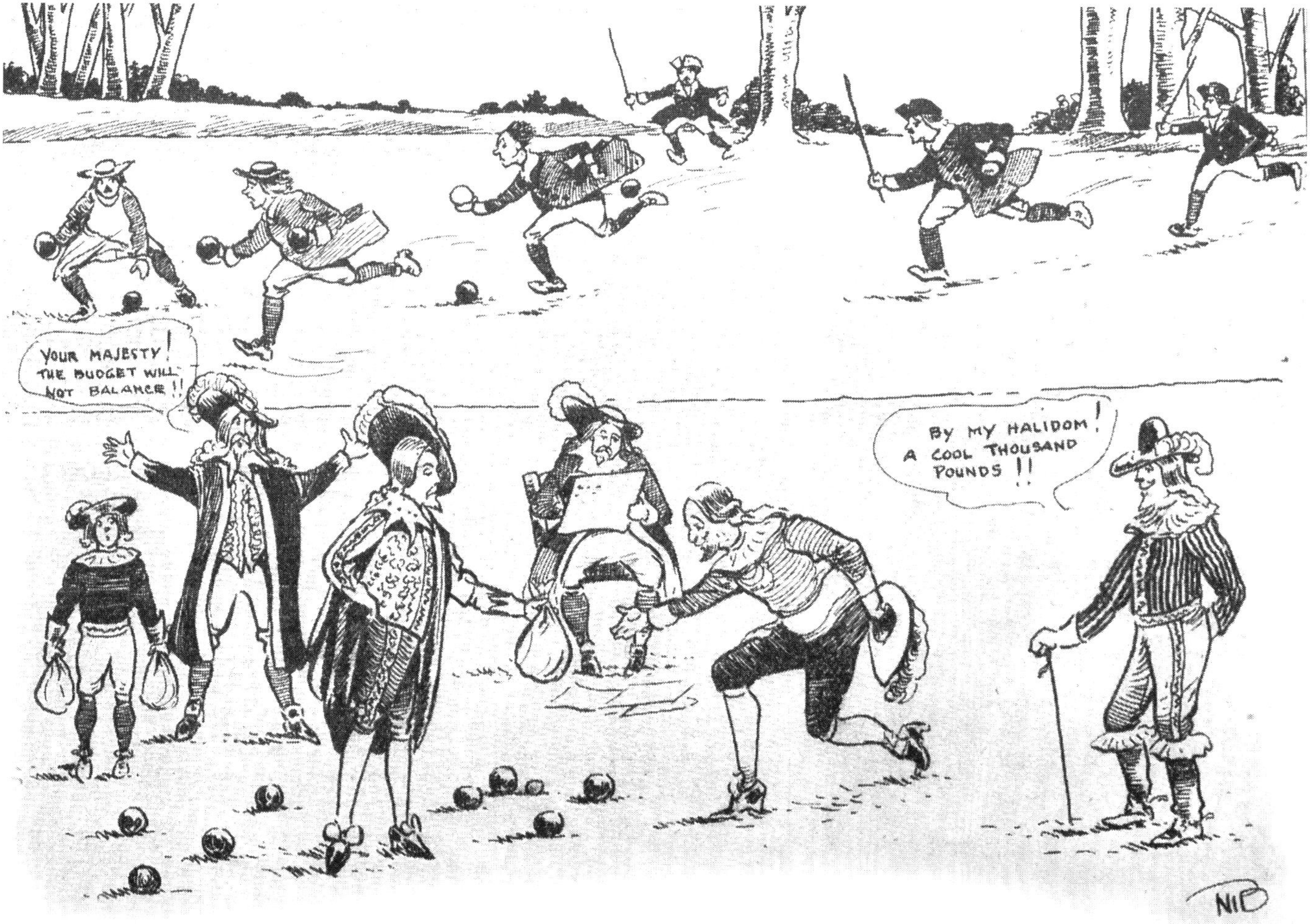
YOUR MAJESTY! THE BUDGET WILL NOT BALANCE!!
BY MY HALIDOM! A COOL THOUSAND POUNDS!!
NIB

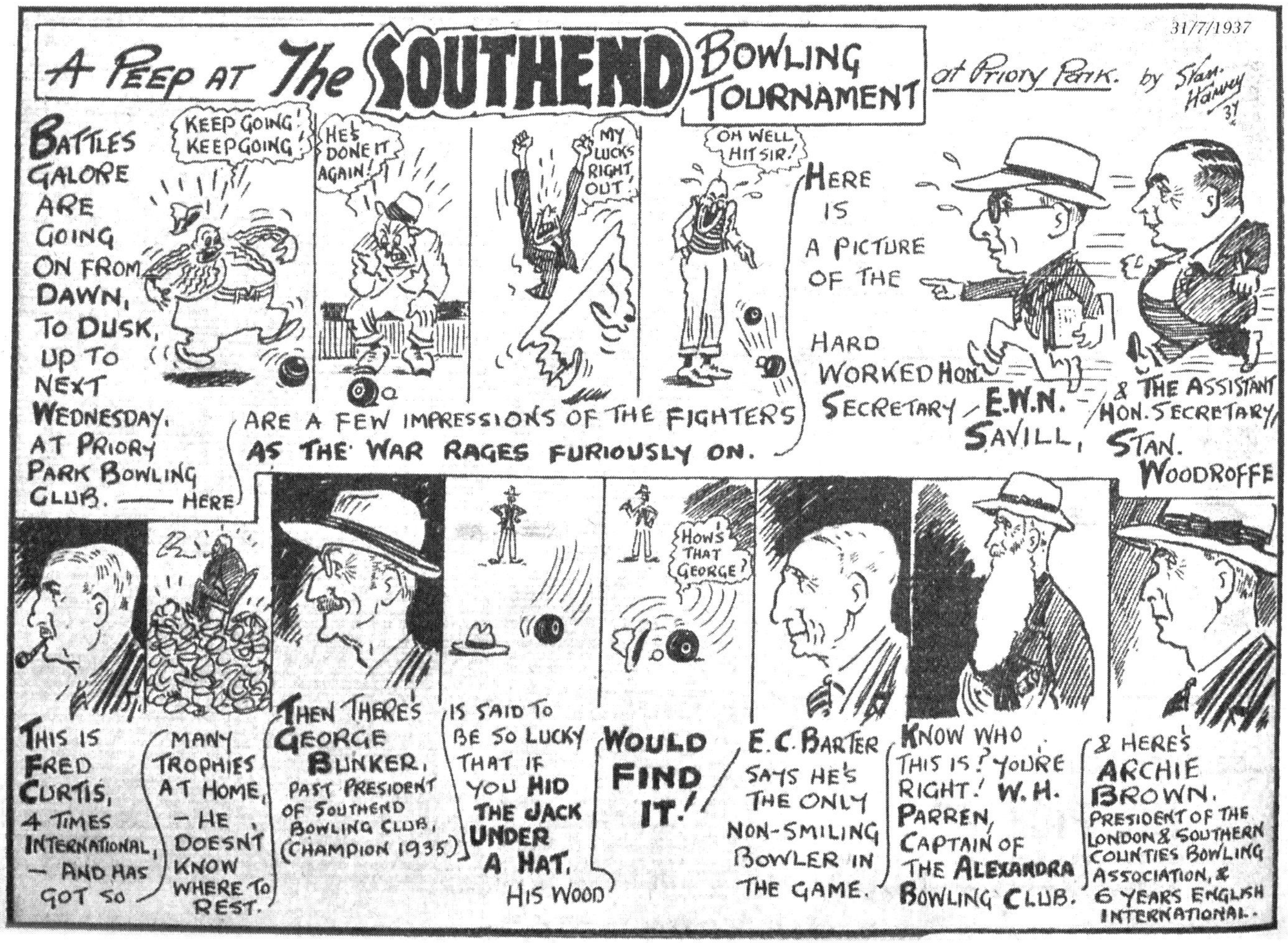
31/7/1937
A PEEP AT The SOUTHEND BOWLING TOURNAMENT at Priory Park. by Stan Harvey 37
BATTLES GALORE ARE GOING ON FROM DAWN, TO DUSK, UP TO NEXT WEDNESDAY. AT PRIORY PARK BOWLING CLUB. —— HERE
KEEP GOING! KEEP GOING!
HE'S DONE IT AGAIN!
MY LUCK'S RIGHT OUT!
OH WELL HIT SIR!
ARE A FEW IMPRESSIONS OF THE FIGHTERS AS THE WAR RAGES FURIOUSLY ON.
HERE IS A PICTURE OF THE HARD WORKED HON. SECRETARY E.W.N. SAVILL, & THE ASSISTANT HON. SECRETARY, STAN. WOODROFFE
THIS IS FRED CURTIS, 4 TIMES INTERNATIONAL, — AND HAS GOT SO
MANY TROPHIES AT HOME, — HE DOESN'T KNOW WHERE TO REST.
THEN THERE'S GEORGE BUNKER, PAST PRESIDENT OF SOUTHEND BOWLING CLUB, (CHAMPION 1935)
IS SAID TO BE SO LUCKY THAT IF YOU HID THE JACK UNDER A HAT, HIS WOOD
HOW'S THAT GEORGE?
WOULD FIND IT!
E.C. BARTER SAYS HE'S THE ONLY NON-SMILING BOWLER IN THE GAME.
KNOW WHO THIS IS? YOU'RE RIGHT! W. H. PARREN, CAPTAIN OF THE ALEXANDRA BOWLING CLUB.
& HERE'S ARCHIE BROWN. PRESIDENT OF THE LONDON & SOUTHERN COUNTIES BOWLING ASSOCIATION, & 6 YEARS ENGLISH INTERNATIONAL.

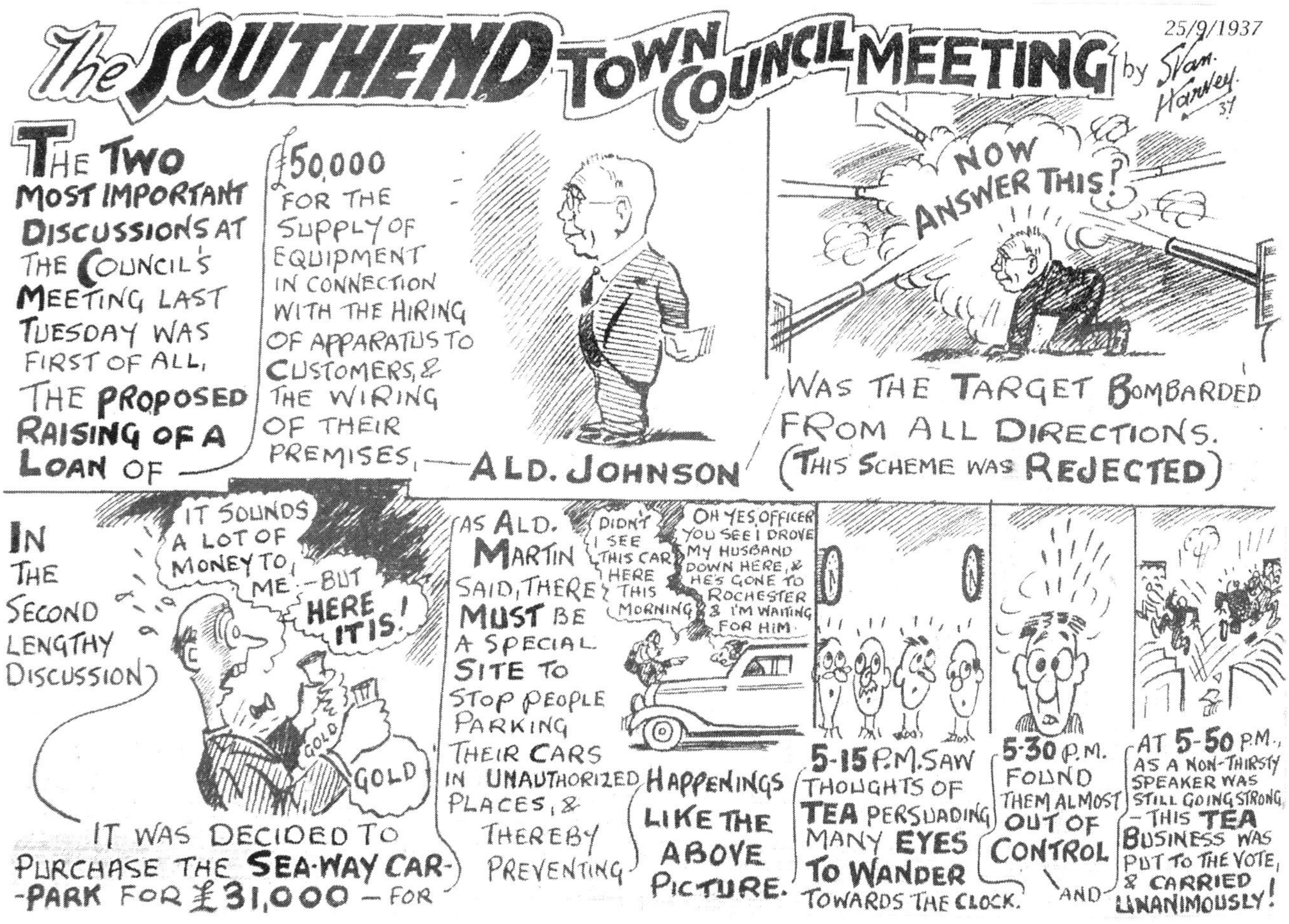

The SOUTHEND TOWN COUNCIL MEETING by Stan. Harvey. 37
25/9/1937
THE TWO MOST IMPORTANT DISCUSSIONS AT THE COUNCIL'S MEETING LAST TUESDAY WAS FIRST OF ALL, THE PROPOSED RAISING OF A LOAN OF
£50,000 FOR THE SUPPLY OF EQUIPMENT IN CONNECTION WITH THE HIRING OF APPARATUS TO CUSTOMERS, & THE WIRING OF THEIR PREMISES,
ALD. JOHNSON
NOW ANSWER THIS?
WAS THE TARGET BOMBARDED FROM ALL DIRECTIONS.
(THIS SCHEME WAS REJECTED)
IN THE SECOND LENGTHY DISCUSSION
IT SOUNDS A LOT OF MONEY TO ME -BUT
HERE IT IS!
GOLD
GOLD
IT WAS DECIDED TO PURCHASE THE SEA-WAY CAR-PARK FOR £31,000 - FOR
AS ALD. MARTIN SAID, THERE MUST BE A SPECIAL SITE TO STOP PEOPLE PARKING THEIR CARS IN UNAUTHORIZED PLACES, & THEREBY PREVENTING
DIDN'T SEE THIS CAR HERE THIS MORNING
OH YES OFFICER YOU SEE I DROVE MY HUSBAND DOWN HERE, & HE'S GONE TO ROCHESTER & I'M WAITING FOR HIM.
HAPPENINGS LIKE THE ABOVE PICTURE.
5-15 P.M. SAW THOUGHTS OF TEA PERSUADING MANY EYES TO WANDER TOWARDS THE CLOCK.
5-30 P.M. FOUND THEM ALMOST OUT OF CONTROL
AND
AT 5-50 P.M., AS A NON-THIRSTY SPEAKER WAS STILL GOING STRONG - THIS TEA BUSINESS WAS PUT TO THE VOTE, & CARRIED UNANIMOUSLY!

Chalkwell Station

Chalkwell station was opened in 1933, four years before this cartoon was created. Naughten imagined the scene opposite in the early part of the 20th century and his caption read:-

Nightingale Dell, the bungalow, crossing and stile is where Chalkwell station stands today. The little hut on the centre left just behind the barrier is where Essex Yacht Club had their first headquarters.

From 1909 to 1939, Arthur Joscelyne leased part of the beach from the railway company. Refreshments were available, changing tents and boats could be hired, bait was sold, and fishing trips arranged. Many still refer to the area as Joscelyne's beach.

Joscelyne's Beach Chalkwell 1930　　　　　　　　LizS

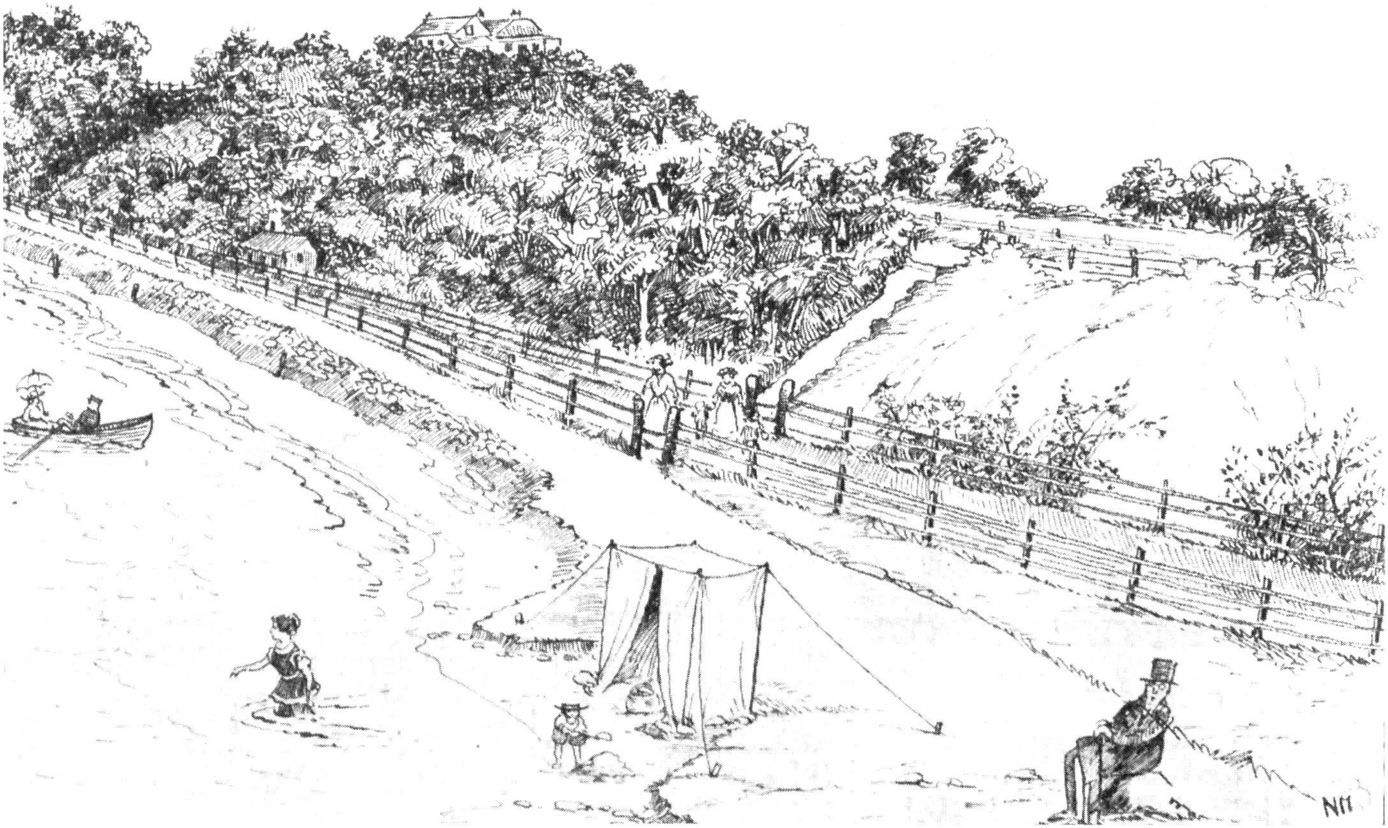

Blackout
Mock Air Raid

The *Southend Pictorial Telegraph* described it as the clock slipping back 20 years. Between midnight on Thursday and 2am on Friday (4/5th November 1937) the whole of the Thames Riverside area was plunged into darkness with residents subjected to the harsh sounds of factory and works sirens for two minutes warning of the approach of 'enemy' aircraft. Happily, no bombs were dropped but the exercise enabled the local communities to test their readiness to deal with the aftermath of aerial bombardment.

For Stan Harvey it was an opportunity for some unusual creativity which resulted in the cartoon opposite.

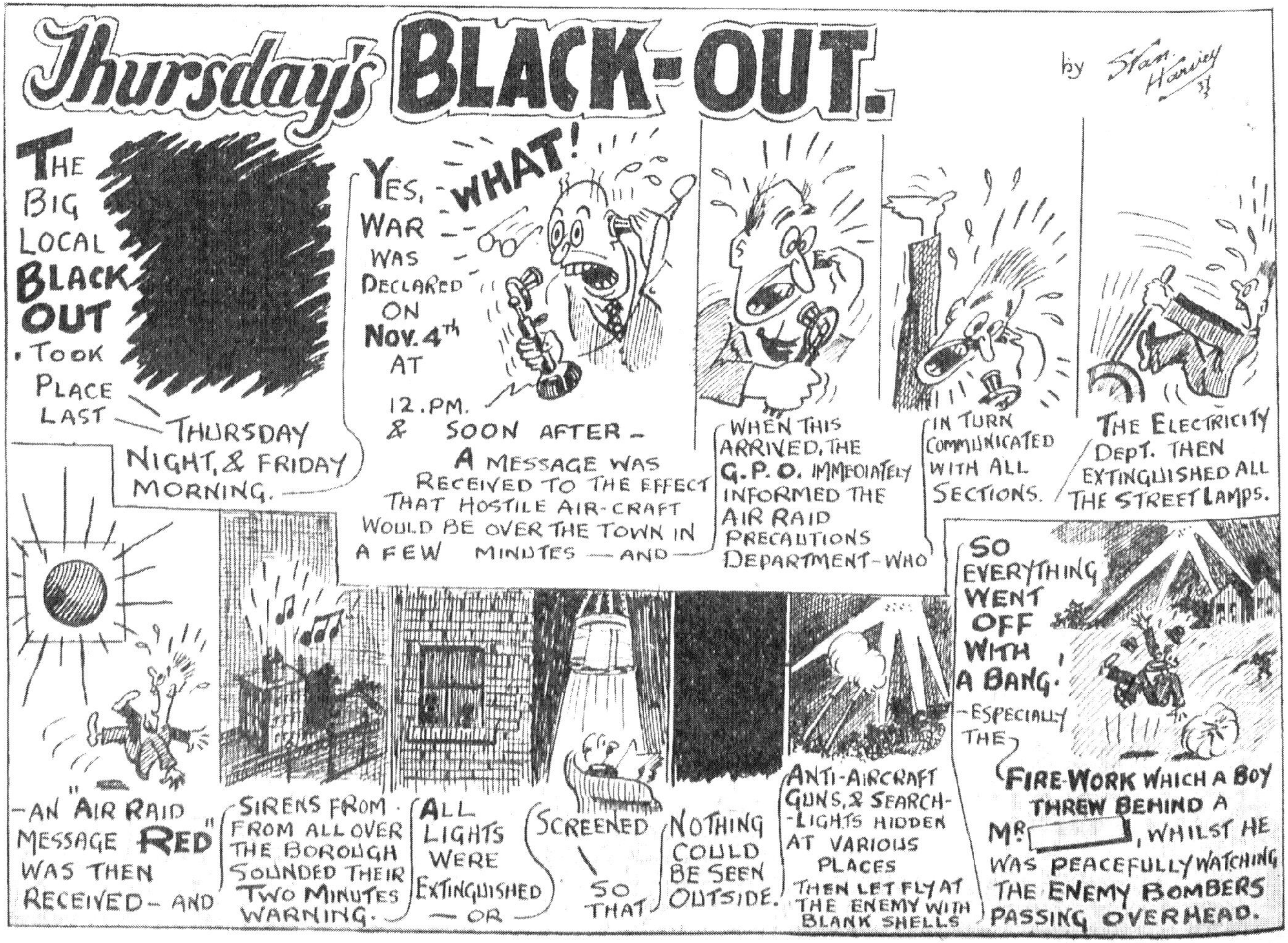

Thursday's BLACK-OUT.
by Stan. Harvey 37
THE BIG LOCAL BLACK OUT TOOK PLACE LAST THURSDAY NIGHT, & FRIDAY MORNING.
YES, WAR WAS DECLARED ON NOV. 4th AT 12. PM.
WHAT!
& SOON AFTER – A MESSAGE WAS RECEIVED TO THE EFFECT THAT HOSTILE AIR-CRAFT WOULD BE OVER THE TOWN IN A FEW MINUTES – AND
WHEN THIS ARRIVED, THE G.P.O. IMMEDIATELY INFORMED THE AIR RAID PRECAUTIONS DEPARTMENT – WHO
IN TURN COMMUNICATED WITH ALL SECTIONS.
THE ELECTRICITY DEPT. THEN EXTINGUISHED ALL THE STREET LAMPS.
SO EVERYTHING WENT OFF WITH A BANG! – ESPECIALLY THE
– AN "AIR RAID MESSAGE RED" WAS THEN RECEIVED – AND
SIRENS FROM FROM ALL OVER THE BOROUGH SOUNDED THEIR TWO MINUTES WARNING.
ALL LIGHTS WERE EXTINGUISHED – OR
SCREENED SO THAT
NOTHING COULD BE SEEN OUTSIDE.
ANTI-AIRCRAFT GUNS, & SEARCH-LIGHTS HIDDEN AT VARIOUS PLACES THEN LET FLY AT THE ENEMY WITH BLANK SHELLS
FIRE-WORK WHICH A BOY THREW BEHIND A MR ___, WHILST HE WAS PEACEFULLY WATCHING THE ENEMY BOMBERS PASSING OVERHEAD.

Press Gangs

According to Fred Naughten, one hundred years previously Canon Robert Stuart King, the rector of St Clements church in Leigh-on-Sea, recorded in some detail the activities of press gangs and smugglers in the late 18th and early 19th centuries. Fred's caption for the image opposite read:-

Smuggling was prevalent and locally at least, no one thought anything of it. Great fun was to be had when there was a shipwreck especially if it contained spirits. More to fear though, by Leigh men, were the dreaded press gangs. Yet the men were a wily bunch and on hearing a shout 'PRESS GANG' they all suddenly disappeared to the sanctuary of Hadleigh or Belfairs woods where they hid for days. In turn their women folk smuggled them food and water until the press gang got fed up with searching and left.

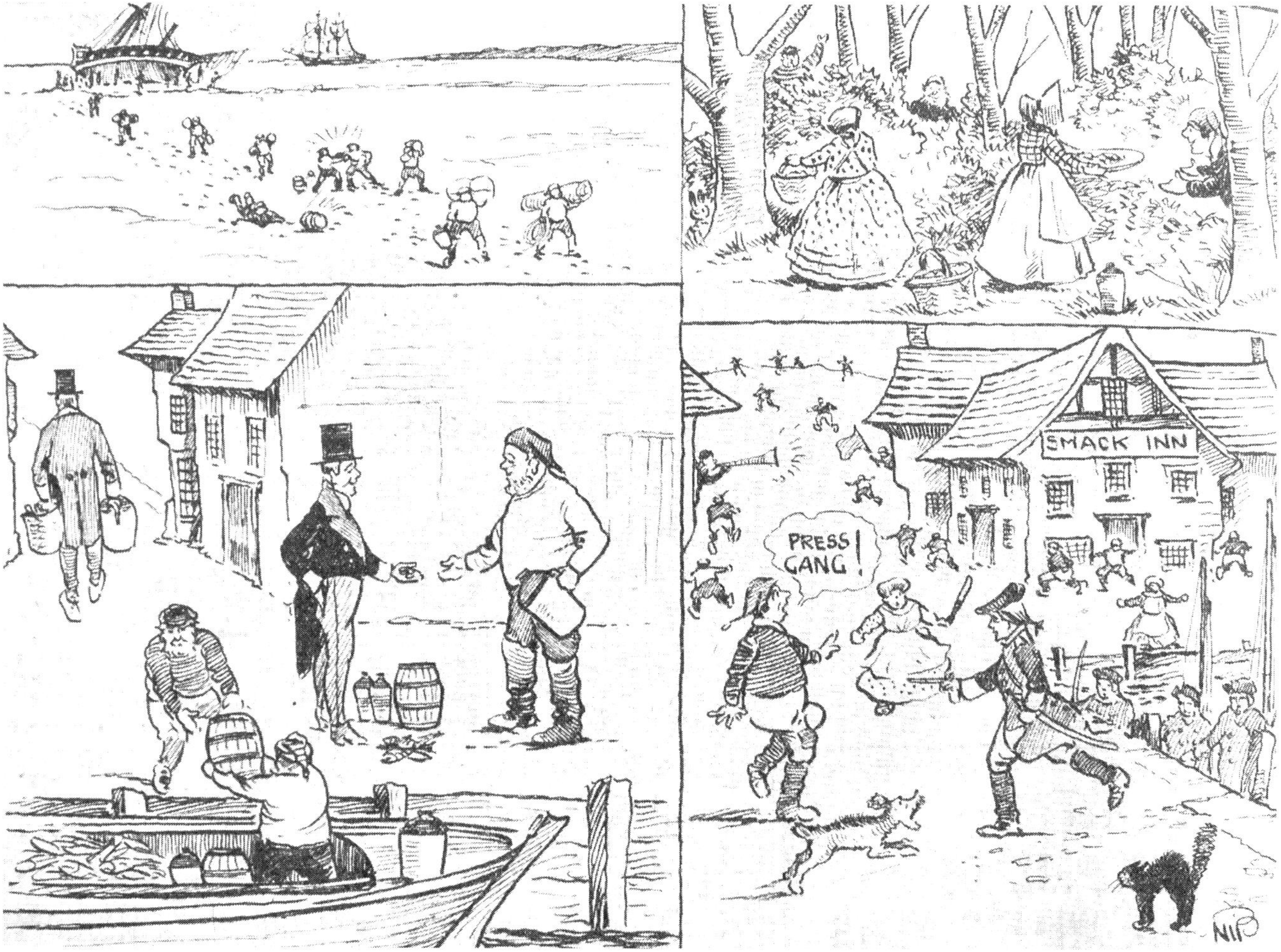
SMACK INN
PRESS GANG!

Dangerous Roads

Fred Naughten returned to one of the themes that seemed to worry him on a regular basis, the subject of dangerous roads. The mid 1930s saw considerable public anxiety about the number of motor vehicle accidents on the roads, especially on the relatively new arterial road to London that was attracting more and more traffic. The cartoon opposite was published in November 1937. The nights were getting longer, fogs were frequent, street lighting on the new arterial road was poor or non-existent and there were few road markings and no crash barriers. A compulsory driving test had only been operating for two years and seat belts and the breathalyser were yet to come. Fred took the opportunity to contrast the 1930s road mayhem with the days of the highwaymen and the dark deeds of the likes of Essex born Dick Turpin.

The caption read:-

November fogs have been the cause of many accidents on the roads of Southend and district, but is a fog today any more dangerous than the roads were a century ago?

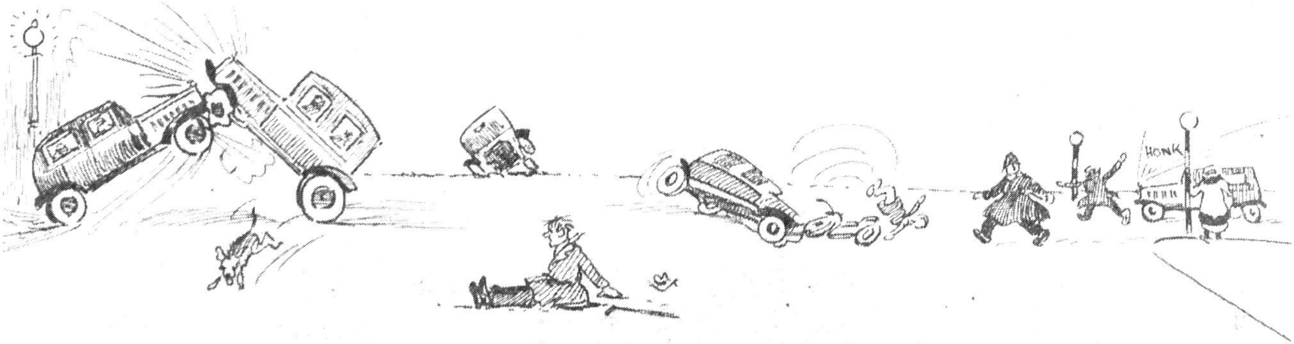
HONK

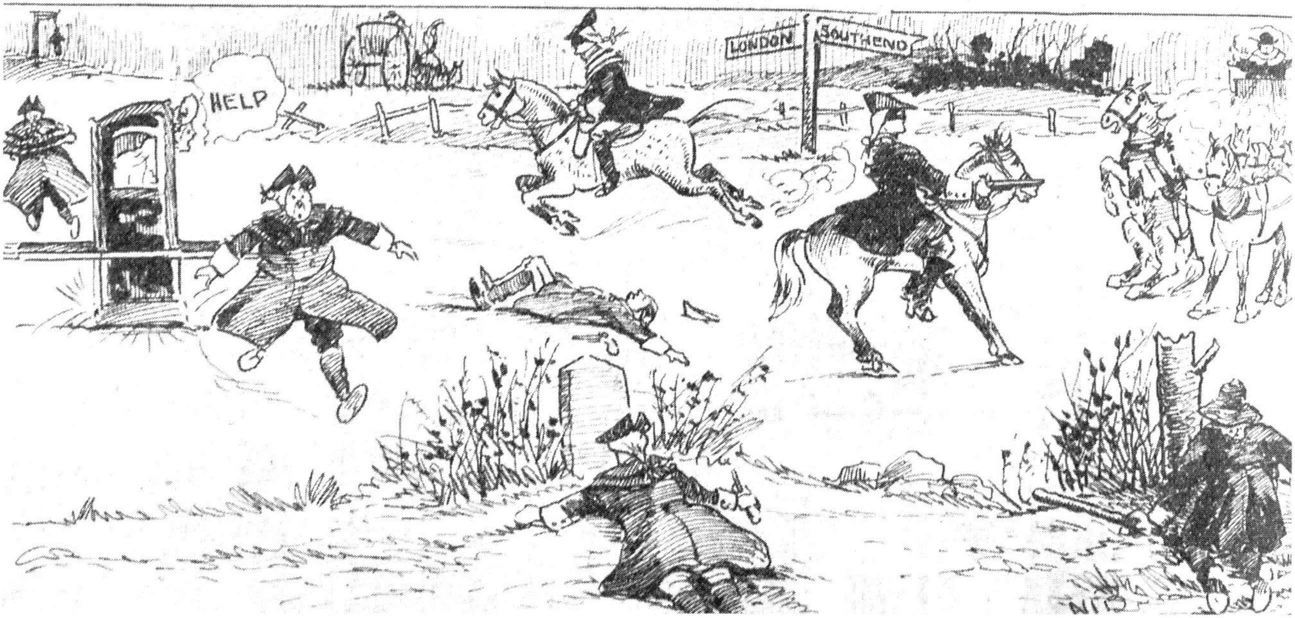
HELP
LONDON
SOUTHEND

Preparing for Christmas a century ago

Christmas away from home is not new. Before the era of getaways to the continent or the Caribbean, Southend was a popular destination over the festive season. Fred wrote the following caption:-

Visitors arriving at Southend by horse-drawn coach, velocipede and steam boat.
Choosing a Christmas turkey, the postmen were not so heavily laden as in modern times.
They didn't forget the mistletoe.

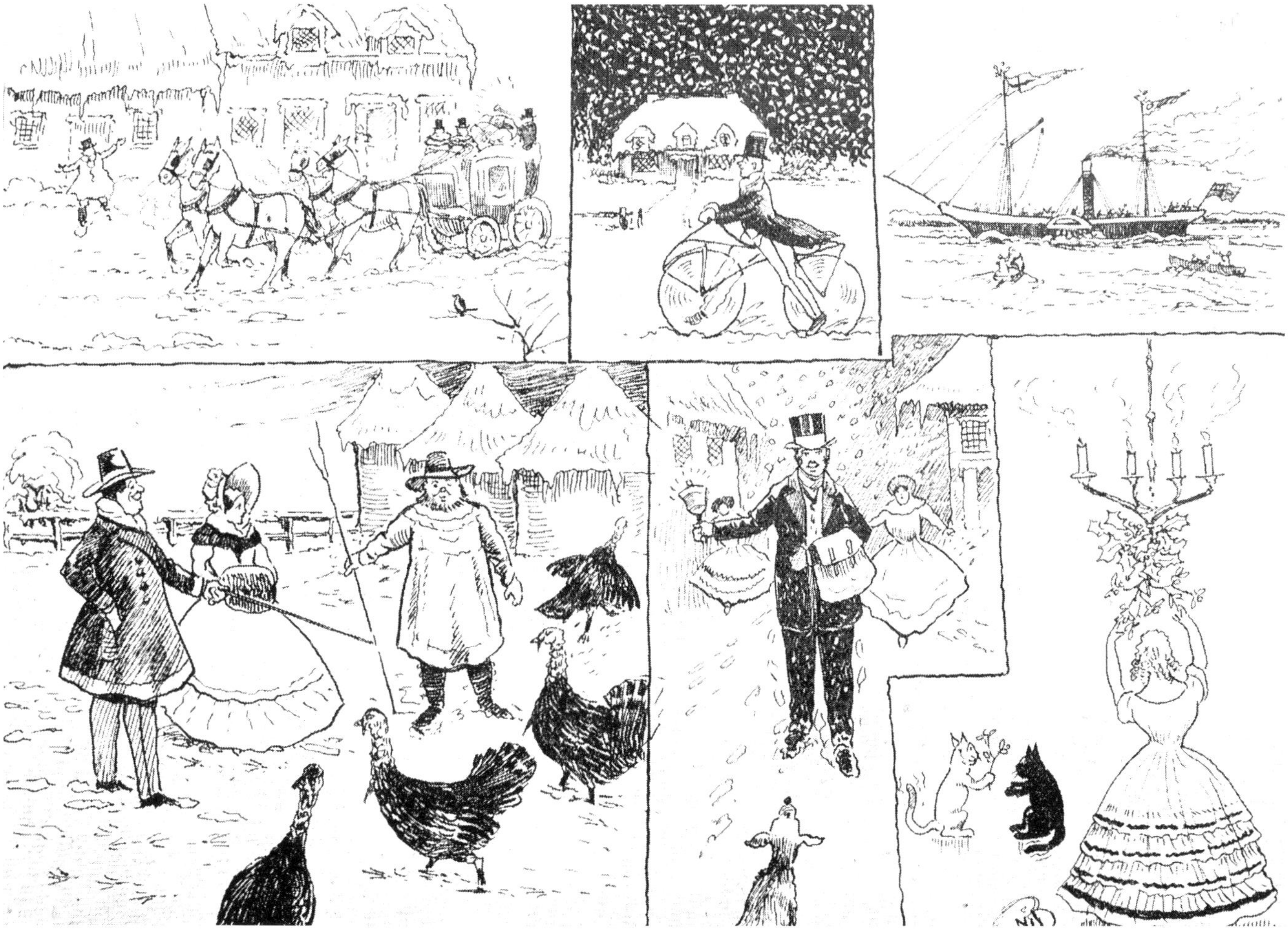

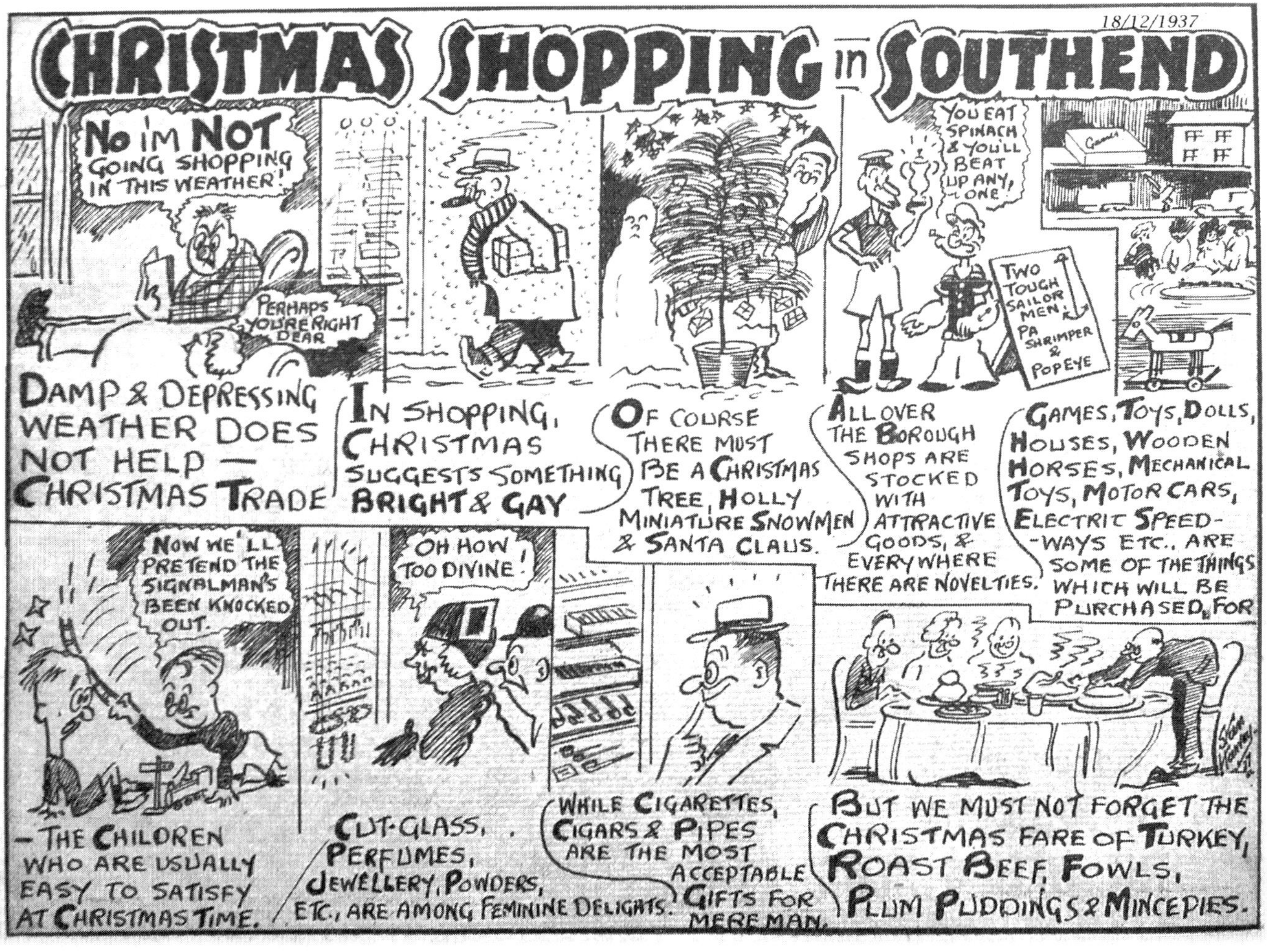
18/12/1937
CHRISTMAS SHOPPING in SOUTHEND
No I'M NOT GOING SHOPPING IN THIS WEATHER!
PERHAPS YOU'RE RIGHT DEAR
YOU EAT SPINACH & YOU'LL BEAT UP ANY ONE!
TWO TOUGH SAILOR MEN, PA SHRIMPER & POPEYE
DAMP & DEPRESSING WEATHER DOES NOT HELP — CHRISTMAS TRADE
IN SHOPPING, CHRISTMAS SUGGESTS SOMETHING BRIGHT & GAY
OF COURSE THERE MUST BE A CHRISTMAS TREE, HOLLY MINIATURE SNOWMEN & SANTA CLAUS.
ALL OVER THE BOROUGH SHOPS ARE STOCKED WITH ATTRACTIVE GOODS, & EVERYWHERE THERE ARE NOVELTIES.
GAMES, TOYS, DOLLS, HOUSES, WOODEN HORSES, MECHANICAL TOYS, MOTOR CARS, ELECTRIC SPEED- -WAYS ETC., ARE SOME OF THE THINGS WHICH WILL BE PURCHASED, FOR
NOW WE'LL PRETEND THE SIGNALMAN'S BEEN KNOCKED OUT.
OH HOW TOO DIVINE!
— THE CHILDREN WHO ARE USUALLY EASY TO SATISFY AT CHRISTMAS TIME.
CUT-GLASS, PERFUMES, JEWELLERY, POWDERS, ETC., ARE AMONG FEMININE DELIGHTS.
WHILE CIGARETTES, CIGARS & PIPES ARE THE MOST ACCEPTABLE GIFTS FOR MERE MAN.
BUT WE MUST NOT FORGET THE CHRISTMAS FARE OF TURKEY, ROAST BEEF, FOWLS, PLUM PUDDINGS & MINCEPIES.

1938

1938

1938 saw the completion of a pilot tunnel under the River Thames between Purfleet and Dartford. Yet it took another 25 years for the first road tunnel to open. Also that year, the highest ever certified speed for a steam locomotive was recorded when the *Mallard* reached a speed of 126 mph. In June the Women's Voluntary Service (WVS) was founded to assist in Civil Defence matters and in July gas masks began to be issued to the civilian population.

In April the *Beano* comic went on sale for the first time featuring the character Lord Snooty and in September *RMS Queen Elizabeth* was launched on Clydebank, the largest ship in the world at that time.

On 30th September, the Prime Minister, Neville Chamberlain, returned to the UK from Munich, Germany and later in Downing Street he gave his famous 'Peace For Our Time' speech. Curiously on 4th November 1938, at a Conservative party meeting in Epping (Essex), future Prime Minister Winston Churchill narrowly survived an attempt by fellow members to remove him from Parliament.

Fred Naughten looked back at New Year resolutions in Southend and District as imagined during the past 800 years with the following caption:-

New Year resolutions in days gone past.

Resolutions. It appears most of them have since come true!

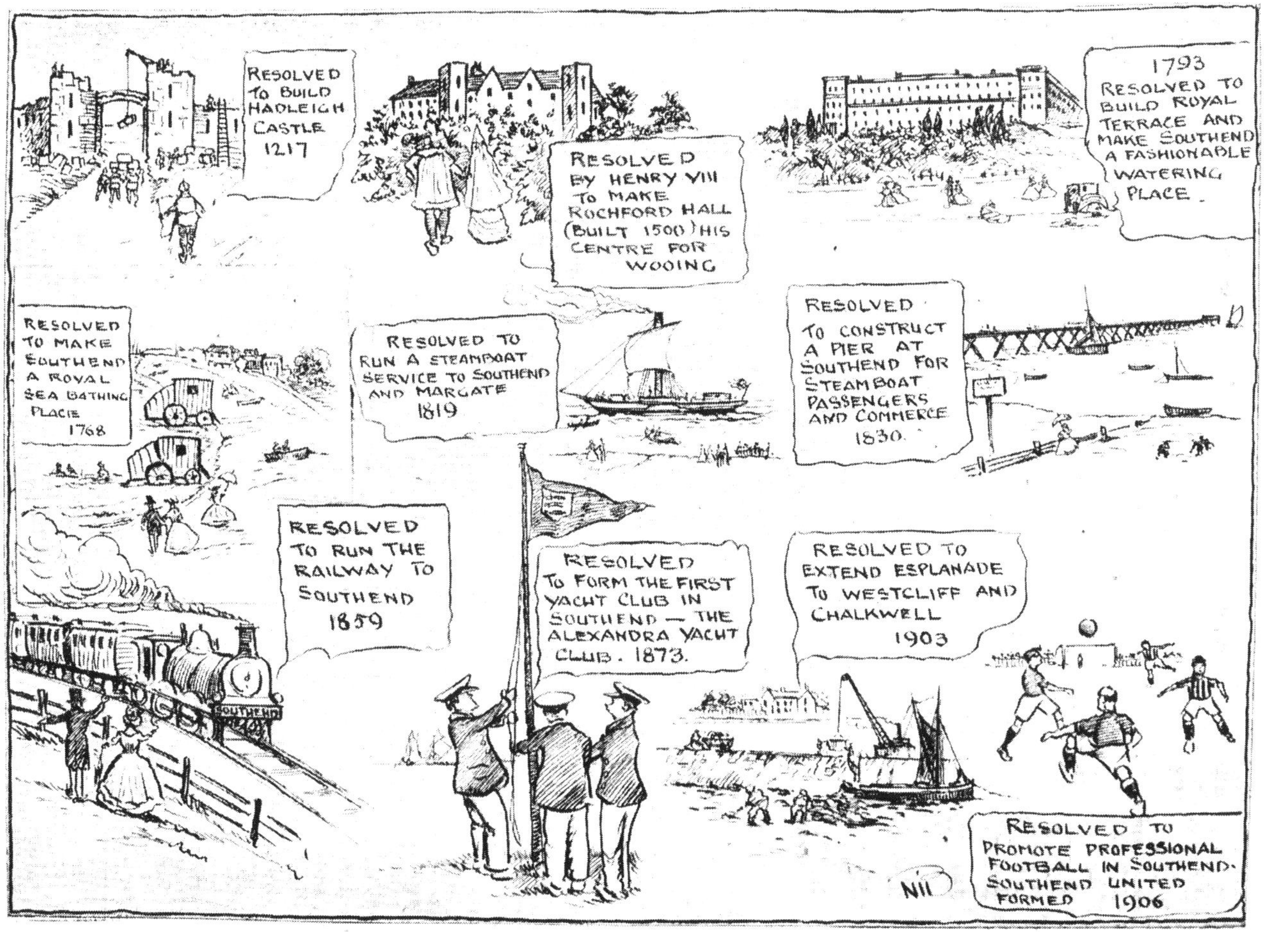
RESOLVED TO BUILD HADLEIGH CASTLE 1217
RESOLVED BY HENRY VIII TO MAKE ROCHFORD HALL (BUILT 1500) HIS CENTRE FOR WOOING
1793 RESOLVED TO BUILD ROYAL TERRACE AND MAKE SOUTHEND A FASHIONABLE WATERING PLACE.
RESOLVED TO MAKE SOUTHEND A ROYAL SEA BATHING PLACE 1768
RESOLVED TO RUN A STEAMBOAT SERVICE TO SOUTHEND AND MARGATE 1819
RESOLVED TO CONSTRUCT A PIER AT SOUTHEND FOR STEAMBOAT PASSENGERS AND COMMERCE 1830.
RESOLVED TO RUN THE RAILWAY TO SOUTHEND 1859
SOUTHEND
RESOLVED TO FORM THE FIRST YACHT CLUB IN SOUTHEND — THE ALEXANDRA YACHT CLUB. 1873.
RESOLVED TO EXTEND ESPLANADE TO WESTCLIFF AND CHALKWELL 1903
RESOLVED TO PROMOTE PROFESSIONAL FOOTBALL IN SOUTHEND. SOUTHEND UNITED FORMED 1906

The Early Nore Lightship

Fred Naughten looked to the sea for his second cartoon of the year.

The caption read:-

The first Nore lightship was placed in position in 1751 and was an old wooden vessel.

The Nore is a sandbank at the mouth of the Thames Estuary that defines the limit of the Thames and the beginning of the North Sea. It follows roughly a line between Shoeburyness, in Essex and the Isle of Sheppey, in Kent.

The Nore is also a major anchorage point for shipping waiting to enter the River Thames to discharge or load cargoes. Until 1964 it marked the seaward limit of the Port of London Authority. The lightship was major seamark. After 1915 the lightship was stood down. The spot is now marked by Sea Reach No. 1 Buoy.

The Nore was the site of a notorious mutiny in 1797. (See also page 32).

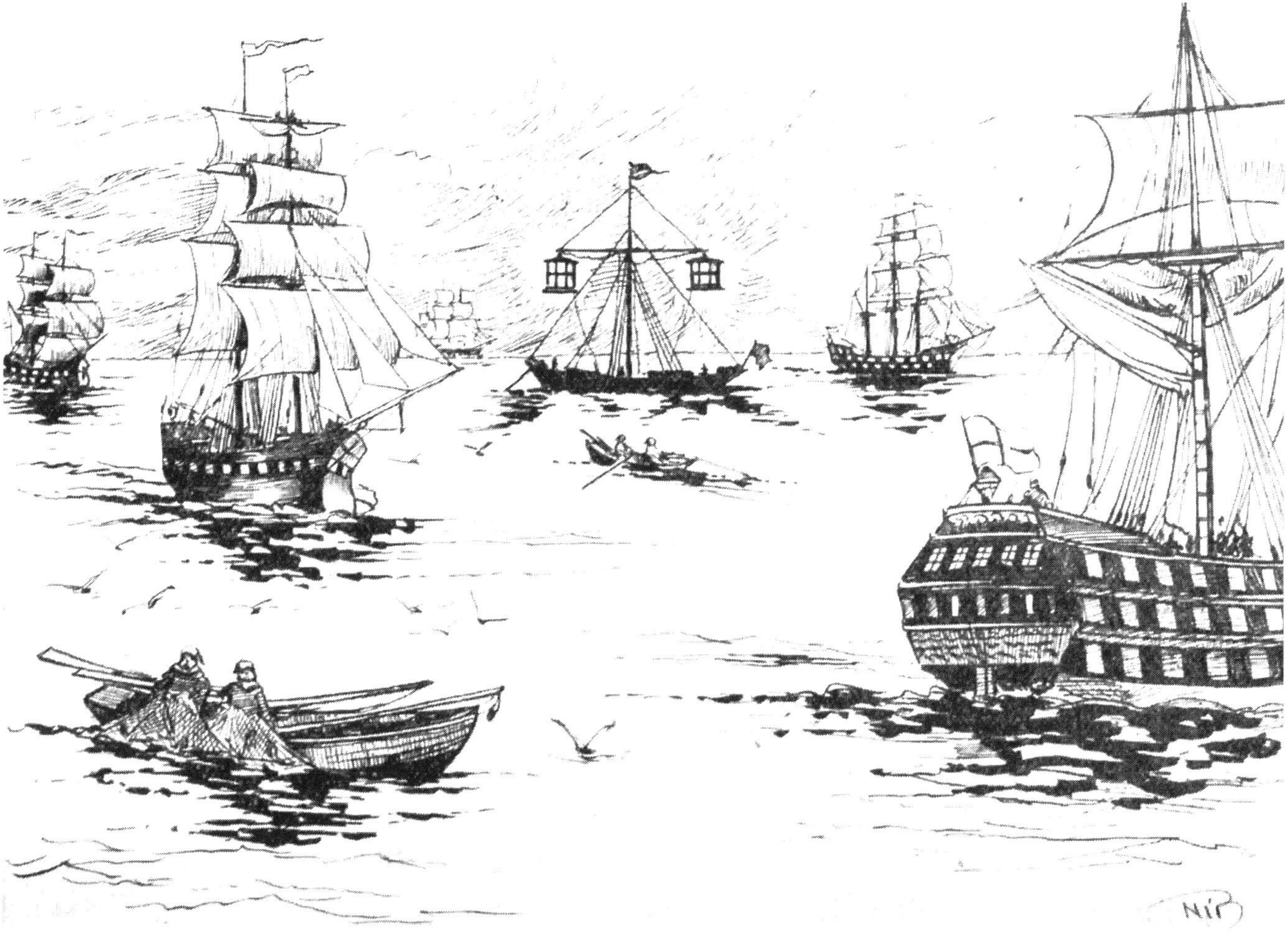

Gales to Remember

The cartoon opposite was published in February 1938 and reflected on the high winds at that time of year, Fred gave the cartoon the caption:-

Memorable Gales. In January 1881, the old Southend Pier was cut in two by the barge West Kent during a gale. In July 1895, a lighter belonging to the Thames Lighterage Company was driven on to the pier in a gale. On December 10th 1898, nearly 100 feet of pier was wrecked during a gale by the ketch Dolphin.

The pier has suffered several other mishaps. In 1907, the hay barge *Robert* damaged 60ft of decking, dislodging 12 piles and, a year later, the Thames Conservancy Hulk *Marlborough* breached the pier between the old and new pier heads. In 1921, the pier was broken in two when hit by the concrete ship *Violette* and twelve years later the pier was damaged by the 75 ton *Matilda* after it dragged anchor during a gale. As recently as June 1986, the pier was again sliced in two by a waste disposal ship the *Kingsabby*.

The pier has experienced several fires too during its existence, notably in 1959, 1976, 1995 and 2005, with the latter causing significant damage to the old pier head and surrounding structures.

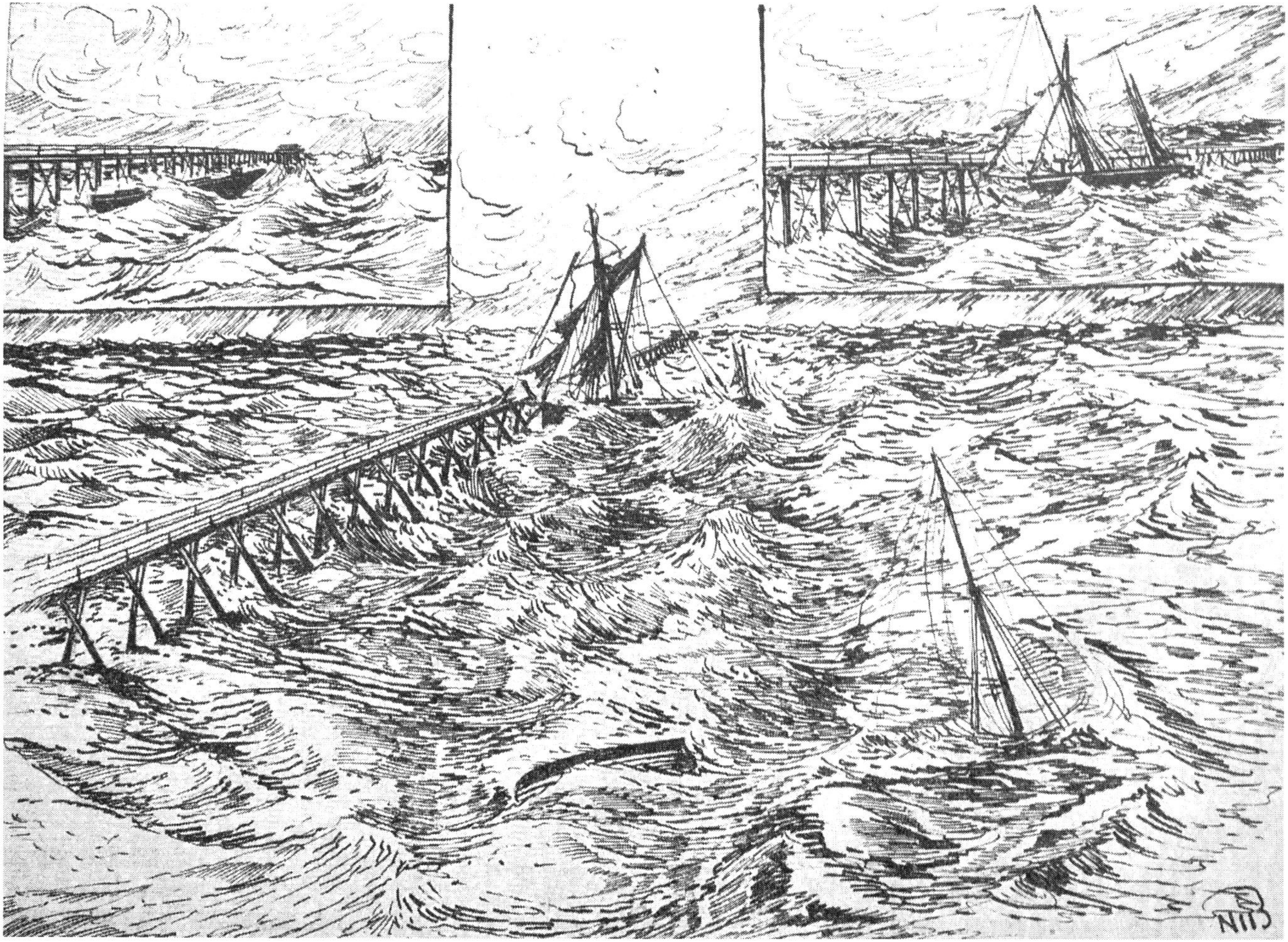

A New Bridge over the River Crouch?

In this cartoon published in February 1938 Fred Naughten turned his attention to bridges, following speculation that another bridge could be built across the river at Fambridge. He penned the following caption to accompany the image opposite:-

A bridge or bridges, if erected during the present century, will not be the first to span the River Crouch. There is evidence that a bridge existed at Hullbridge in the Fifteenth Century. There are also records of bridges at Fambridge, North and South, which joined on a small island in mid-stream. The island was subsequently washed away by the tide. Ferries have existed at Hullbridge, Fambridge and Creeksea from time immemorial.

Today the only bridge on the lower River Crouch is at Battlesbridge. There is also a summer ferry service across the Crouch from Wallasea Island to Burnham.

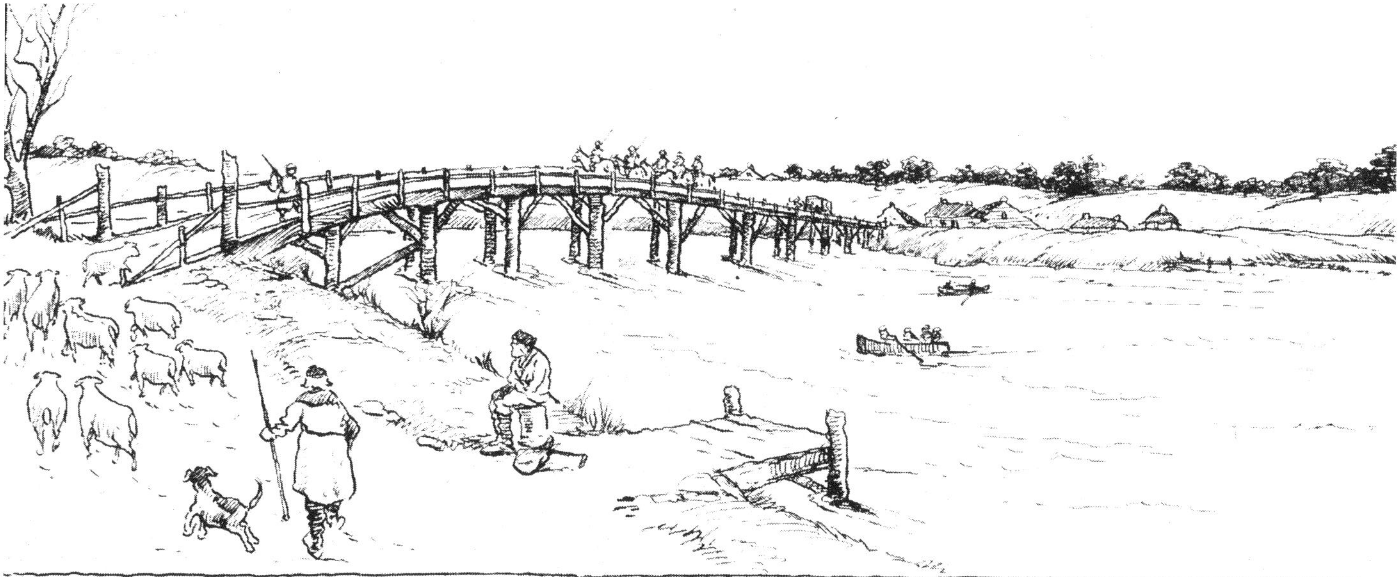

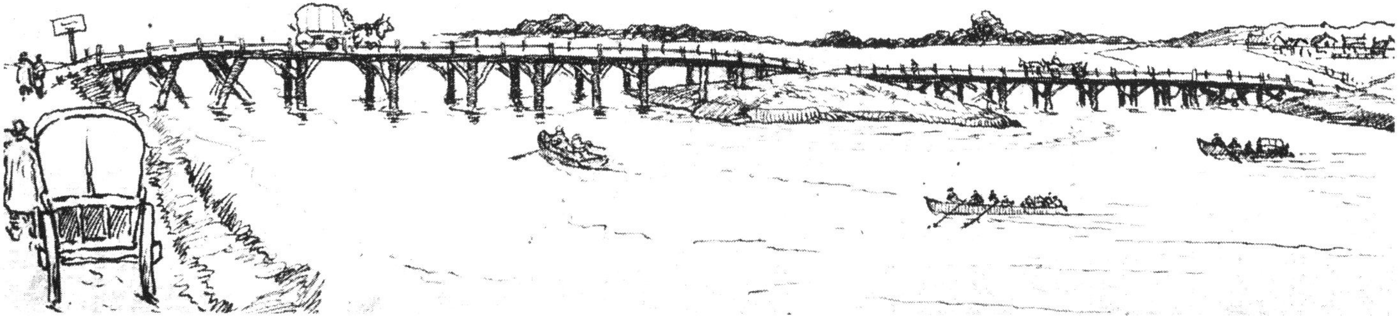

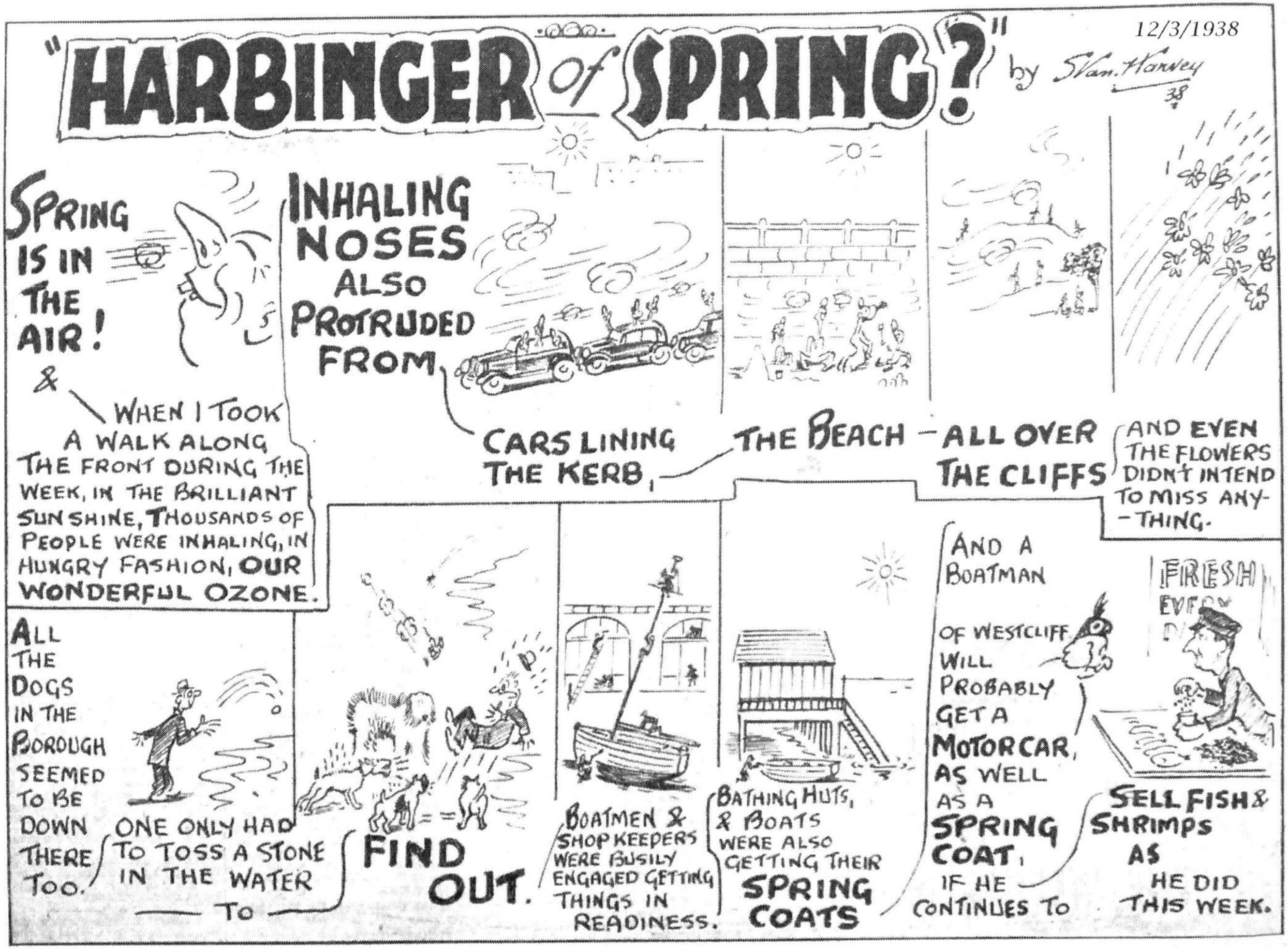
12/3/1938
"HARBINGER of SPRING?"
by Stan. Harvey 38
SPRING IS IN THE AIR!
& WHEN I TOOK A WALK ALONG THE FRONT DURING THE WEEK, IN THE BRILLIANT SUN SHINE, THOUSANDS OF PEOPLE WERE INHALING, IN HUNGRY FASHION, OUR WONDERFUL OZONE.
INHALING NOSES ALSO PROTRUDED FROM
CARS LINING THE KERB,
THE BEACH
ALL OVER THE CLIFFS
AND EVEN THE FLOWERS DIDN'T INTEND TO MISS ANY-THING.
ALL THE DOGS IN THE BOROUGH SEEMED TO BE DOWN THERE TOO.
ONE ONLY HAD TO TOSS A STONE IN THE WATER
TO
FIND OUT.
BOATMEN & SHOP KEEPERS WERE BUSILY ENGAGED GETTING THINGS IN READINESS.
BATHING HUTS, & BOATS WERE ALSO GETTING THEIR SPRING COATS
AND A BOATMAN OF WESTCLIFF WILL PROBABLY GET A MOTOR CAR, AS WELL AS A SPRING COAT,
IF HE CONTINUES TO
SELL FISH & SHRIMPS AS HE DID THIS WEEK.
FRESH

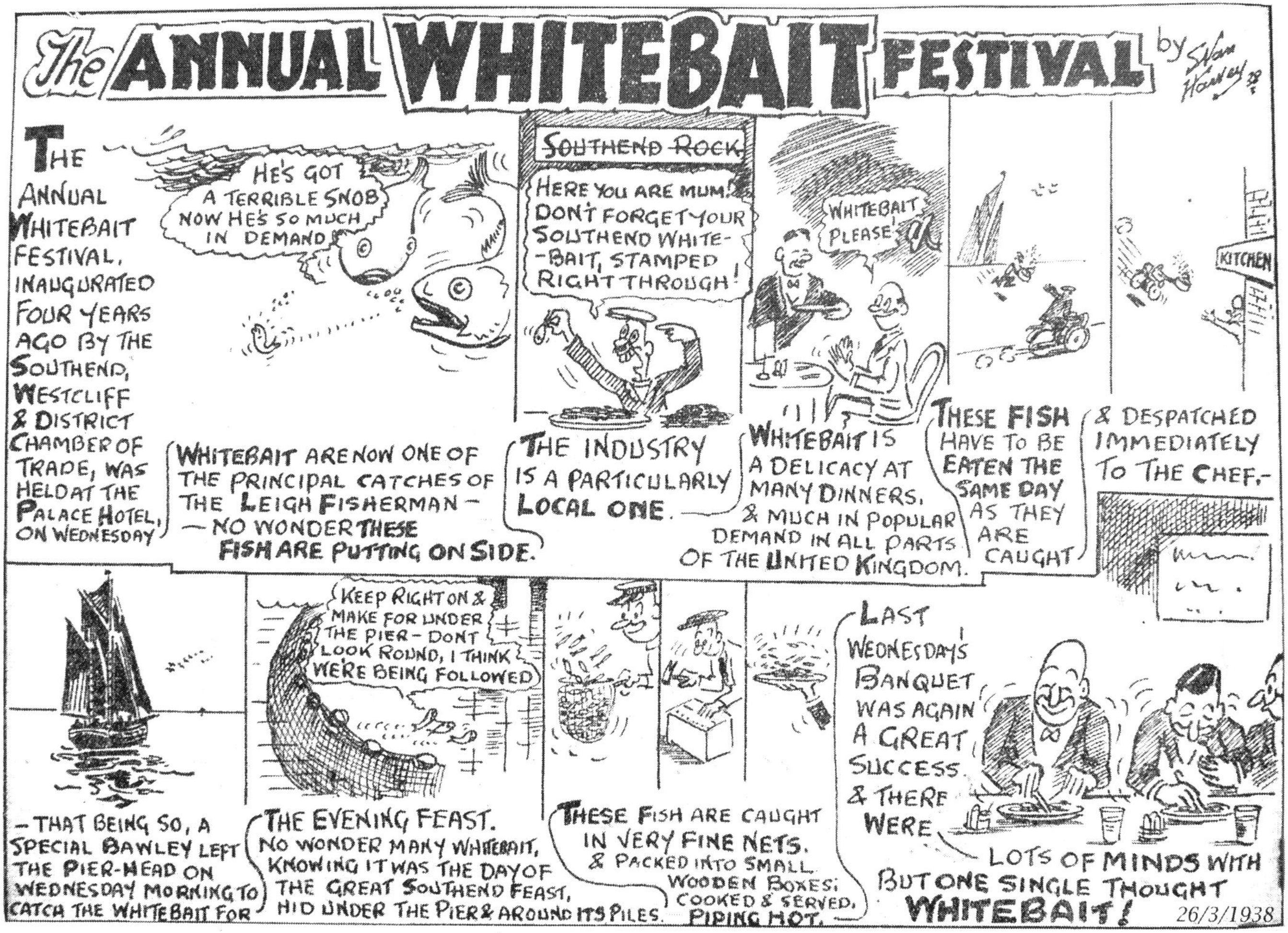

The Annual WHITEBAIT Festival
by Stan Hawley 38
The Annual Whitebait Festival, inaugurated four years ago by the Southend, Westcliff & District Chamber of Trade, was held at the Palace Hotel, on Wednesday
He's got a terrible snob now he's so much in demand
Whitebait are now one of the principal catches of the Leigh Fisherman — no wonder these fish are putting on side.
Southend Rock
Here you are mum! Don't forget your Southend white-bait, stamped right through!
The industry is a particularly local one.
Whitebait please!
Whitebait is a delicacy at many dinners, & much in popular demand in all parts of the United Kingdom.
These fish have to be eaten the same day as they are caught
Kitchen
& despatched immediately to the chef.-
-That being so, a special Bawley left the Pier-head on Wednesday morning to catch the whitebait for
Keep right on & make for under the pier - dont look round, I think we're being followed
The evening feast. No wonder many whitebait, knowing it was the day of the great Southend feast, hid under the pier & around its piles.
These fish are caught in very fine nets. & packed into small wooden boxes; cooked & served, piping hot.
Last Wednesday's banquet was again a great success & there were — lots of minds with but one single thought Whitebait!
26/3/1938

Air Raid Precautions

In April 1938, a new war in Europe seemed a real possibility. Military bomber technology had advanced substantially since the First World War, so taking defensive measures against threat seemed appropriate.

In his characteristic way and always looking at the lighter side Fred Naughten created the image opposite with the following caption:-

Air raid precautions date back to the Neolithic Age. In many part of the country Celtic burrows have been discovered. These were not air raid shelters, but burial places.
Still, we might learn something from the Celts about air raid precautions.

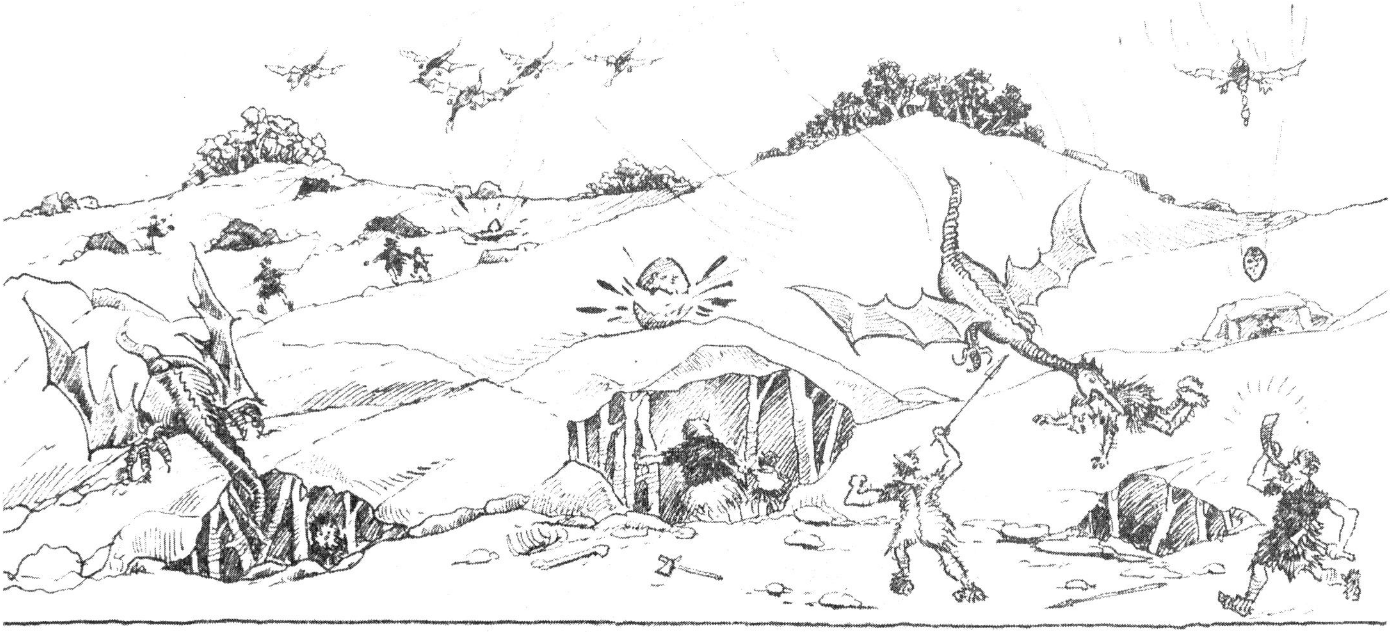

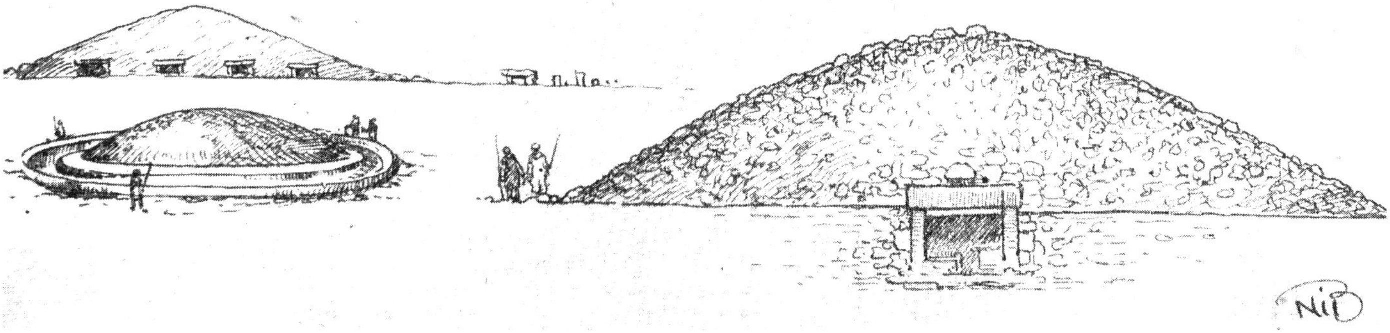

May Day

Fred Naughten captioned the cartoon opposite for May Day 1938 with the following:-

In Medieval and Tudor England, May Day was a great public holiday and may-poles were erected in every town and village. When the Puritans came into power, may-poles were forbidden and cut down but came once more into favour at Restoration. The last to be erected in London was in 1661. This was of cedar and 134ft high. It was taken down in 1757 and set up in Wanstead Park.

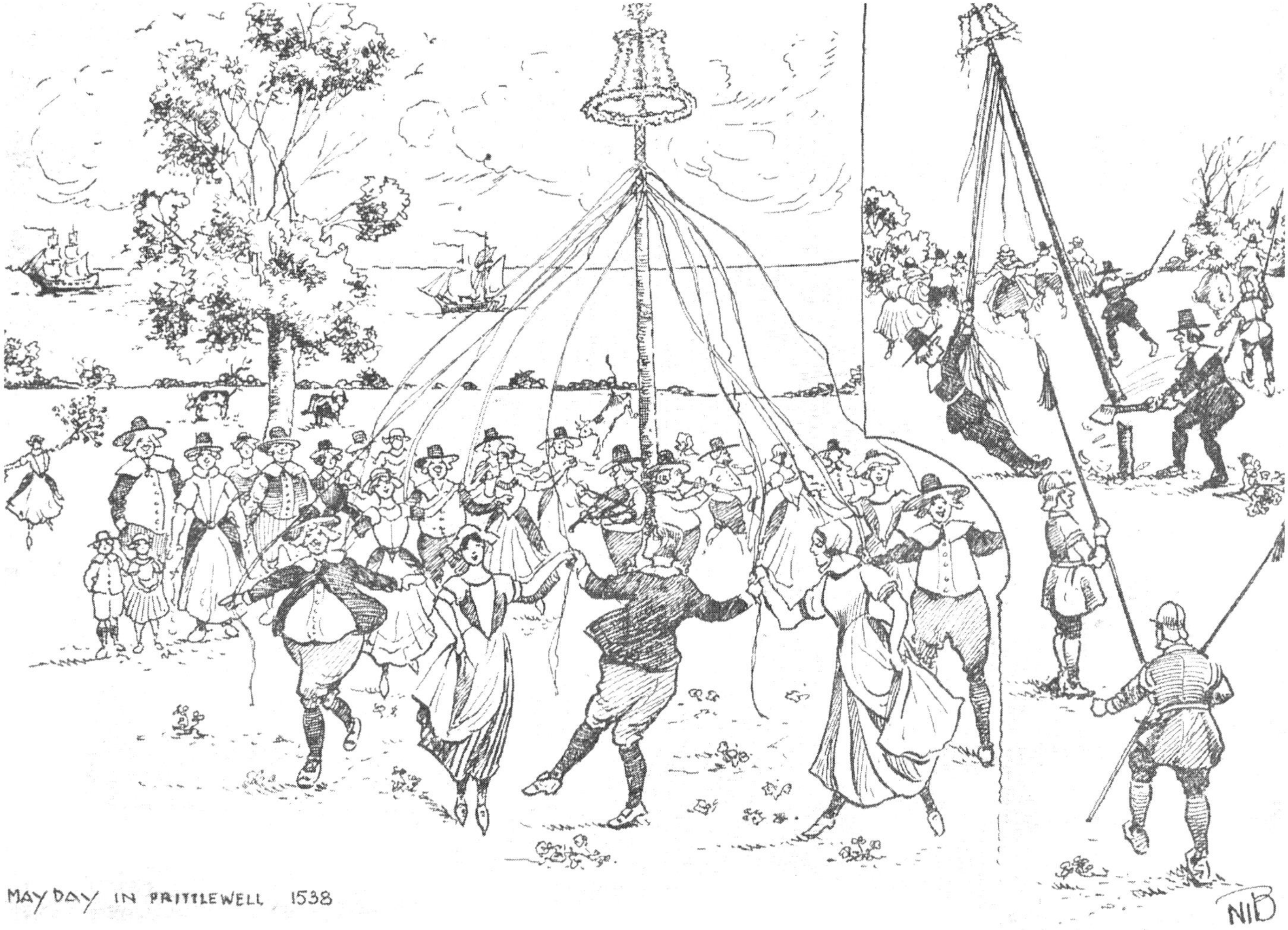
MAY DAY IN PRITTLEWELL 1538
NIB

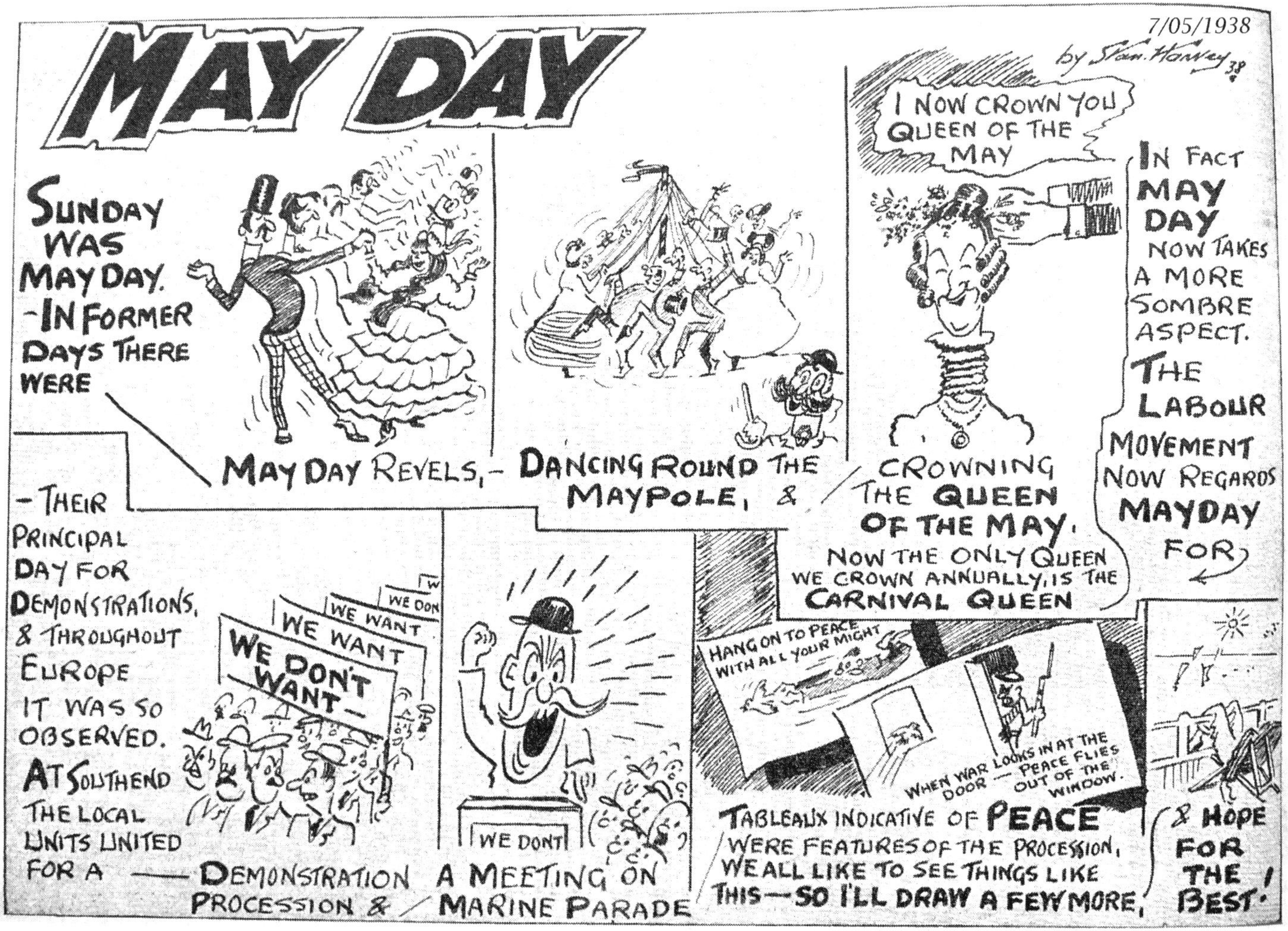
7/05/1938
MAY DAY
by Stan. Harvey 38
SUNDAY WAS MAY DAY. - IN FORMER DAYS THERE WERE
MAY DAY REVELS, - DANCING ROUND THE MAYPOLE, &
I NOW CROWN YOU QUEEN OF THE MAY
CROWNING THE QUEEN OF THE MAY.
NOW THE ONLY QUEEN WE CROWN ANNUALLY, IS THE CARNIVAL QUEEN
IN FACT MAY DAY NOW TAKES A MORE SOMBRE ASPECT. THE LABOUR MOVEMENT NOW REGARDS MAYDAY FOR
- THEIR PRINCIPAL DAY FOR DEMONSTRATIONS, & THROUGHOUT EUROPE IT WAS SO OBSERVED. AT SOUTHEND THE LOCAL UNITS UNITED FOR A
WE WANT
WE WANT
WE DON'T WANT -
WE DON
DEMONSTRATION PROCESSION &
WE DONT
A MEETING ON MARINE PARADE
HANG ON TO PEACE WITH ALL YOUR MIGHT
WHEN WAR LOOKS IN AT THE DOOR - PEACE FLIES OUT OF THE WINDOW.
TABLEAUX INDICATIVE OF PEACE WERE FEATURES OF THE PROCESSION, WE ALL LIKE TO SEE THINGS LIKE THIS - SO I'LL DRAW A FEW MORE,
& HOPE FOR THE BEST!

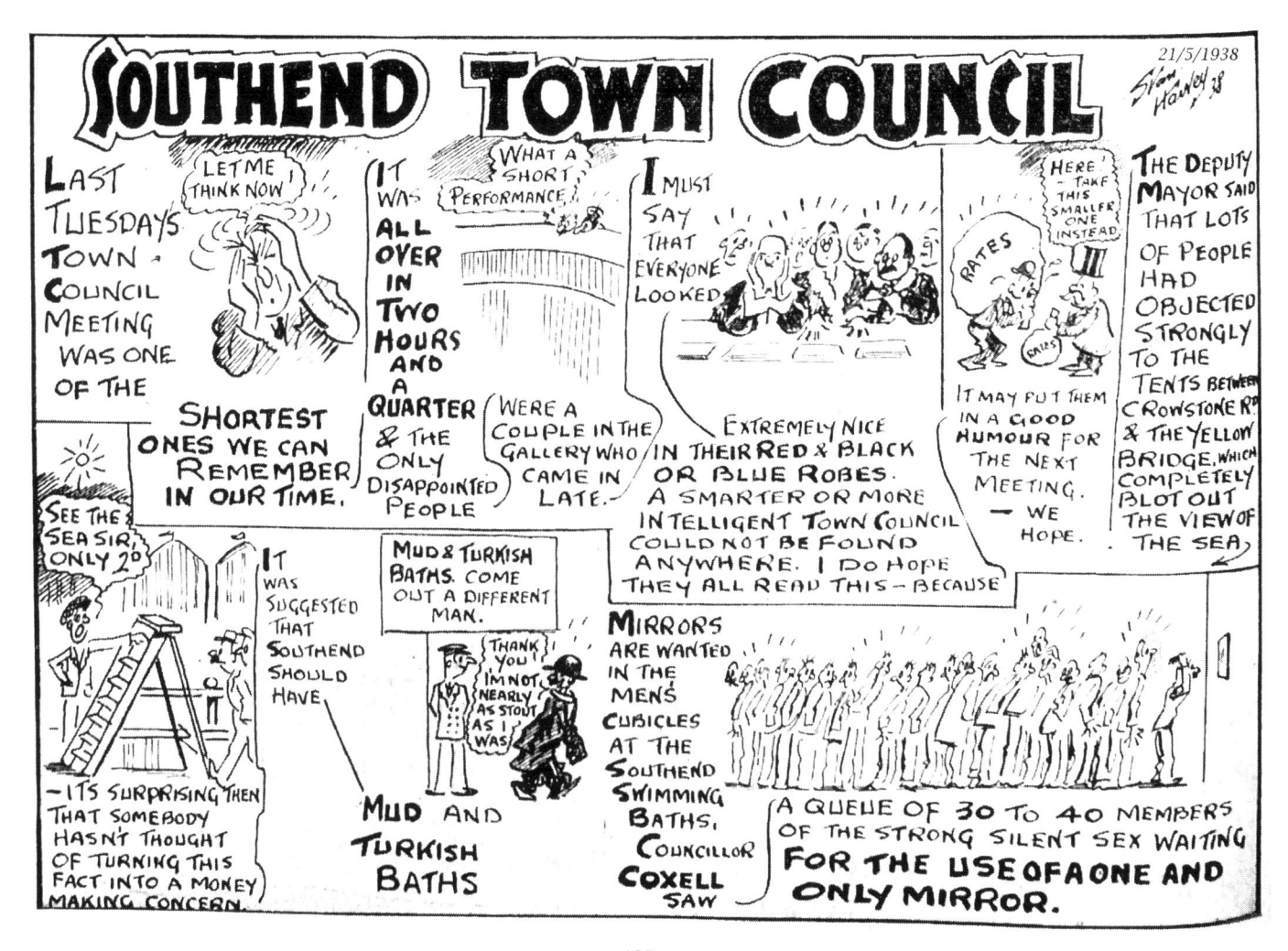

SOUTHEND TOWN COUNCIL

21/5/1938 — Stan Harvey '38

Last Tuesday's Town Council Meeting was one of the shortest ones we can remember in our time.

"Let me think now"

It was all over in two hours and a quarter & the only disappointed people

"What a short performance"

were a couple in the gallery who came in late.

I must say that everyone looked extremely nice in their red & black or blue robes. A smarter or more intelligent Town Council could not be found anywhere. I do hope they all read this — because

"Here — take this smaller one instead" (RATES)

It may put them in a good humour for the next meeting. — We hope.

The Deputy Mayor said that lots of people had objected strongly to the tents between Crowstone Rd & the Yellow Bridge, which completely blot out the view of the sea.

"See the sea sir, only 2d"

— It's surprising then that somebody hasn't thought of turning this fact into a money making concern.

It was suggested that Southend should have

"Mud & Turkish Baths. Come out a different man."

"Thank you! I'm not nearly as stout as I was."

Mud and Turkish Baths

Mirrors are wanted in the men's cubicles at the Southend Swimming Baths. Councillor Coxell saw

a queue of 30 to 40 members of the strong silent sex waiting for the use of a one and only mirror.

Beacons

As rumours swirled around of the possibility of another war and possible invasion, Fred drew this cartoon.

Lighting beacons are not new and were used by the peasants during the great revolt of 1381 as a call to arms (by the peasants). They were also lit to warn of the enemy at the time of the Spanish Armada and again at the time of a threatened Napoleonic invasion.

Fred's caption read:-

The Thames estuary has always been a danger area when invasion threatened. When Napoleon was massing his forces to effect a landing on our coasts they had black-out rehearsals. Beacons were built ready to be lighted as a warning that the enemy fleet arrived.

In less threatening times beacons have also been lit to celebrate events such as the crowning of the monarch or a jubilee.

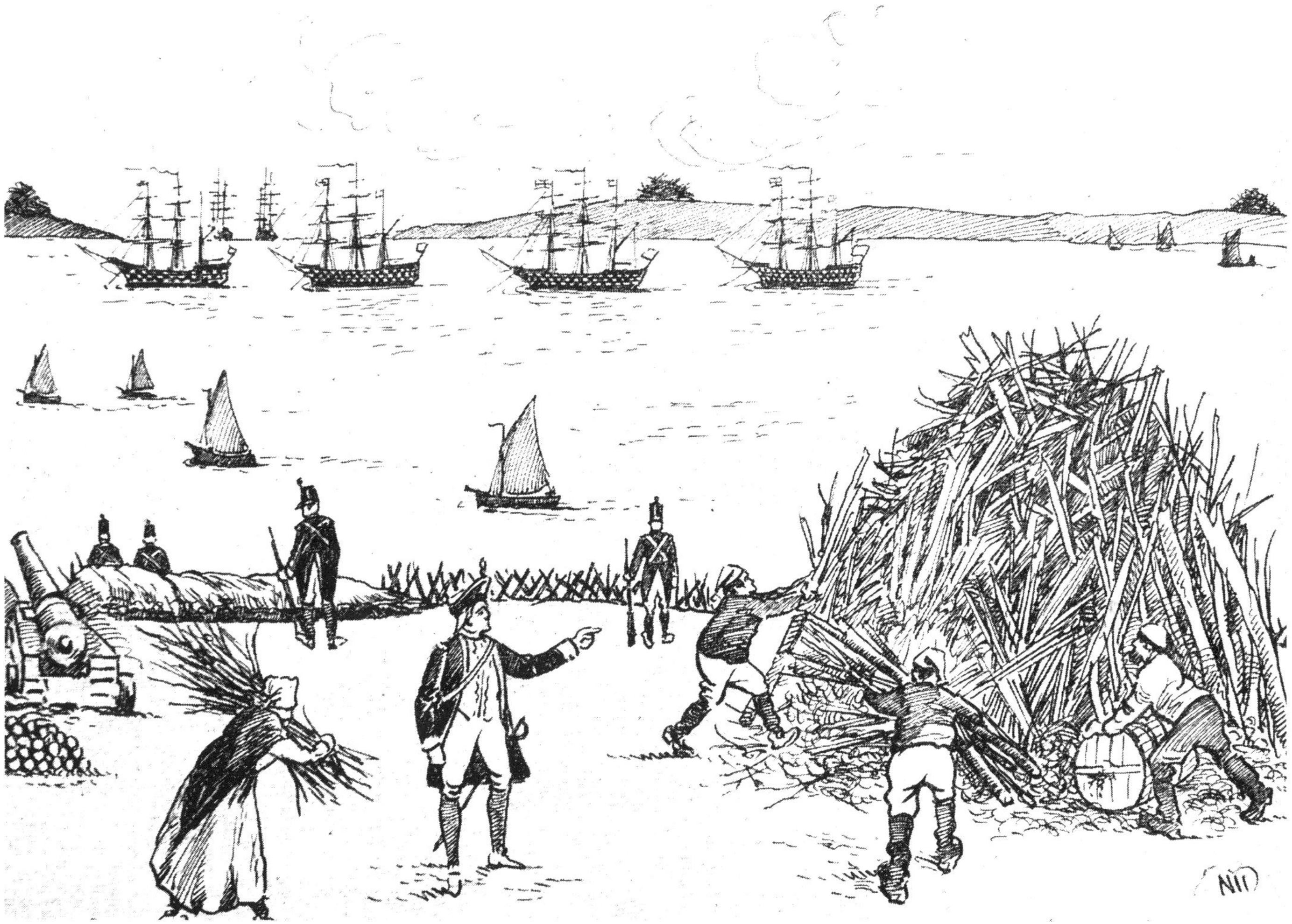
NID

Darts Down The Ages

Fred Naughten reflected on the increasing national popularity of darts, which was no longer confined to smoke filled pubs. The game was being played in what he described as 'Mayfair mansions' and even in the House of Commons. Private ownership of dart boards was booming. In 1938 there were local and national leagues, ladies' and gentlemen's teams and even international matches were planned. The cartoonist looked back at the history of darts, all explained in the cartoon opposite with the following caption:-

Darts have proved a highly popular game in Southend. The pastime was enjoyed many centuries before Southend became a borough. The early Southenders, the Danes and the Romans all played darts, but in a different form from that now adopted by the Southend Darts league.

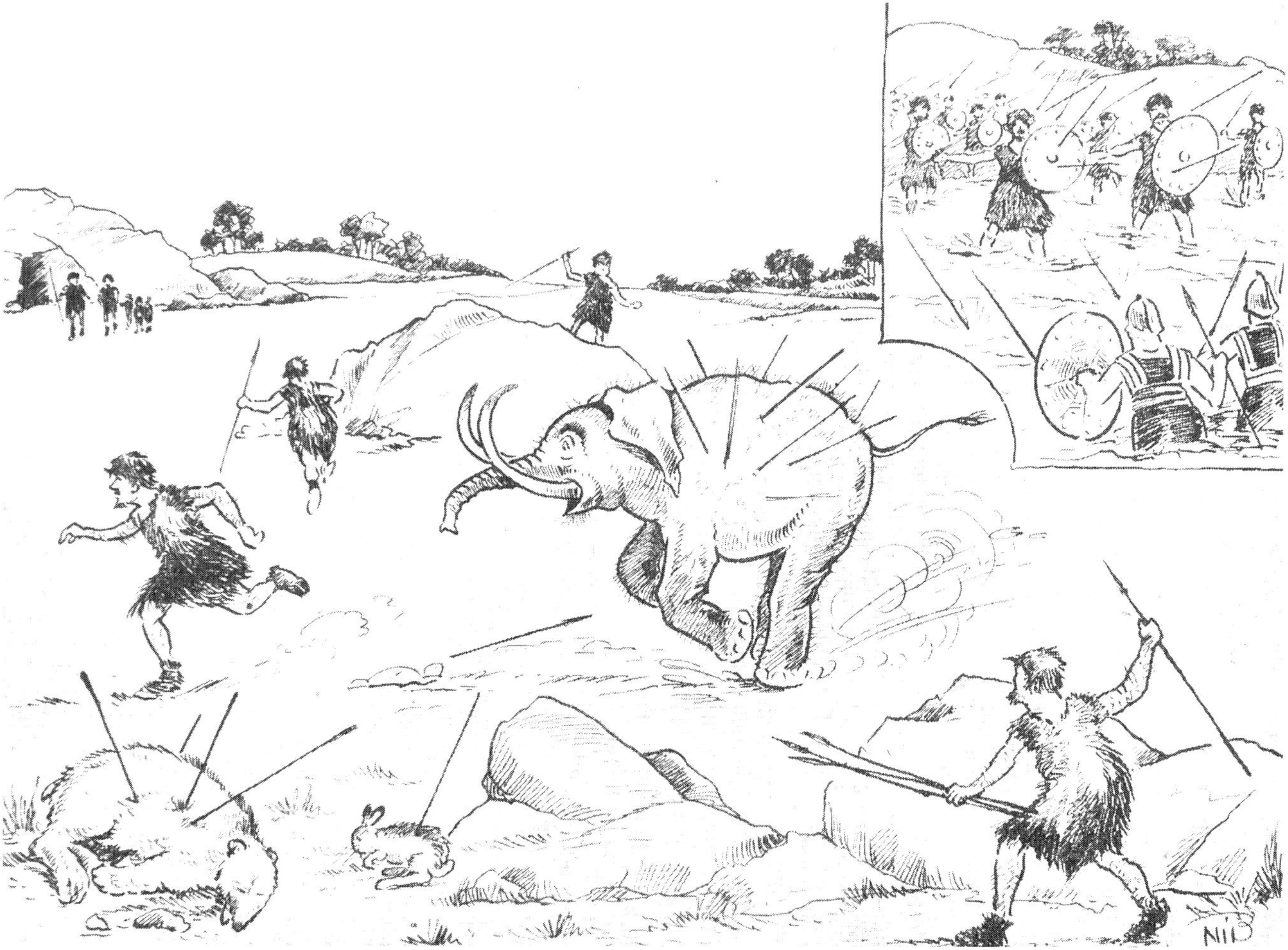

The Cricket Festival

The Visitors

For the first time in 17 years, (on 4th June 1938) at Southchurch Park in Southend, Essex played Australia. It was fortunate the match went ahead as two days earlier Southend had experienced its worst gales in many years. Much damage was caused on the seafront and seven sailing barges and two large motor vessels were driven ashore, badly damaging the Camper Road Jetty. At Southchurch Park on 3rd June, daylight revealed widespread destruction of the cricket marquees. The park had to be closed to prevent pilfering. Luckily, the storm abated by match day. Sadly, Essex lost by 97 runs. Stan Harvey's take on the match is opposite.

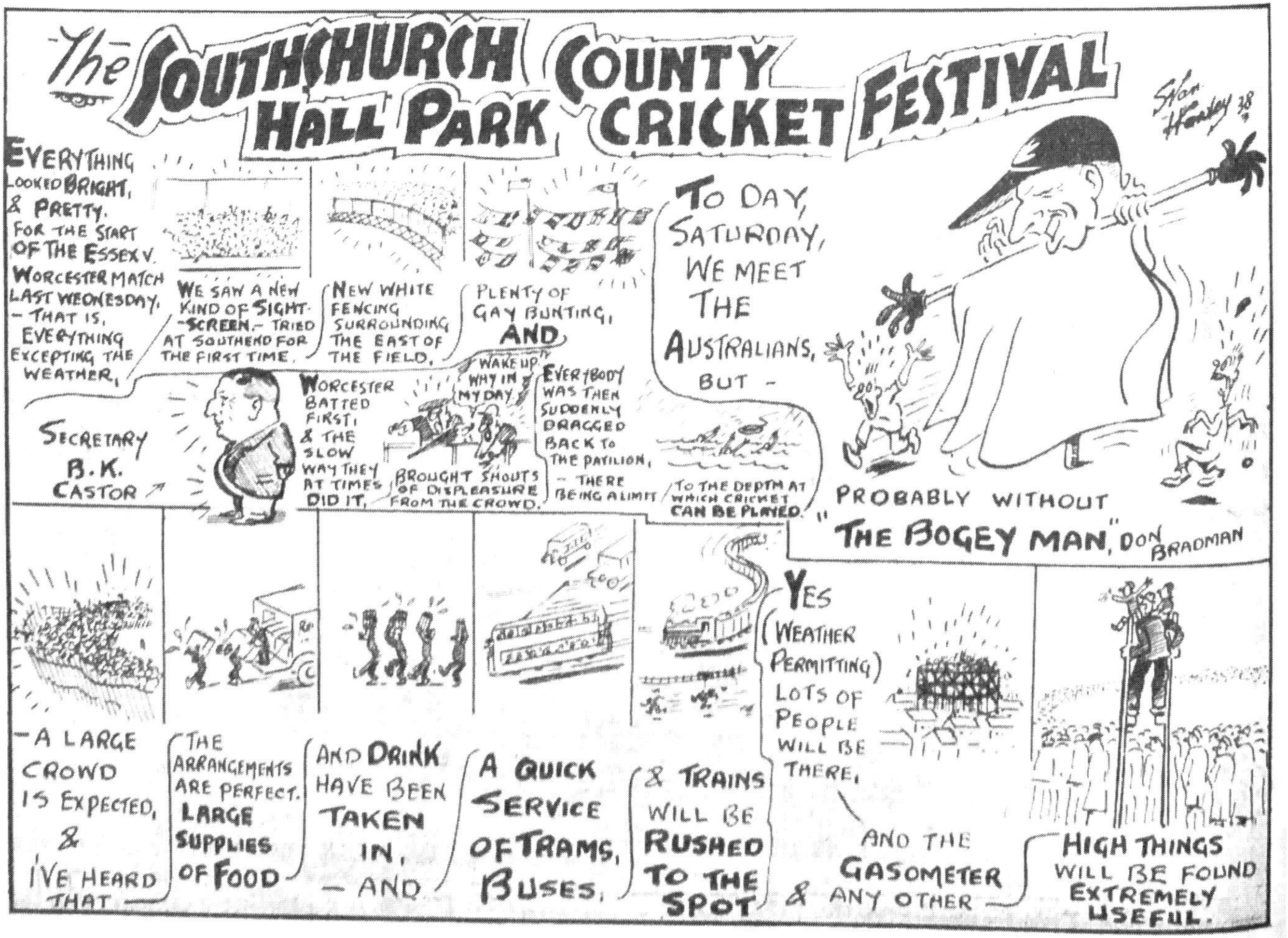
The Southchurch Hall Park County Cricket Festival
Stan Hanley 38
Everything looked bright, & pretty, for the start of the Essex v. Worcester match last Wednesday, - that is, everything excepting the weather,
We saw a new kind of sight-screen - tried at Southend for the first time.
New white fencing surrounding the east of the field,
Plenty of gay bunting, and
To day, Saturday, we meet the Australians, but -
probably without "The Bogey Man," Don Bradman
Secretary B.K. Castor
Worcester batted first, & the slow way they at times did it,
Wake up why in my day
brought shouts of displeasure from the crowd.
Everybody was then suddenly dragged back to the pavilion, - there being a limit
to the depth at which cricket can be played.
- A large crowd is expected, & I've heard that -
The arrangements are perfect. Large supplies of food
and drink have been taken in, - and
a quick service of trams, buses,
& trains will be rushed to the spot
Yes (weather permitting) lots of people will be there,
and the gasometer & any other -
High things will be found extremely useful.

Southend's New Drill Hall

Southend's new Drill Hall, in Eastwood Road, Leigh-on-Sea, was opened with great fanfare on 15th June 1938 by the Secretary of State for War, the Rt. Hon. L. Hore-Belisha MP. The hall was the home to the recently formed 193rd A.A. (Anti-Aircraft) battery of the Royal Artillery.

Stan Harvey was on hand to review the opening with one of his matchless cartoons, shown opposite.

The Drill Hall was built despite some misgivings locally. Apart from the cost many worried that in the event of war a military drill hall and anything surrounding it would become a target. At the same time the Government was insisting there would be no war.

In the summer of 2000 the hall was demolished and replaced by housing.

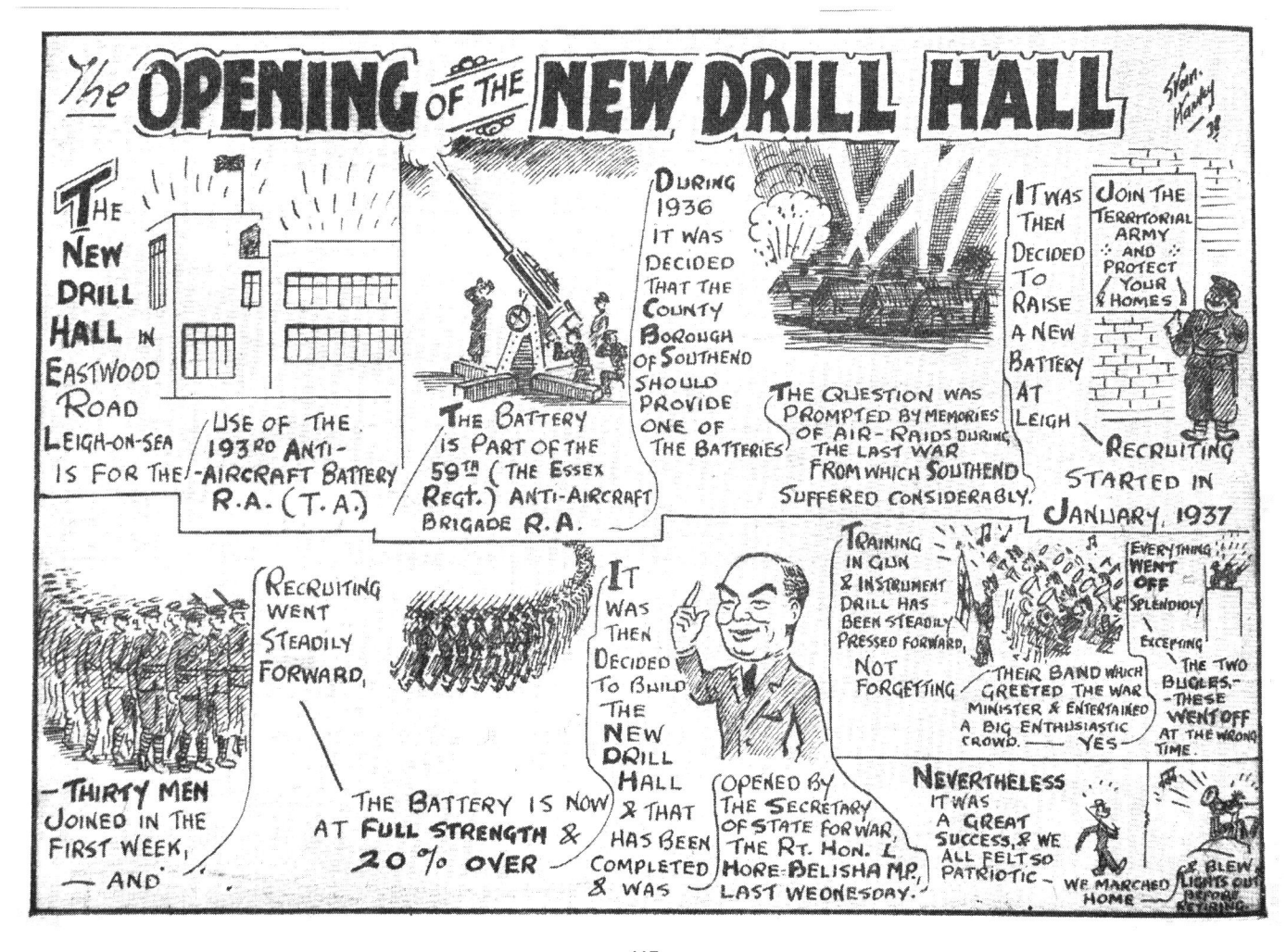

The Opening of the New Drill Hall

The New Drill Hall in Eastwood Road Leigh-on-Sea is for the use of the 193rd Anti-Aircraft Battery R.A. (T.A.)

The Battery is part of the 59th (The Essex Regt.) Anti-Aircraft Brigade R.A.

During 1936 it was decided that the County Borough of Southend should provide one of the batteries.

The question was prompted by memories of air-raids during the last war from which Southend suffered considerably.

It was then decided to raise a new battery at Leigh.

Join the Territorial Army and protect your homes

Recruiting started in January, 1937.

Recruiting went steadily forward, — thirty men joined in the first week, — and the Battery is now at **full strength & 20% over**.

It was then decided to build the new Drill Hall & that has been completed & was opened by the Secretary of State for War, the Rt. Hon. L. Hore-Belisha M.P., last Wednesday.

Training in gun & instrument drill has been steadily pressed forward, not forgetting their band which greeted the War Minister & entertained a big enthusiastic crowd. — Yes Everything went off splendidly excepting the two bugles, — these went off at the wrong time.

Nevertheless it was a great success, & we all felt so patriotic — we marched home — & blew lights out before retiring.

Under Threat

As the clouds of war grew darker Fred Naughten had the cartoon opposite published in July 1938 with the following caption:-

When Britain was threatened by invasion by Napoleon, Leigh was called on to provide 21 men and Southend 29 for defence. Owing to unwillingness to volunteer for service and training, the force became useless and was disbanded. In 1938 volunteers to serve the Leigh Anti-Aircraft battery were so numerous that the establishment was over-strength.

In the late 17th century, when Napoleon threatened invasion, Fred may have had in mind the *Essex Sea Fencibles*, a rag tag band of coastal dwellers who were encouraged to join a coastal defence force - a sort of maritime 'Dads Army'. The Fencibles never saw action but found the weapons supplied by the navy quite useful for their day job which involved much smuggling. The Fencibles were disbanded when the threatened Napoleonic invasion receded and the *Essex Sea Fencibles* have been largely forgotten ever since.

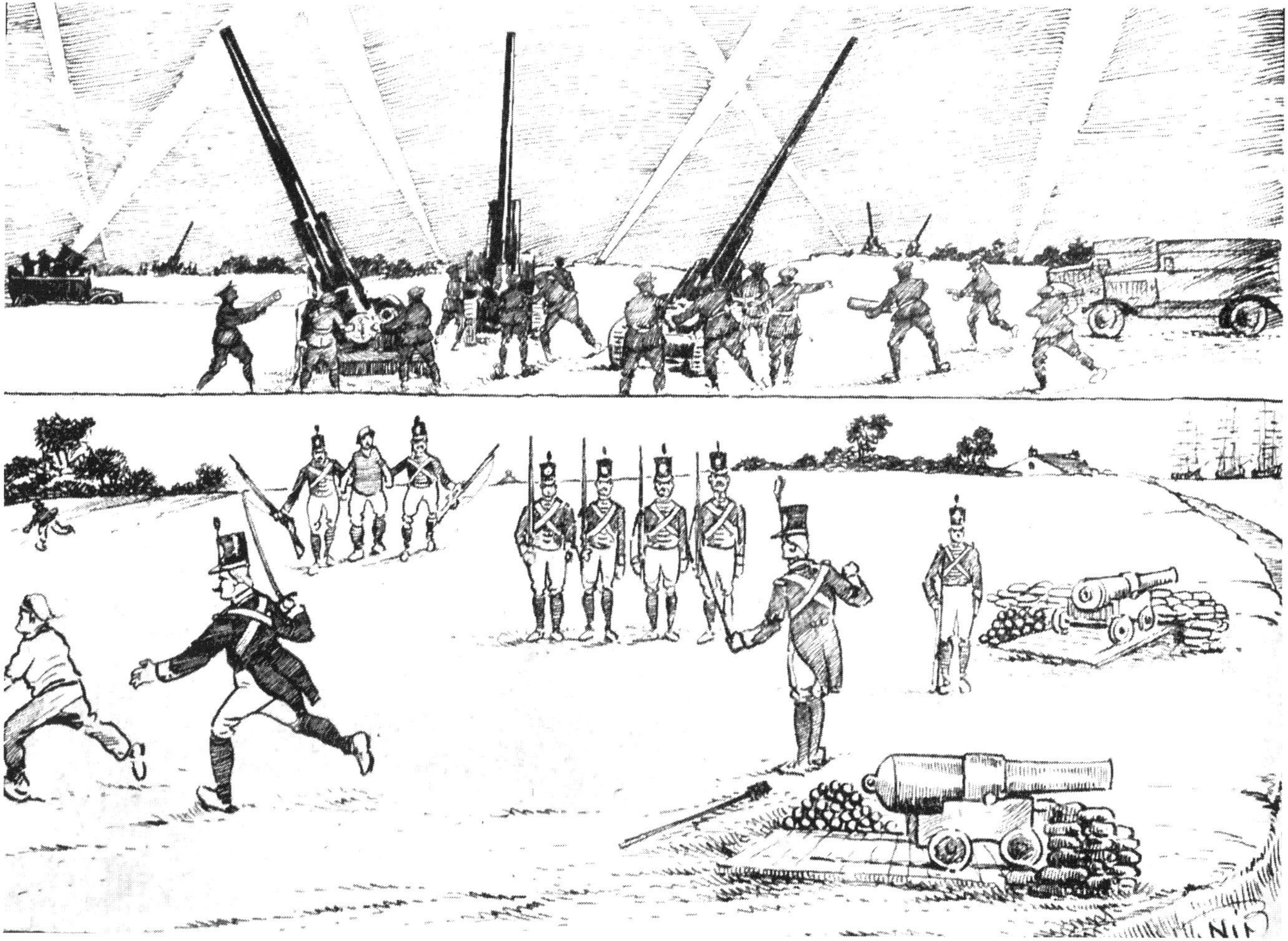

A New Town Hall?

In July 1938, Southend Council held another of its special meetings to discuss building a new town hall. The question had been talked about for years. After lengthy, and at times acrimonious, debate a motion was passed to build a new town hall, police headquarters and court on Victoria Avenue. The estimated cost was £194,216 of which Southend hoped to get 50% of the cost from the government for the police headquarters and court. However, Southend had to wait almost another thirty years to get the new civic centre, police headquarters and courts and the cost was considerably in excess of £194,216.

In a classic cartoon, Fred Naughten created the image opposite adding the caption:-

When the Romans were in occupation in Essex, they would have saved the present generation a lot of controversy and expense if they had built a Town Hall in Southend.

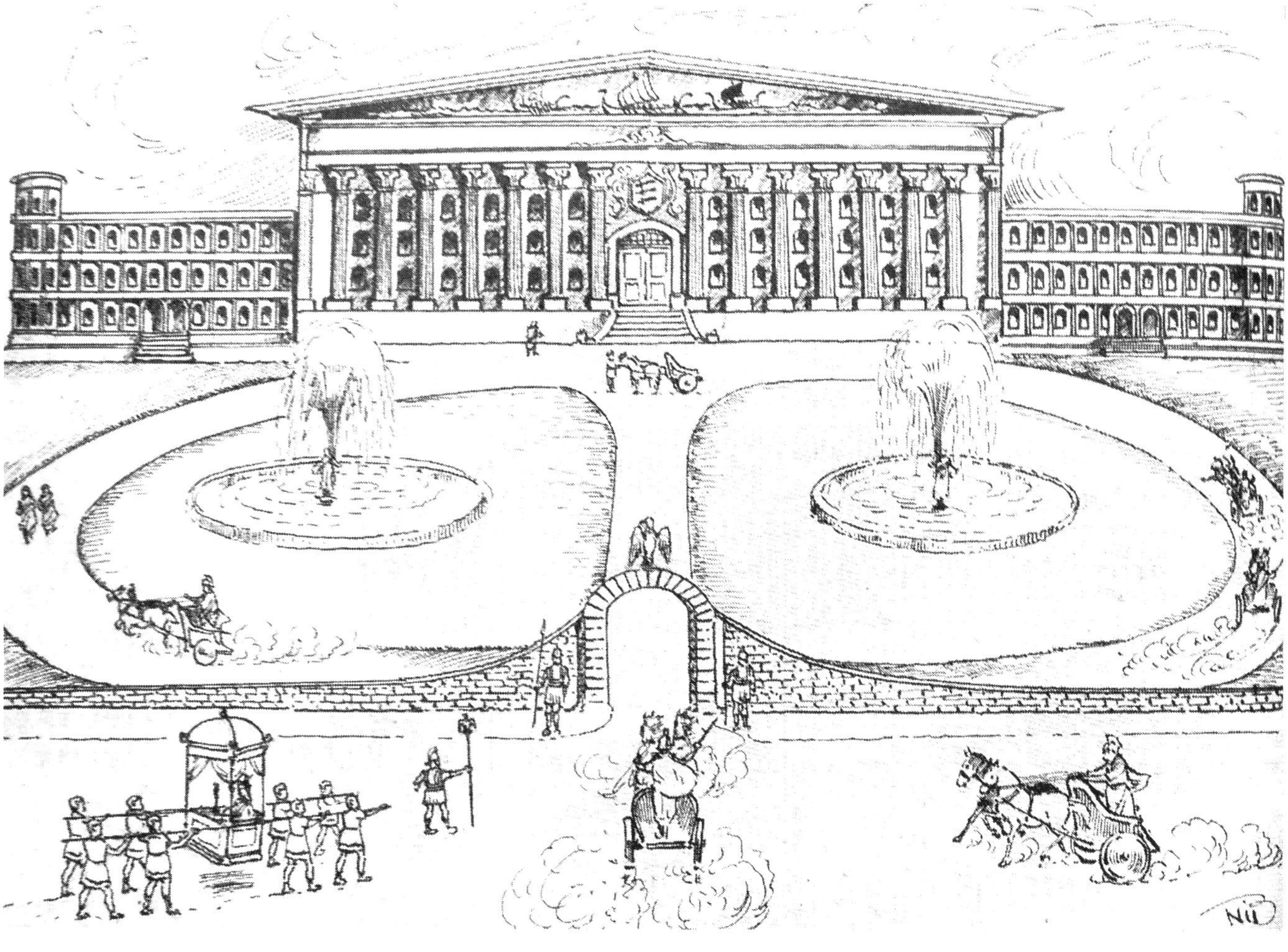

The Essex Regiment

In September 1938, Fred Naughten looked back at the history of the Essex Regiment and imagined seven stages with the following caption for the image opposite:-

The origin and evolution of the Essex Regiment Stone age – Eve of World War II.

Despite Fred's admirable efforts we can't trace the Essex Regiment back to the Stone, Roman or Tudor ages. In 1782 the army's 44th Regiment of Foot became the East Essex Regiment and the 56th became the West Essex Regiment. Ninety-nine years later these two regiments were brought together as the 1st and 2nd Battalions of the newly formed Essex Regiment.

The Essex Regiment survived in name until 1964 when the remaining 1st Battalion became part of the 3rd Battalion of the Royal Anglian Regiment.

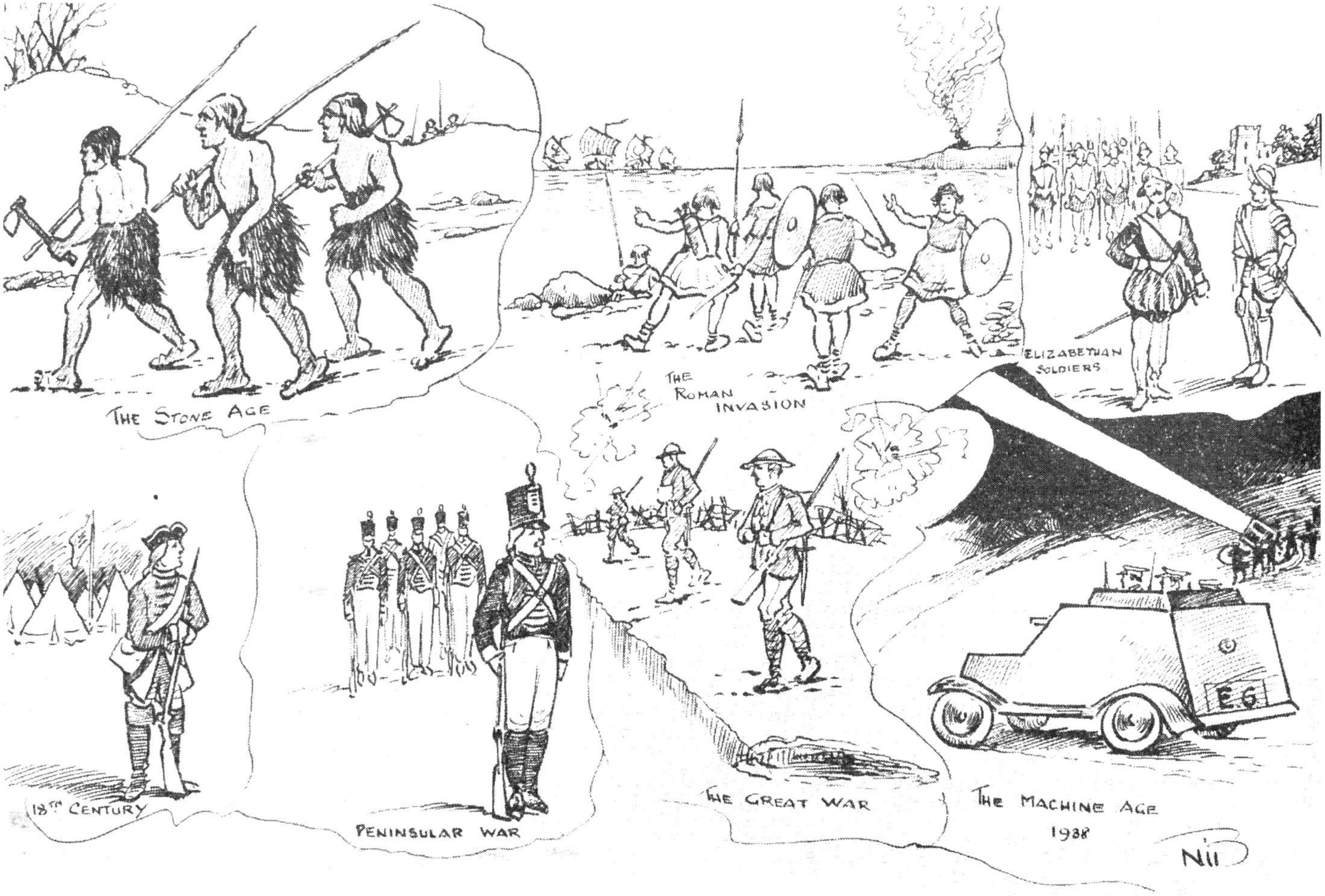
THE STONE AGE
THE ROMAN INVASION
ELIZABETHAN SOLDIERS
18TH CENTURY
PENINSULAR WAR
THE GREAT WAR
E.G
THE MACHINE AGE
1938
Nil

Where have all the salmon gone?

The autumn angling festival reminded Fred of fish and fishing in the River Thames with this cartoon that appeared with the following caption:-

A century ago, fish were so plentiful in the Thames estuary that flounders and haddock could be caught in great quantities from Bell Wharf. In the upper reaches of the Thames, as far as Maidenhead, salmon were caught up to the year 1812, when they disappeared.

The River Thames was historically well stocked with salmon and was mentioned as far back as the time of the Magna Carta in 1215. However, increasing pollution created as a result of the industrial revolution led to salmon (and most other fish) being wiped out by the 1830s. Despite huge efforts to upgrade water quality, attempts to restore sustainable salmon stocks to the Thames have been largely unsuccessful.

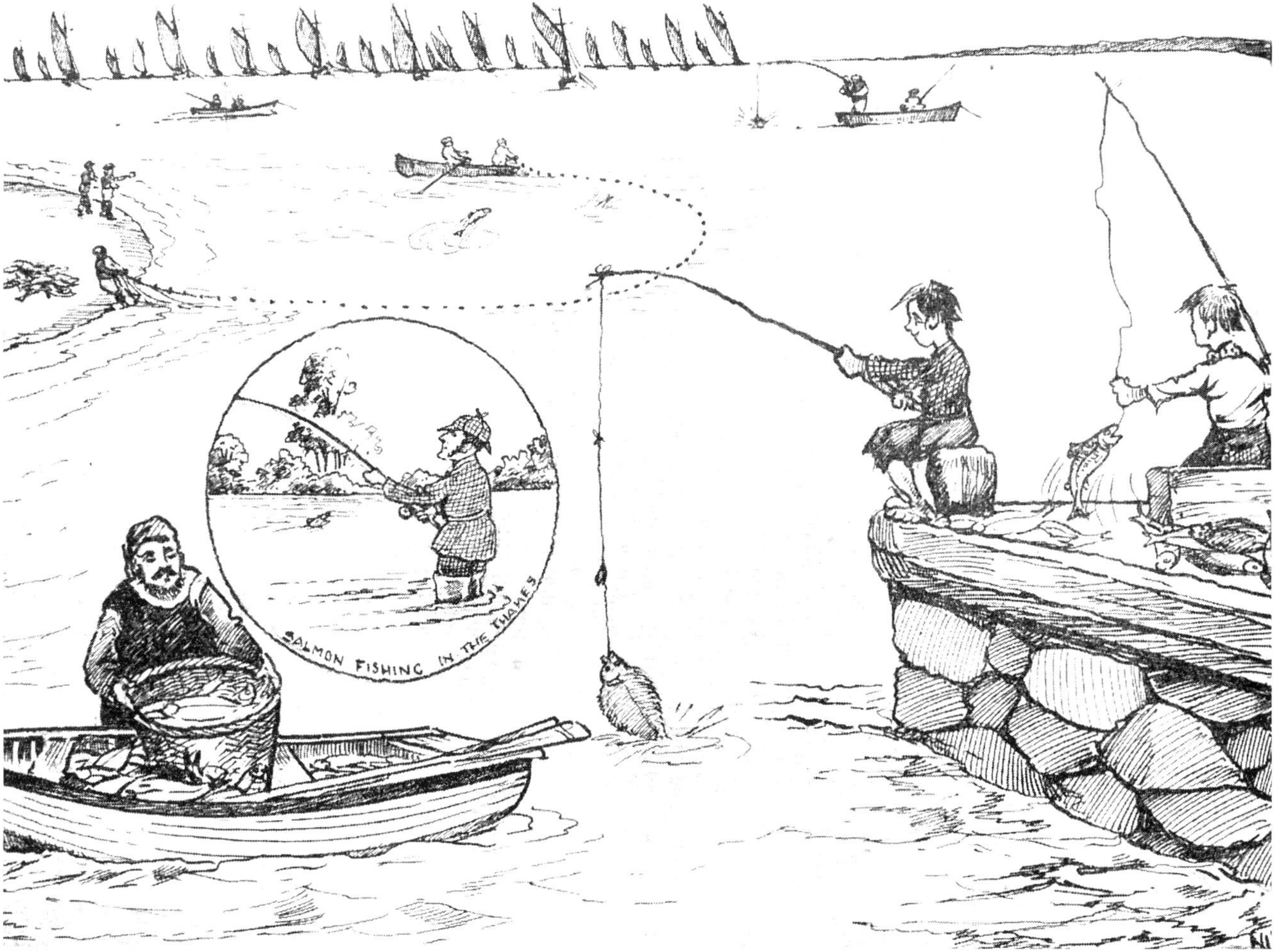
SALMON FISHING IN THE THAMES

Education. An elementary school in the Neolithic age and one in 1938.

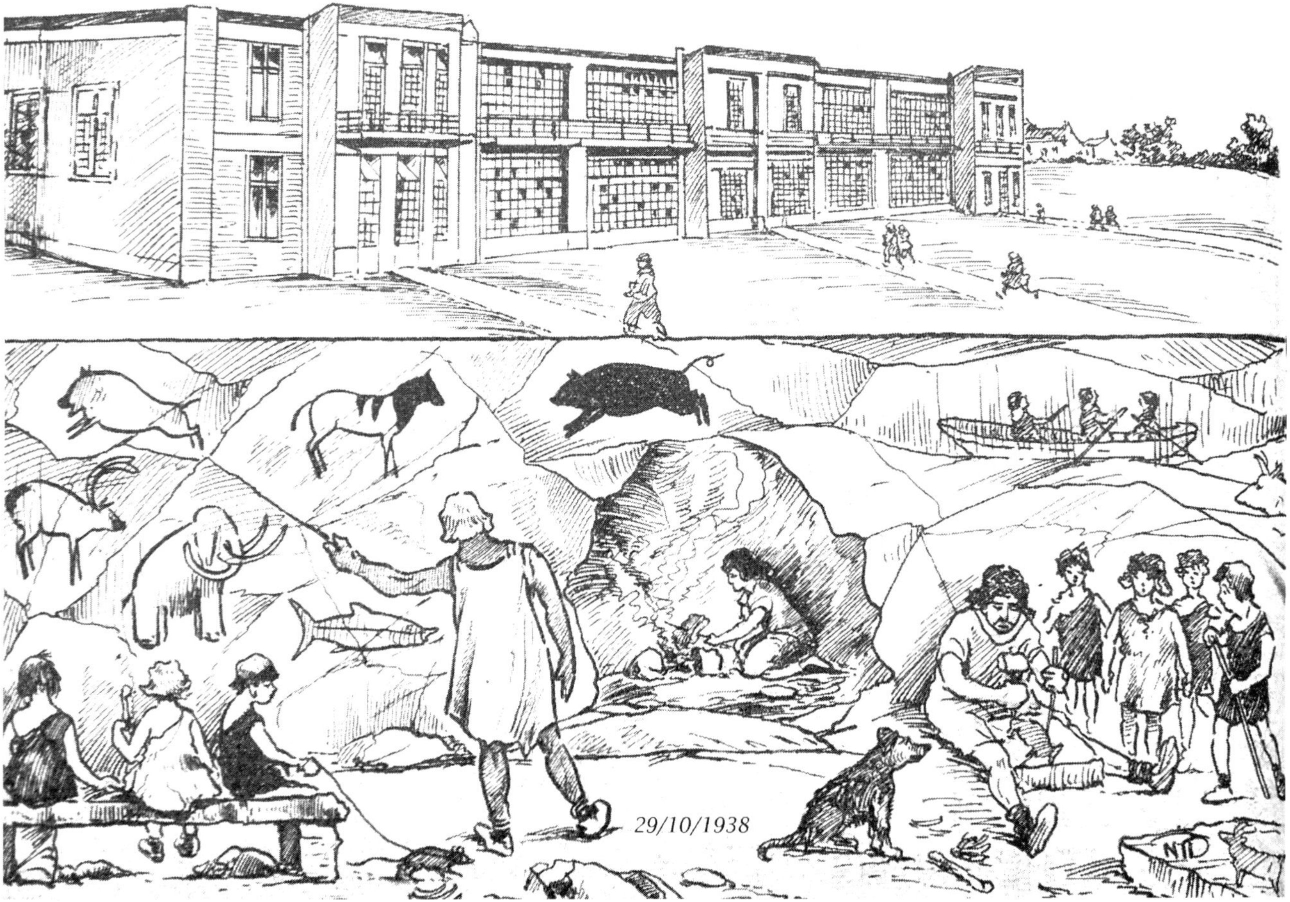
29/10/1938
NTD

*With War Clouds looming a reminder of the past,
Zeppelin L15 was shot down and crashed in the Thames in March 1916.*

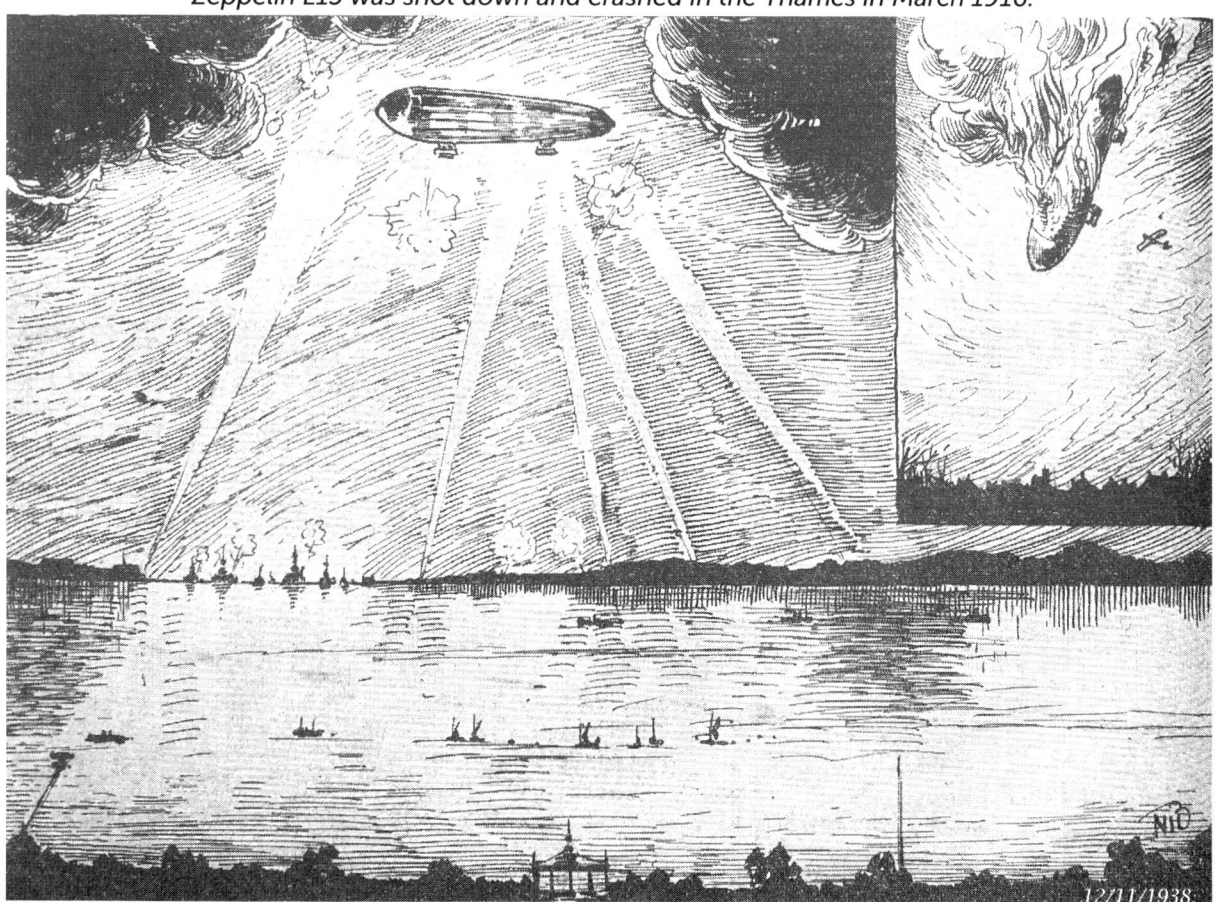

Sea Monsters

This Naughten cartoon was published in December 1938 after the sighting of a whale in the estuary the previous week. It had the following caption:-

Sea Monsters are not new to the Leigh foreshore. About fifty years ago a beak-nosed whale was caught on the Nore sands, brought to Leigh and exhibited. After a few days in the hot sun it became objectionable and was finally buried.

What was described in the caption was not unique as the Victorians were far less respectful of marine life than we are today. In 1849, a finback whale was caught at Grays, dragged ashore and put on display at sixpence a head admission. Fifty years later a female rorqual whale appeared in the Thames at North Woolwich. It was rammed by a steam tug and dragged ashore before being killed with hatchets and crowbars. Again, it was put on display and admission charged.

By 1962 society was more compassionate. At Brightlingsea a whale followed a boat into the river Colne and was later found dead near Bateman's tower. The whale was buried at East End Green. In 2006, a northern blue nose whale was spotted in the River Thames close to the Thames Barrier. Efforts to save it became the focus of international attention but alas they were in vain.

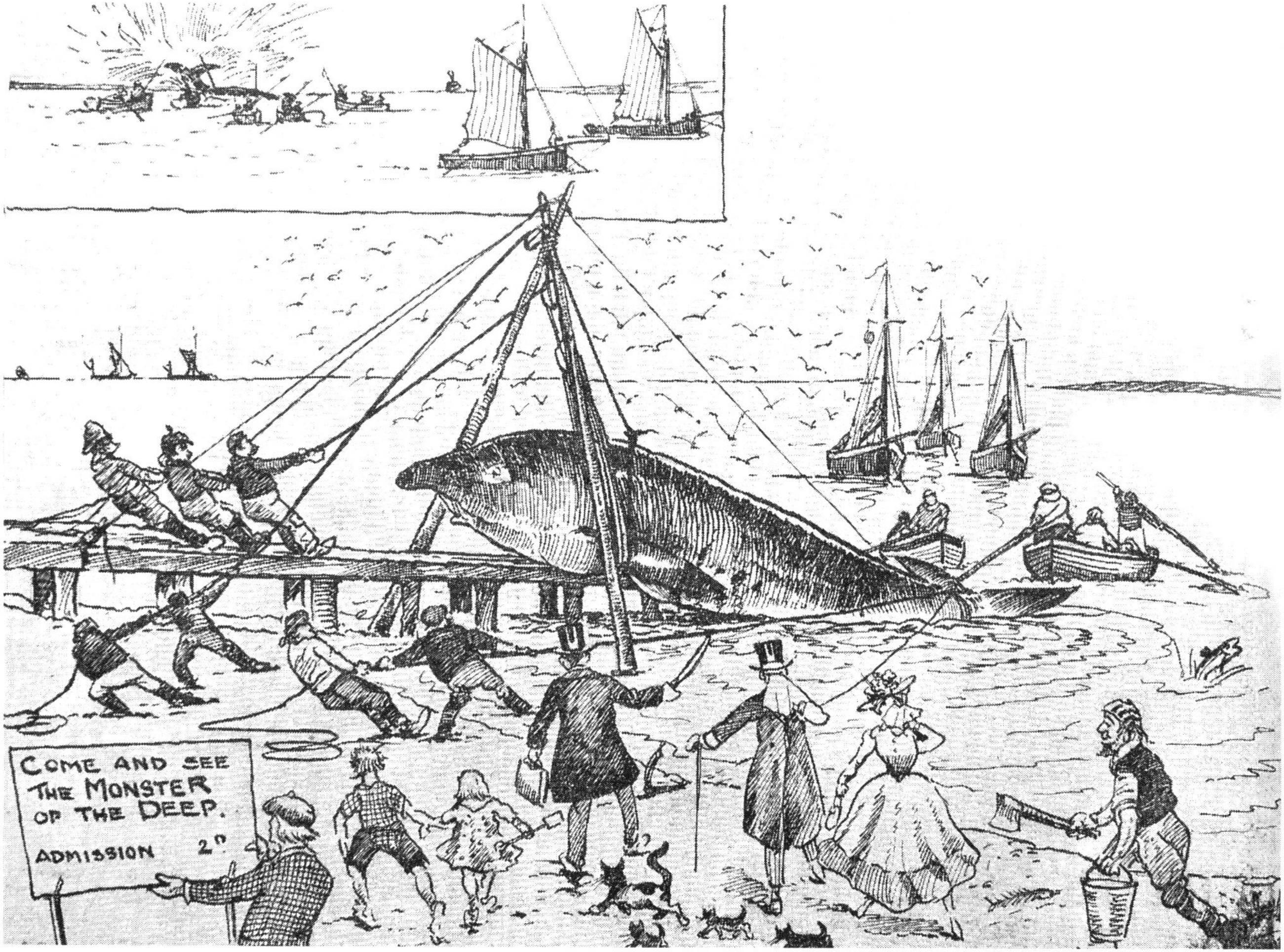
COME AND SEE
THE MONSTER
OF THE DEEP.
ADMISSION 2D

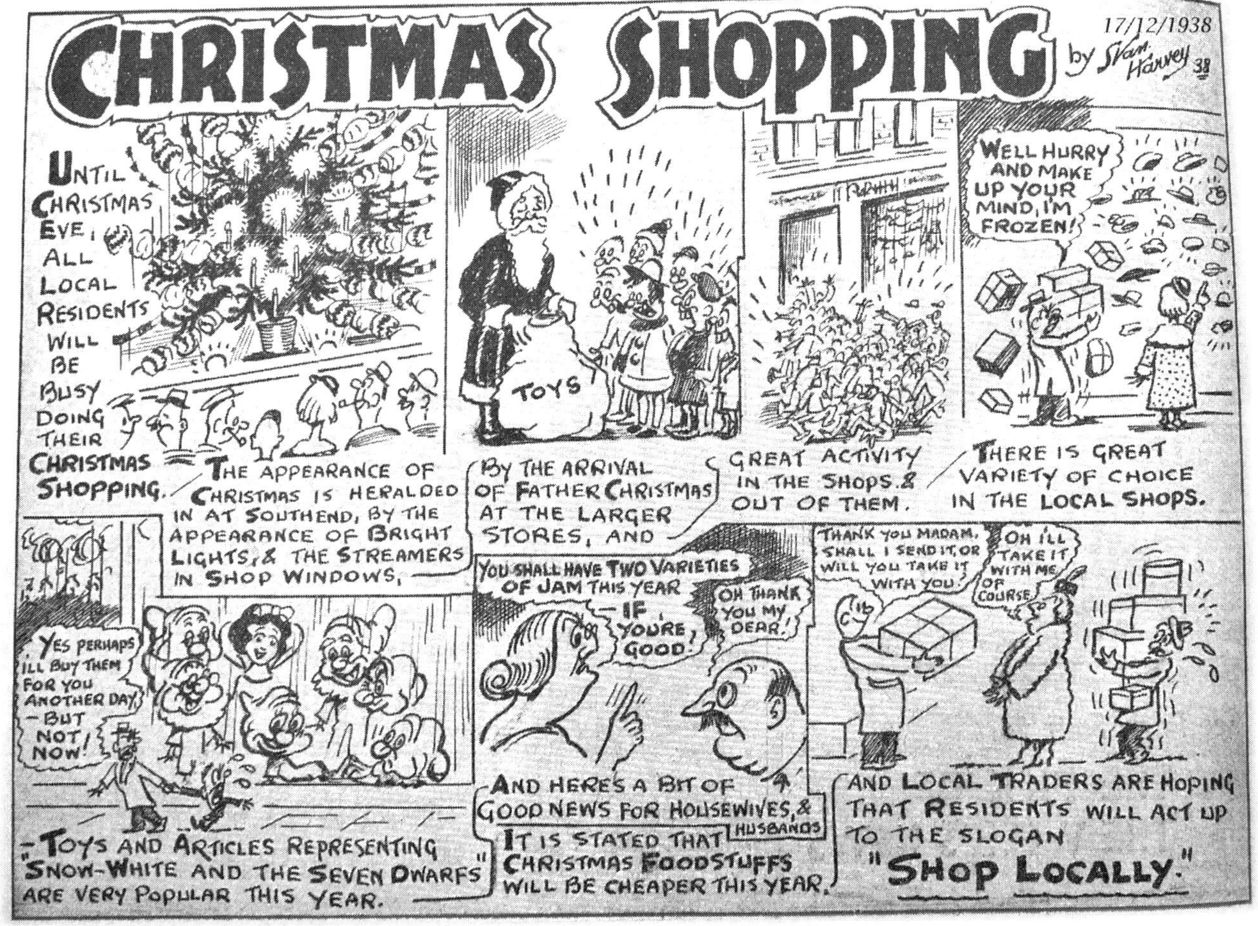
CHRISTMAS SHOPPING
17/12/1938
by S. Van Harvey 38
UNTIL CHRISTMAS EVE, ALL LOCAL RESIDENTS WILL BE BUSY DOING THEIR CHRISTMAS SHOPPING.
THE APPEARANCE OF CHRISTMAS IS HERALDED IN AT SOUTHEND, BY THE APPEARANCE OF BRIGHT LIGHTS, & THE STREAMERS IN SHOP WINDOWS,
TOYS
BY THE ARRIVAL OF FATHER CHRISTMAS AT THE LARGER STORES, AND
GREAT ACTIVITY IN THE SHOPS & OUT OF THEM.
WELL HURRY AND MAKE UP YOUR MIND, I'M FROZEN!
THERE IS GREAT VARIETY OF CHOICE IN THE LOCAL SHOPS.
YES PERHAPS I'LL BUY THEM FOR YOU ANOTHER DAY - BUT NOT NOW!
- TOYS AND ARTICLES REPRESENTING "SNOW-WHITE AND THE SEVEN DWARFS" ARE VERY POPULAR THIS YEAR.
YOU SHALL HAVE TWO VARIETIES OF JAM THIS YEAR - IF YOU'RE GOOD!
OH THANK YOU MY DEAR!
AND HERE'S A BIT OF GOOD NEWS FOR HOUSEWIVES, & HUSBANDS
IT IS STATED THAT CHRISTMAS FOODSTUFFS WILL BE CHEAPER THIS YEAR.
THANK YOU MADAM. SHALL I SEND IT, OR WILL YOU TAKE IT WITH YOU?
OH I'LL TAKE IT WITH ME OF COURSE.
AND LOCAL TRADERS ARE HOPING THAT RESIDENTS WILL ACT UP TO THE SLOGAN "SHOP LOCALLY."

1939

1939

Unfortunately, the original papers, physical and electronic records for the months January to April 1939 are lost so we do not know what gems Stan Harvey and Fred Naughten created during that time. By May 1939 *Southend Pictorial Telegraph* had disappeared and been replaced by *Southend-on-Sea & County Pictorial.*

The latter part of 1939 was dominated by the outbreak of the Second World War. However, some of the other notable events of the year were as follows. In February, what was described as the most haunted house in England, Borley Rectory in the north of Essex, mysteriously burned down. Sensational newspaper reporting suggested the fire was caused by resident ghosts. Yet, following a detailed investigation, the fire was deemed to have been caused by the occupant as part of an insurance scam. May 1939 saw the appearance of *Batman* in comic form and in August MGM's classic musical *The Wizard of Oz*, starring Judy Garland as Dorothy, premiered in Hollywood. Perhaps an unusual escape story was that of the Dagenham Girl Pipers, thirty of whom set off under the supervision of Reverend Graves in late July for a six-week tour of Germany.

The tour was cut short on the advice of the British Consul in Friedrichshafen and the Pipers, many of whom protested, returned to the UK in great secrecy just before war was declared.

In 1939 the *Royal Daffodil* was launched. It was described as the fastest and finest new pleasure boat around. It was a regular sight in the waters off Southend plying its trade between Tilbury, Southend and the continent. After the war, the *Daffodil* returned to service but was withdrawn in 1966 and later scrapped.

Southend on Sea
A Cultured town

Casting war and doom aside and seemingly without a care in the world, Fred Naughten reflected on 200 years of Southend in a gentler time – perhaps?

To accompany the cartoon opposite he wrote:-

Southend on Sea as a health and pleasure resort has a history of nearly two hundred years. In the first quarter of the Nineteenth century, it held an assured position in the esteem of cultured visitors to the seaside.

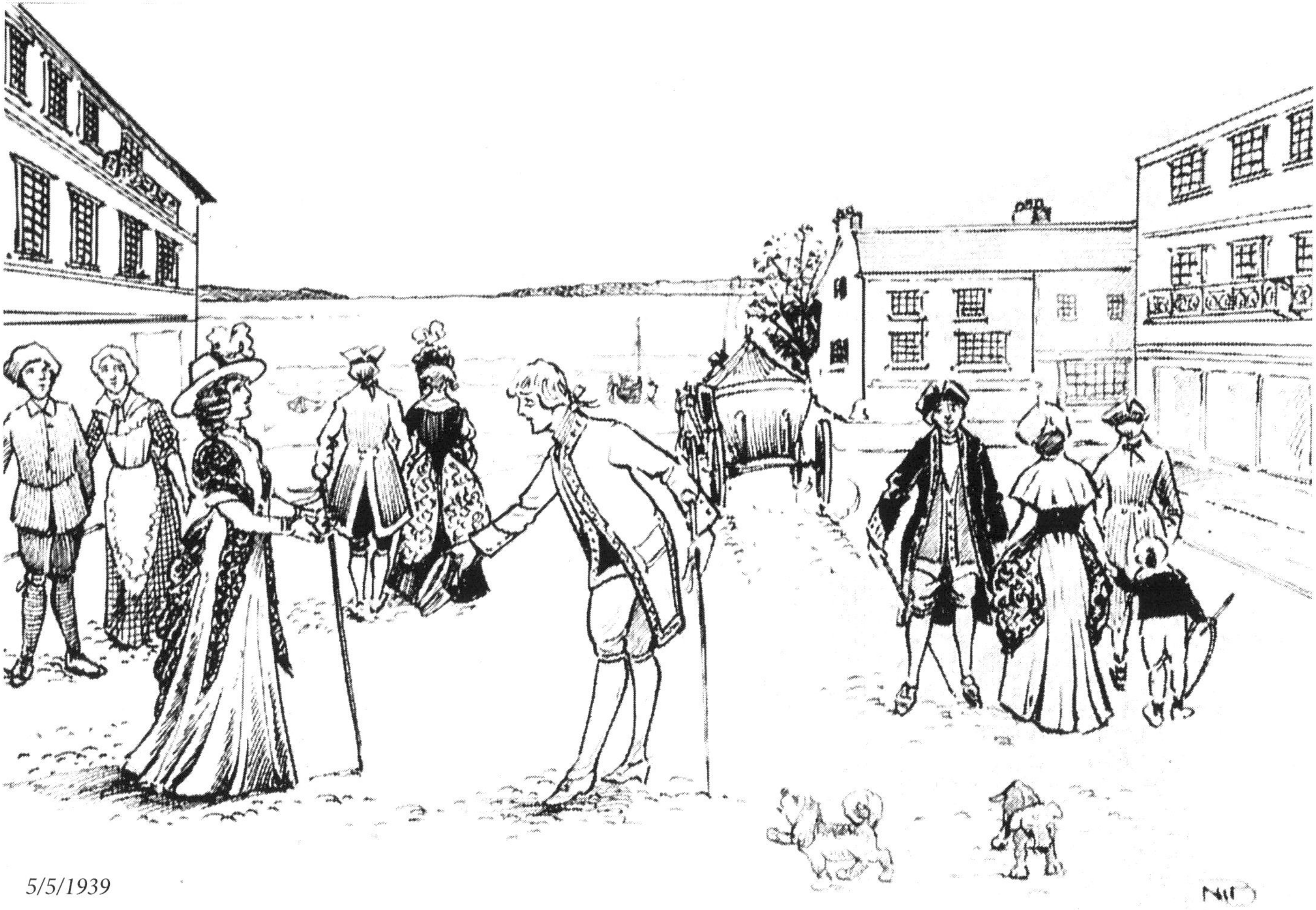
NHO

5/5/1939

A good Whitsun Holiday in Southend the Stone Age.

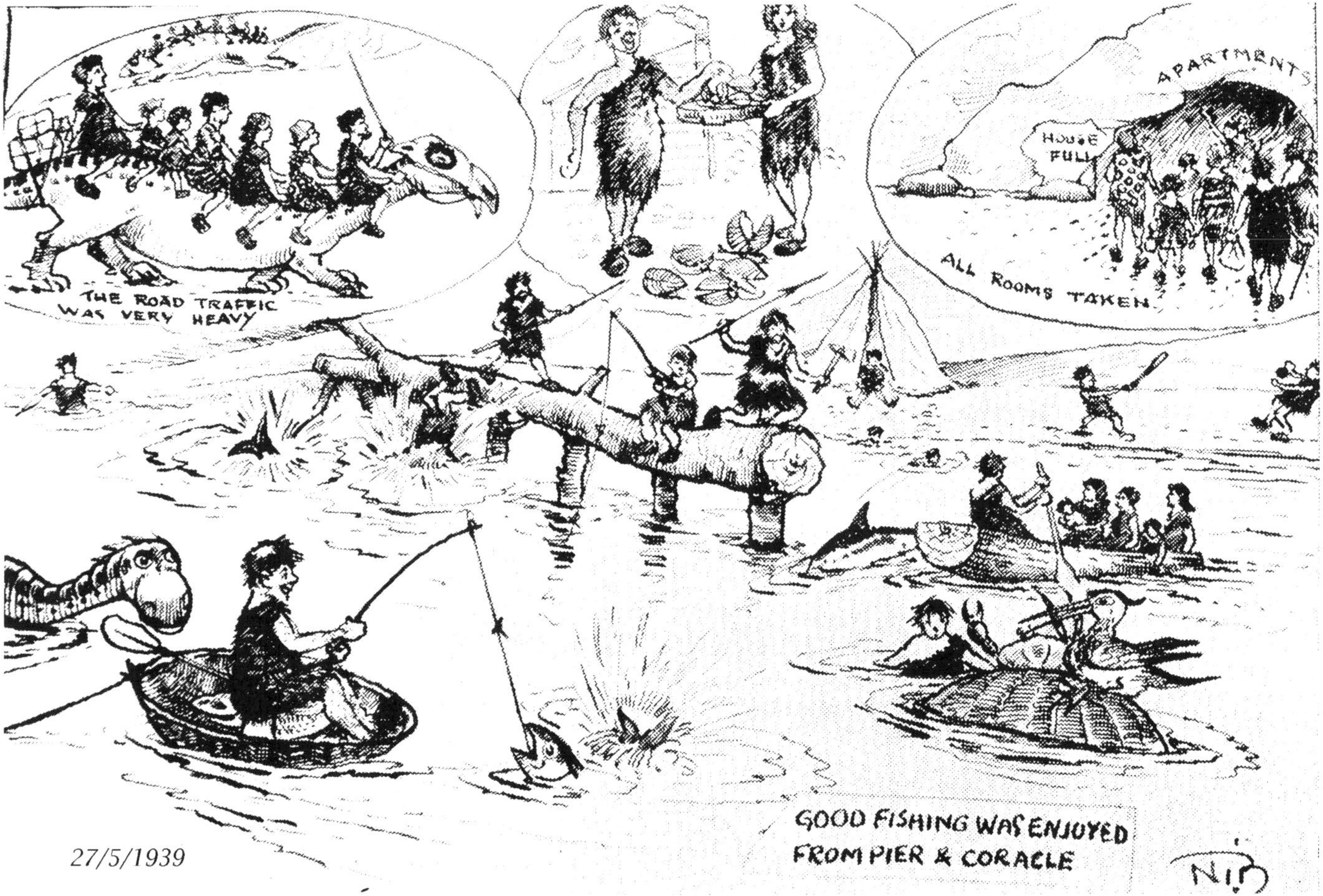
THE ROAD TRAFFIC WAS VERY HEAVY
HOUSE FULL
APARTMENTS
ALL ROOMS TAKEN
GOOD FISHING WAS ENJOYED FROM PIER & CORACLE
27/5/1939

Southend Yachting Week in the Roman era. A close finish in the one-design Galley Race.

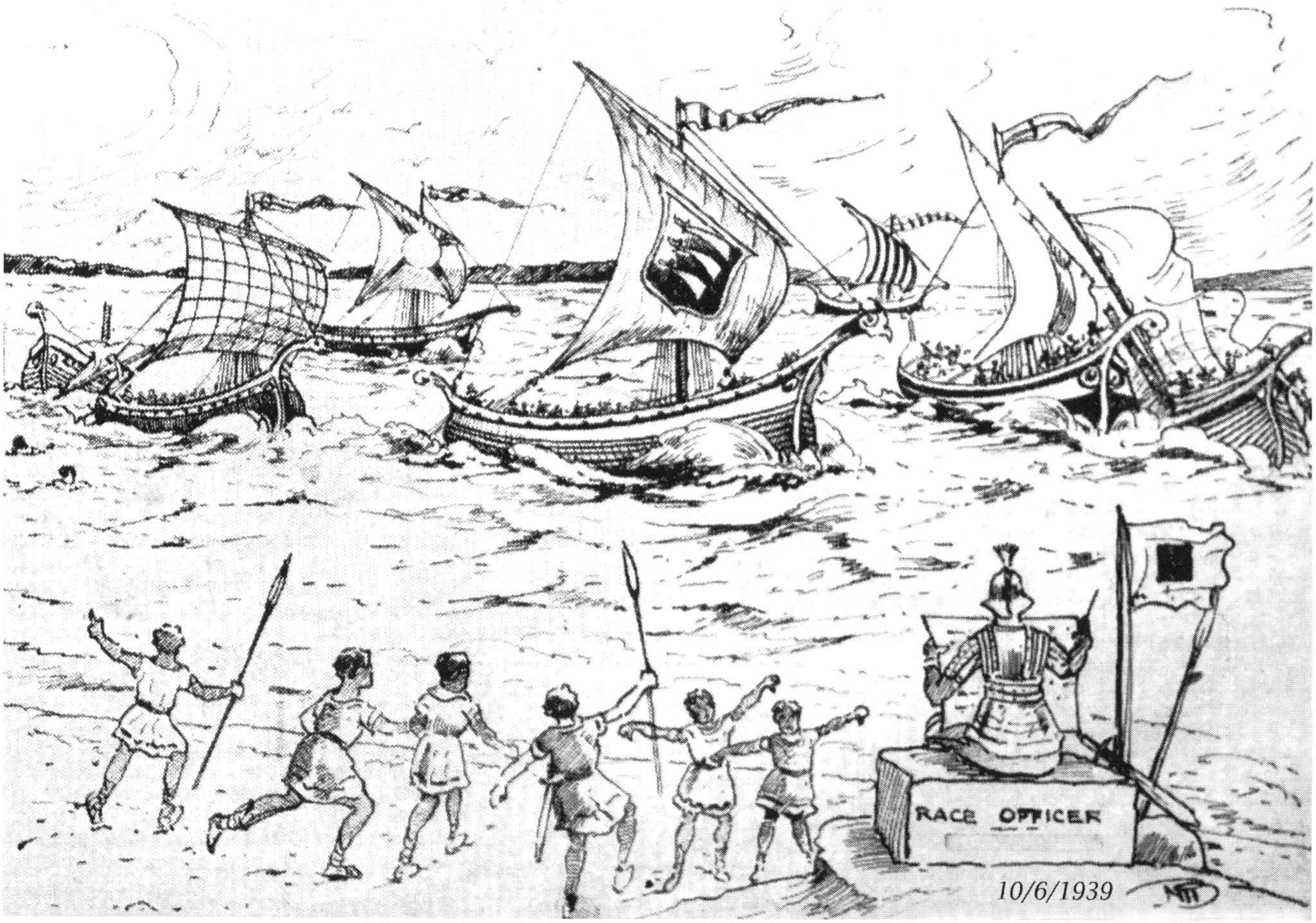
RACE OFFICER
10/6/1939

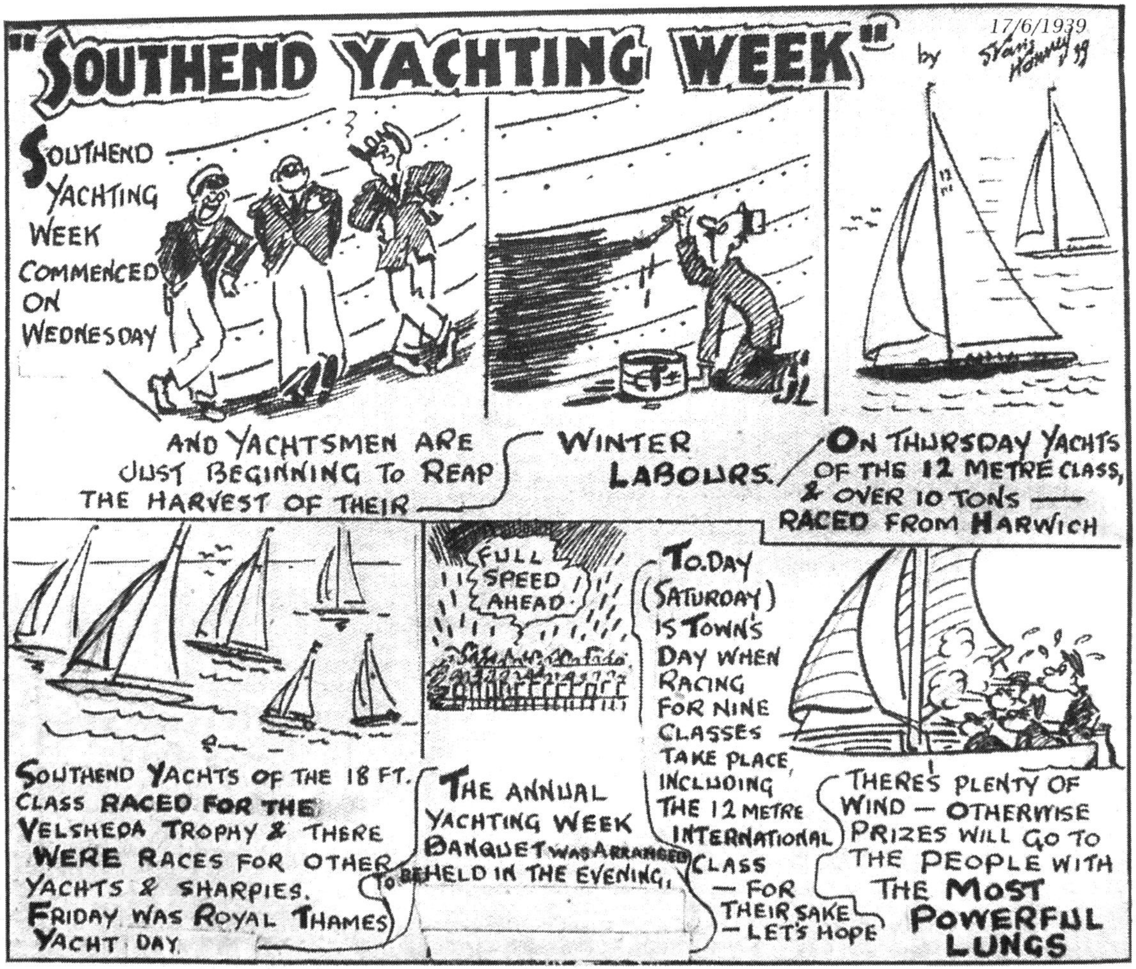
17/6/1939
"SOUTHEND YACHTING WEEK"
by
SOUTHEND YACHTING WEEK COMMENCED ON WEDNESDAY
AND YACHTSMEN ARE JUST BEGINNING TO REAP THE HARVEST OF THEIR
WINTER LABOURS.
ON THURSDAY YACHTS OF THE 12 METRE CLASS, & OVER 10 TONS — RACED FROM HARWICH
SOUTHEND YACHTS OF THE 18 FT. CLASS RACED FOR THE VELSHEDA TROPHY & THERE WERE RACES FOR OTHER YACHTS & SHARPIES.
FRIDAY WAS ROYAL THAMES YACHT DAY.
FULL SPEED AHEAD
THE ANNUAL YACHTING WEEK BANQUET WAS ARRANGED TO BE HELD IN THE EVENING.
TO.DAY (SATURDAY) IS TOWN'S DAY WHEN RACING FOR NINE CLASSES TAKE PLACE, INCLUDING THE 12 METRE INTERNATIONAL CLASS — FOR THEIR SAKE — LET'S HOPE
THERE'S PLENTY OF WIND — OTHERWISE PRIZES WILL GO TO THE PEOPLE WITH THE MOST POWERFUL LUNGS

A century ago it did not take three days to decide a local cricket match.

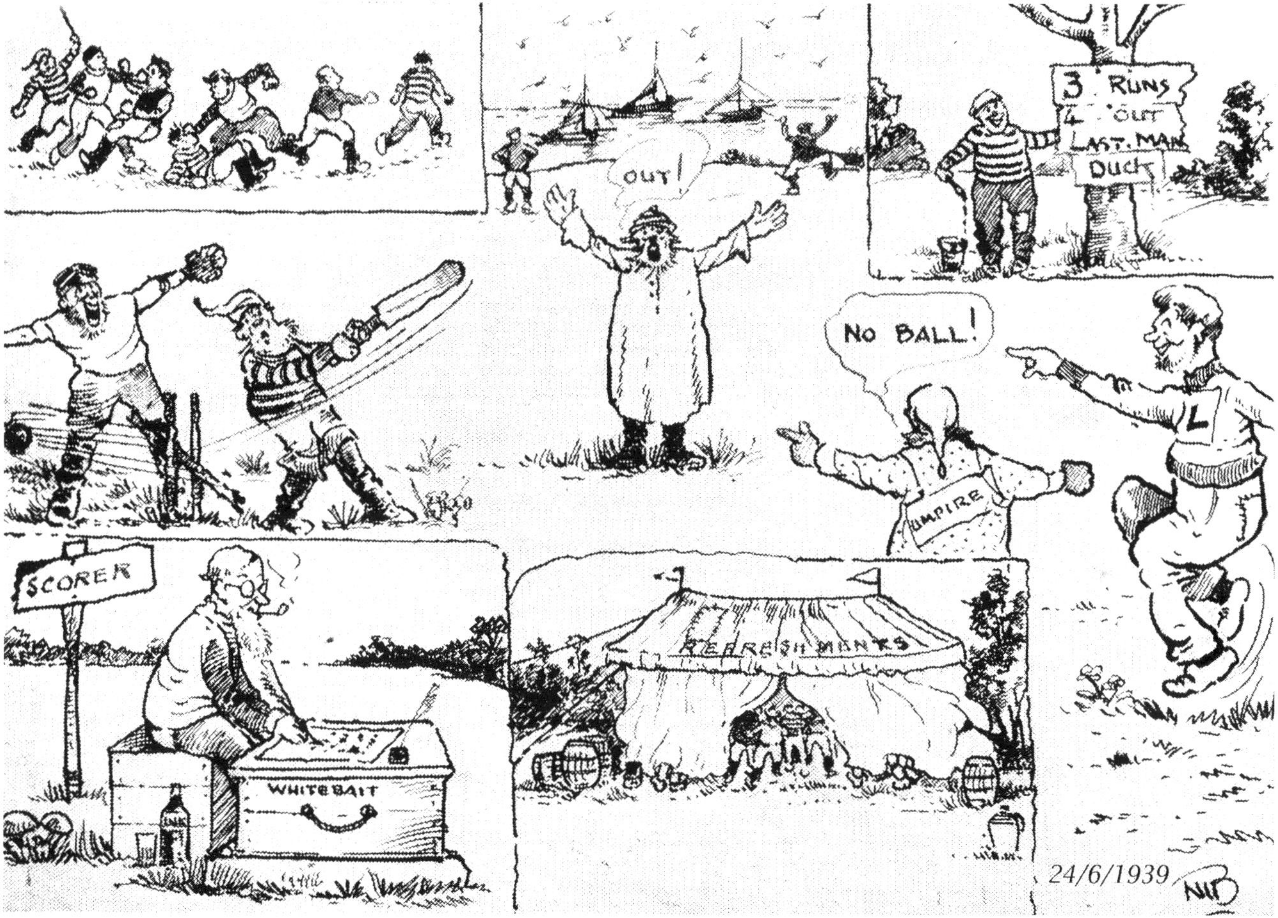

OUT!
3 RUNS
4 OUT
LAST MAN
DUCK
NO BALL!
UMPIRE
L
SCORER
WHITEBAIT
INK
REFRESHMENTS
24/6/1939

1/7/1939

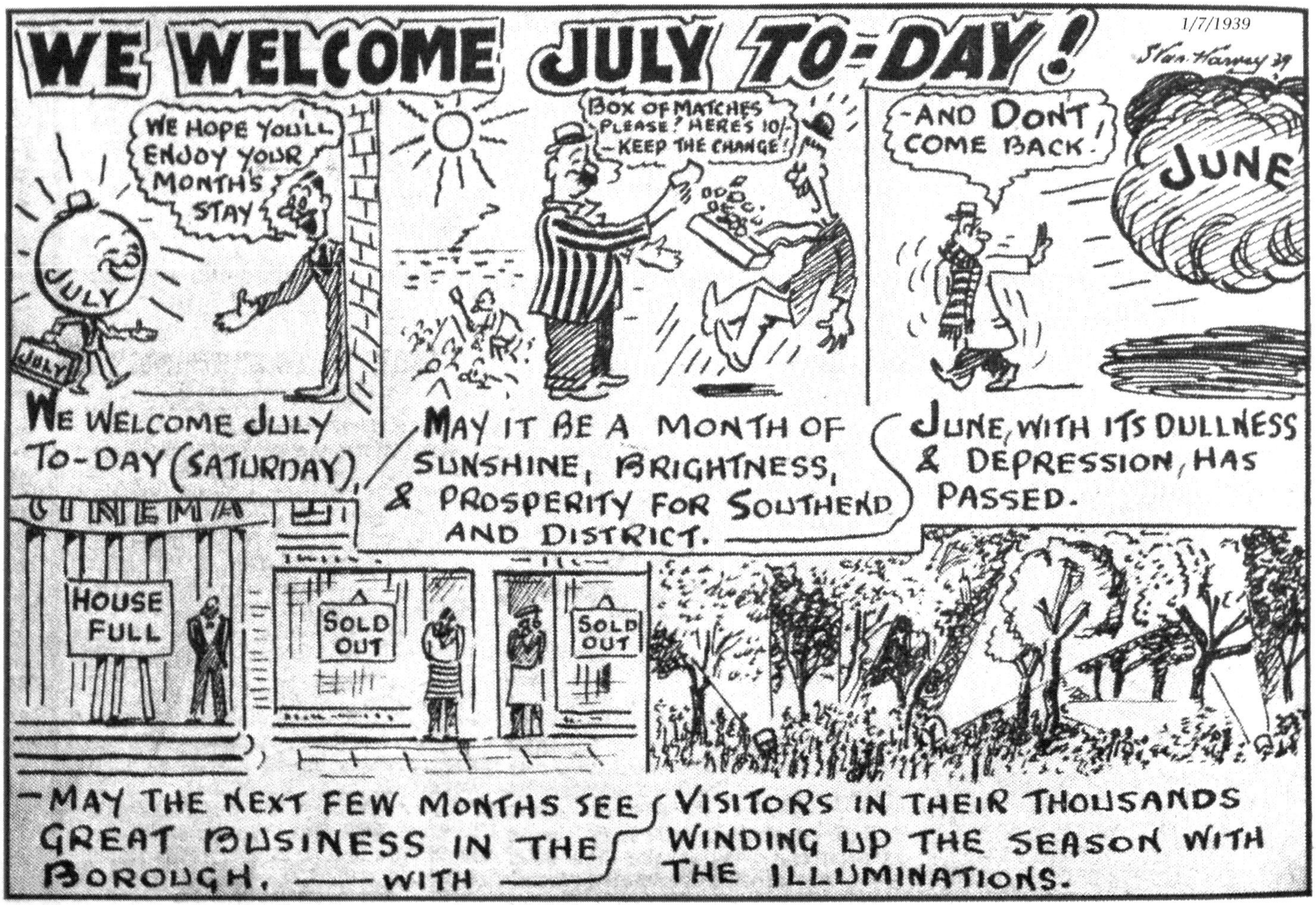

WE WELCOME JULY TO-DAY!
Stan Harvey 39
WE HOPE YOU'LL ENJOY YOUR MONTH'S STAY
JULY
JULY
BOX OF MATCHES PLEASE? HERE'S 10/- KEEP THE CHANGE!
-AND DON'T COME BACK
JUNE
WE WELCOME JULY TO-DAY (SATURDAY)
MAY IT BE A MONTH OF SUNSHINE, BRIGHTNESS, & PROSPERITY FOR SOUTHEND AND DISTRICT.
JUNE, WITH ITS DULLNESS & DEPRESSION, HAS PASSED.
CINEMA
HOUSE FULL
SOLD OUT
SOLD OUT
-MAY THE NEXT FEW MONTHS SEE GREAT BUSINESS IN THE BOROUGH. —— WITH
VISITORS IN THEIR THOUSANDS WINDING UP THE SEASON WITH THE ILLUMINATIONS.

Southend and district re-discovered two centuries hence – relics of a bygone bombing age.

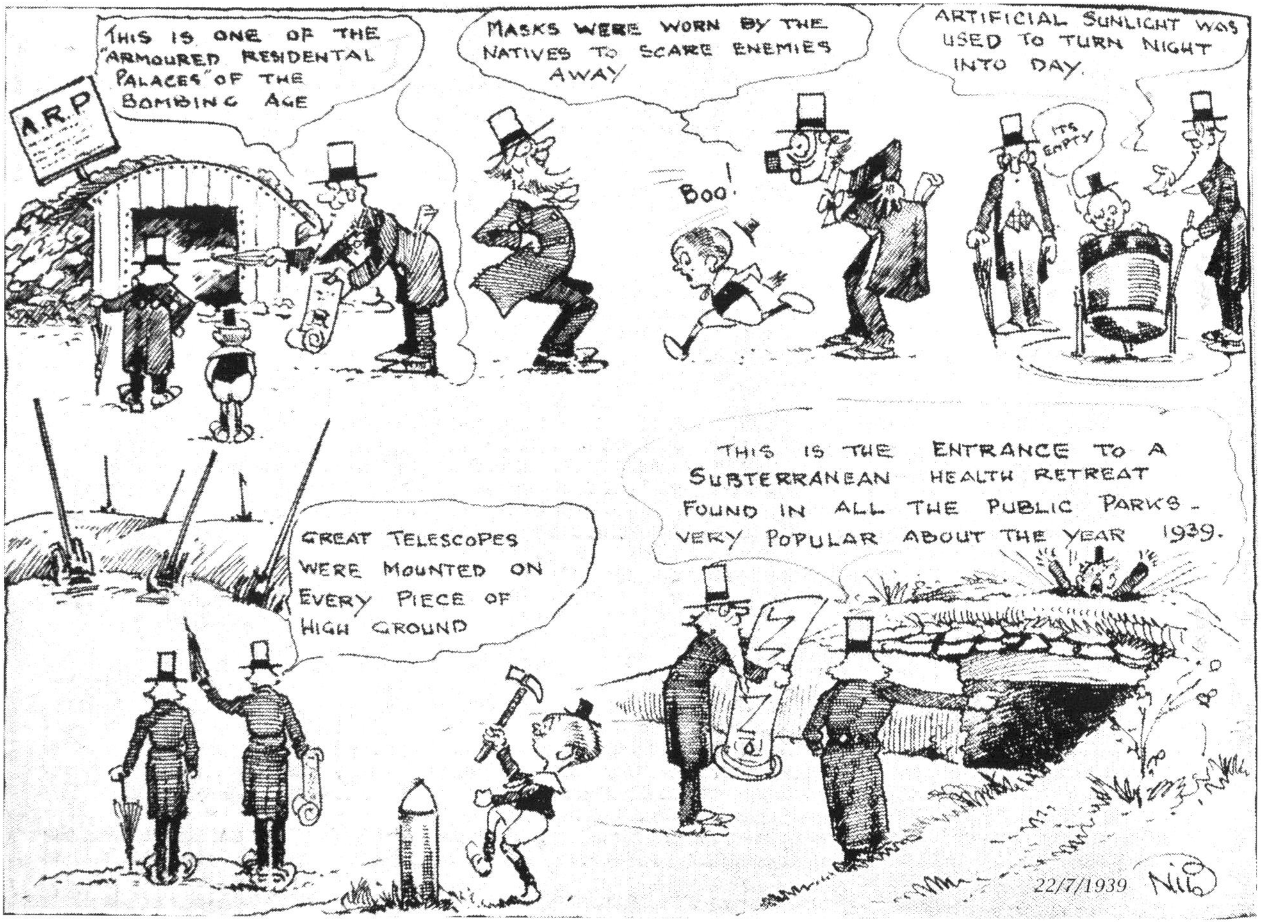
THIS IS ONE OF THE "ARMOURED RESIDENTAL PALACES" OF THE BOMBING AGE
A.R.P
MASKS WERE WORN BY THE NATIVES TO SCARE ENEMIES AWAY
BOO!
ARTIFICIAL SUNLIGHT WAS USED TO TURN NIGHT INTO DAY.
ITS EMPTY
GREAT TELESCOPES WERE MOUNTED ON EVERY PIECE OF HIGH GROUND
THIS IS THE ENTRANCE TO A SUBTERRANEAN HEALTH RETREAT FOUND IN ALL THE PUBLIC PARKS - VERY POPULAR ABOUT THE YEAR 1939.
22/7/1939
Nib

Golden Hinds

This image of the two Golden Hinds (opposite) by Fred Naughten was published in July 1939 with the following caption: -

The Golden Hind launched on the Medway 300 years ago and the Golden Hind launched this month.

The *Golden Hind* was best known as an English galleon that circumnavigated the globe between 1577 and 1580, captained by Sir Francis Drake. The ship was originally known as the *Pelican*. There have been several replicas. One was constructed in 1947 on the east side of the Southend Pier. It survived 50 years until 1997 when it was broken up. 1939 was a time of rapid development in the aviation world and that year the aircraft maker Shorts launched the *Golden Hind,* a flying boat that could carry 40 passengers. We are not sure where the original *Golden Hind* was built, the Medway? Records today indicate the ship was laid and registered in Plymouth. However, the Flying boat *Golden Hind* was launched from the Short Works in Rochester, Kent on the Medway.

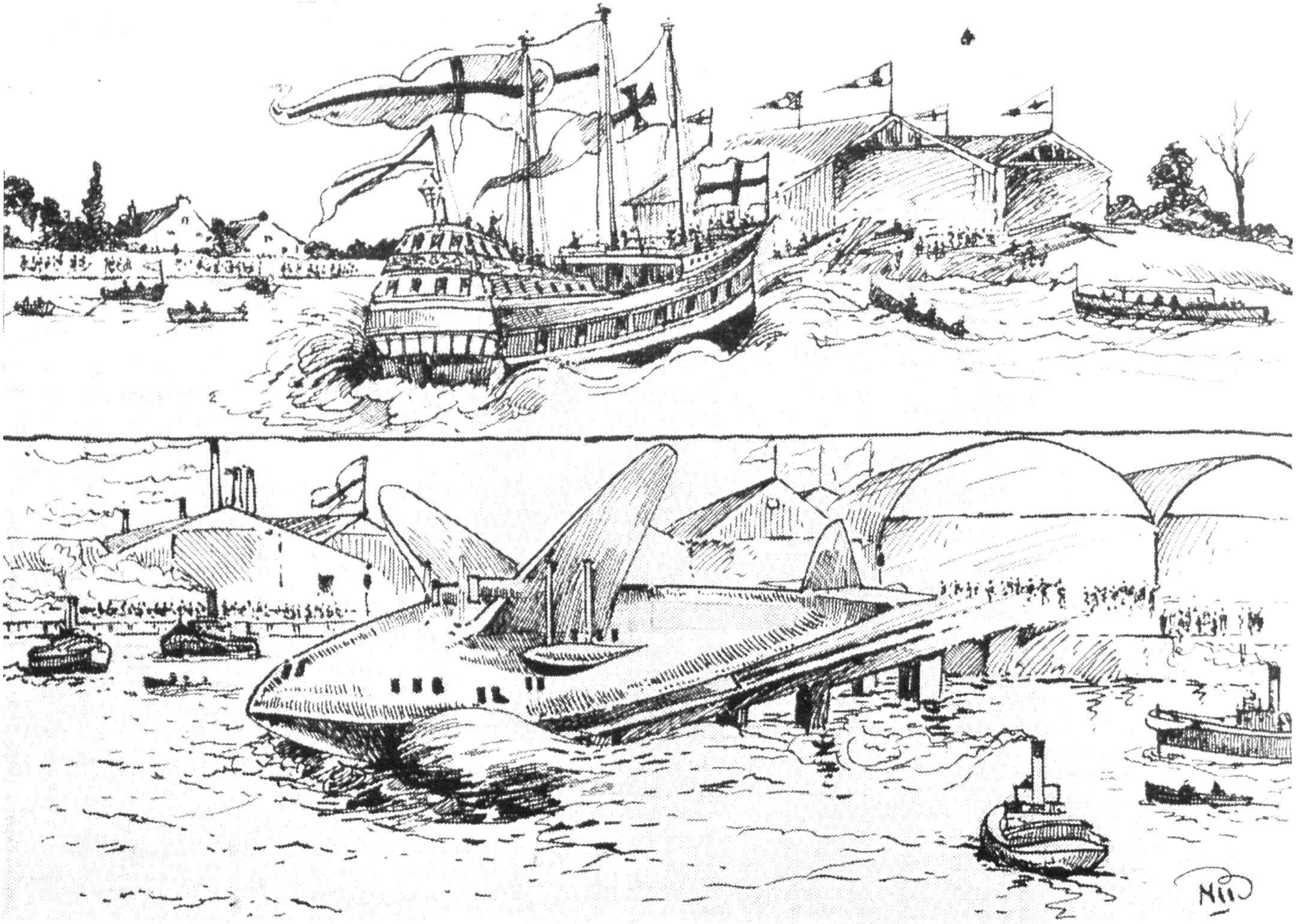

Normality?

With the declaration of war just over a month away, in July 1939, Stan Harvey reflected on the children's summer holiday (featured opposite). Everything seemed almost normal – sports days took place and prize givings were held.

The Mayor's Garden party was well attended and sailing trips continued across the channel without interruption. The summer show at the end of the pier was sold out and preparations were well in hand for the carnival season. At the end of the month the new Southend United team was unveiled for the 1939/40 season.

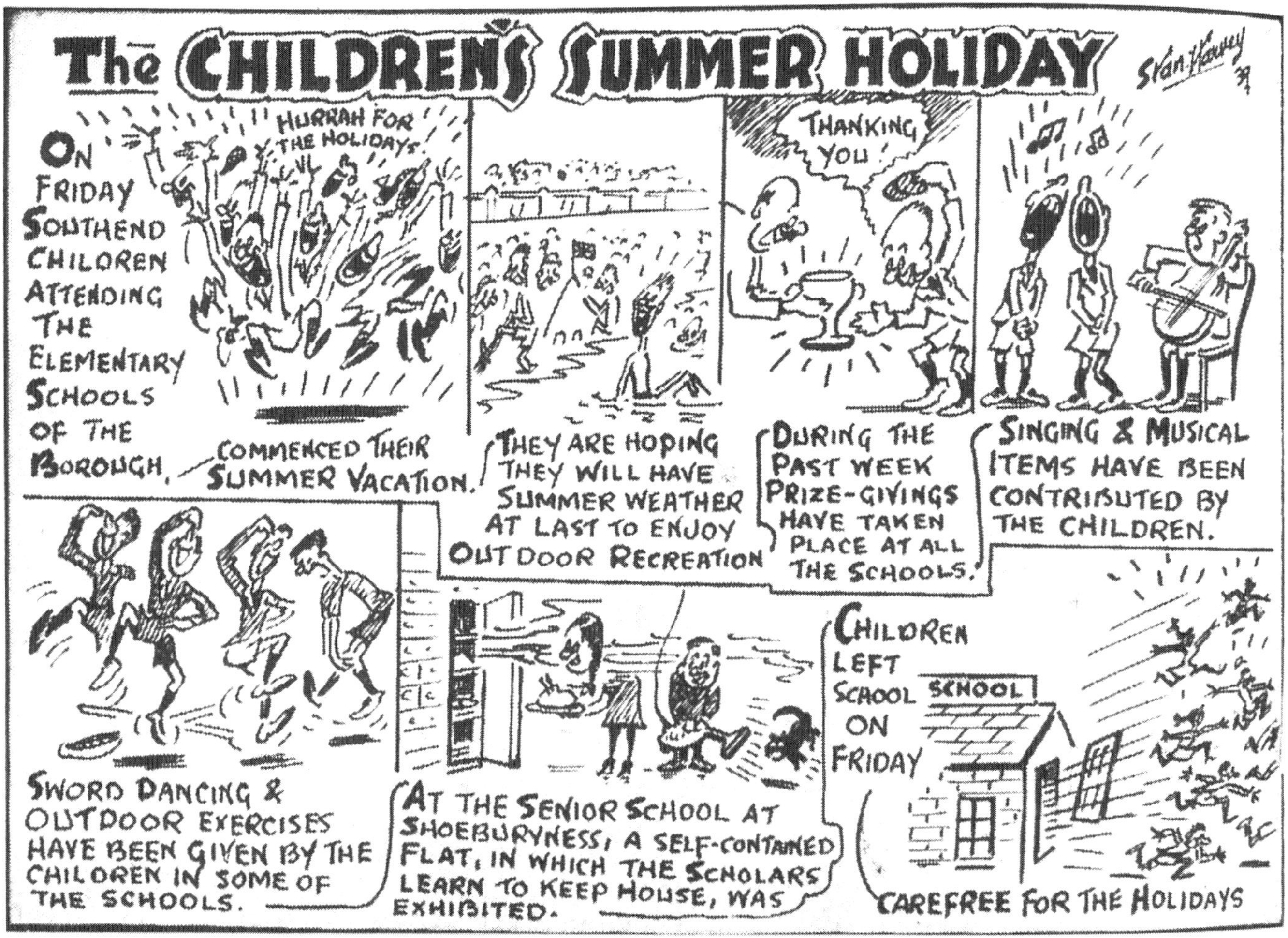
The CHILDREN'S SUMMER HOLIDAY
Stan Harvey 37
HURRAH FOR THE HOLIDAYS!
ON FRIDAY SOUTHEND CHILDREN ATTENDING THE ELEMENTARY SCHOOLS OF THE BOROUGH, — COMMENCED THEIR SUMMER VACATION.
THEY ARE HOPING THEY WILL HAVE SUMMER WEATHER AT LAST TO ENJOY OUTDOOR RECREATION
THANKING YOU!
DURING THE PAST WEEK PRIZE-GIVINGS HAVE TAKEN PLACE AT ALL THE SCHOOLS.
SINGING & MUSICAL ITEMS HAVE BEEN CONTRIBUTED BY THE CHILDREN.
SWORD DANCING & OUTDOOR EXERCISES HAVE BEEN GIVEN BY THE CHILDREN IN SOME OF THE SCHOOLS.
AT THE SENIOR SCHOOL AT SHOEBURYNESS, A SELF-CONTAINED FLAT, IN WHICH THE SCHOLARS LEARN TO KEEP HOUSE, WAS EXHIBITED.
CHILDREN LEFT SCHOOL ON FRIDAY
SCHOOL
CAREFREE FOR THE HOLIDAYS

SRP Blackout

By August 1939 war seemed inevitable. Locally and nationally defensive measures were rapidly put in place. Evacuation plans were drawn up, air raid shelter construction continued apace and anti-aircraft defences beefed up.

Fred Naughten was always keen to relate contemporary news with historical events. He especially liked the Viking era. The constant black out rehearsals inspired the cartoon opposite carrying the following caption:-

SRP – Sea Raid Precautions. A black-out at Southend follows the warning of an impending raid by the Danes in the ninth Century.

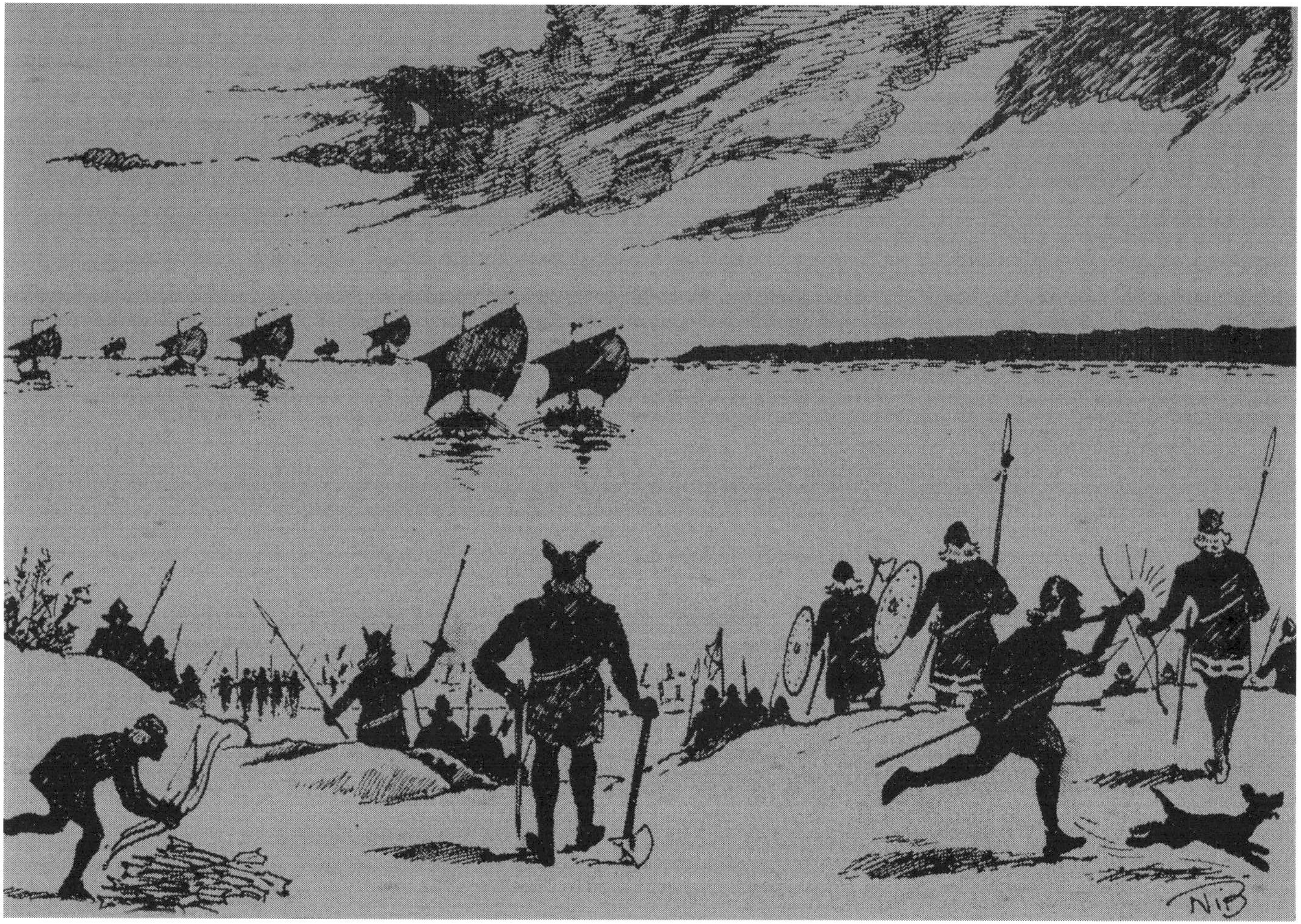

Strong Women to the Rescue in Time of Need

Fred Naughten used a fair degree of artistic (and historical) licence to create the image opposite. The caption read:-

Queens in ages past and how they came to Southend. Anne Boleyn rode over from Rochford Hall. Queen Elizabeth I came down the Thames in her Royal Barge. Queen Boadicea arrived on her chariot.

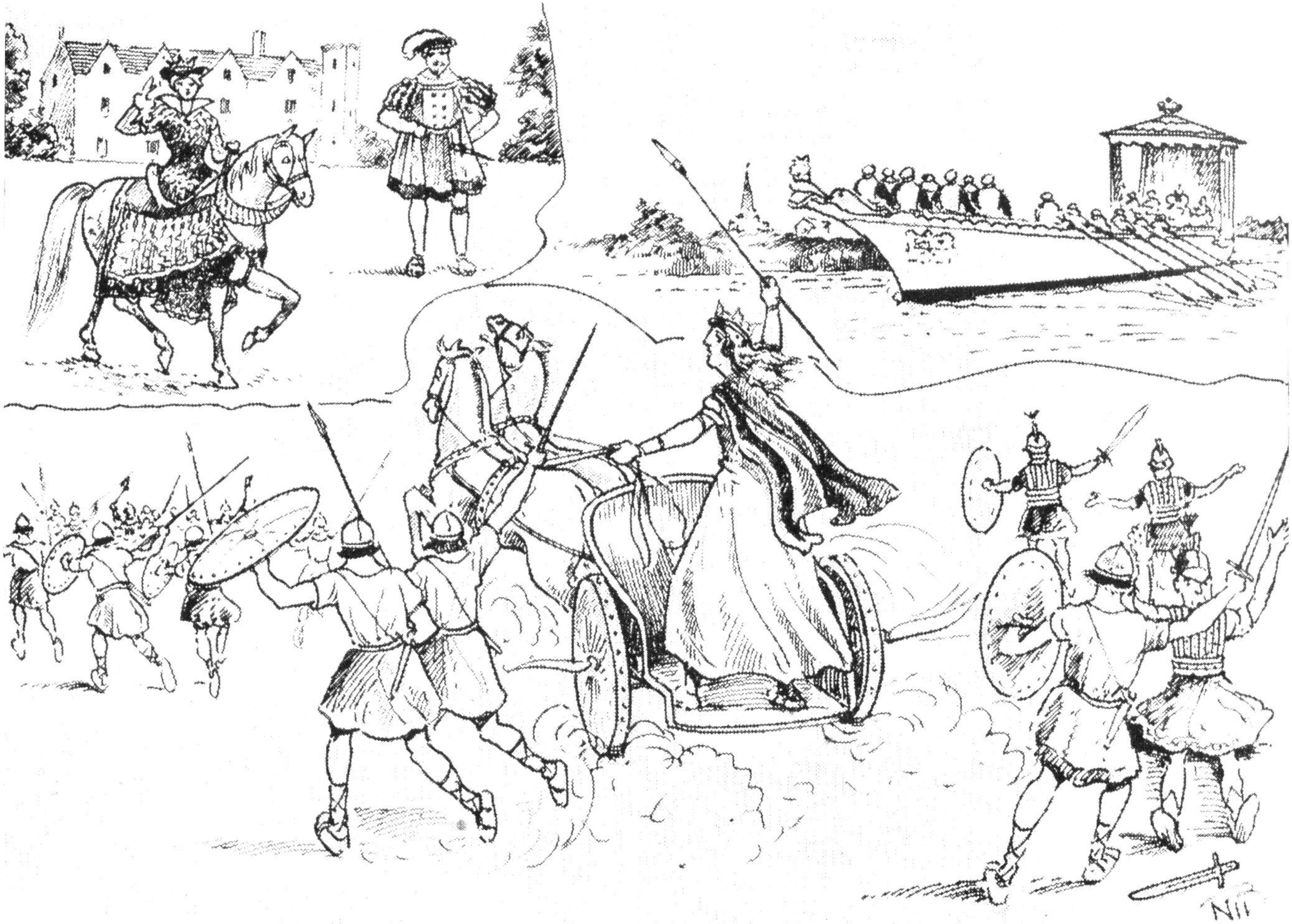

Dark Days

On the eve of war, with the bank holiday and carnival season over, Fred created this poignant cartoon which was published on September 2nd 1939.

We have been menaced in the past by dictators who would have enslaved us, but they came to an untimely end. History has a habit of repeating itself.

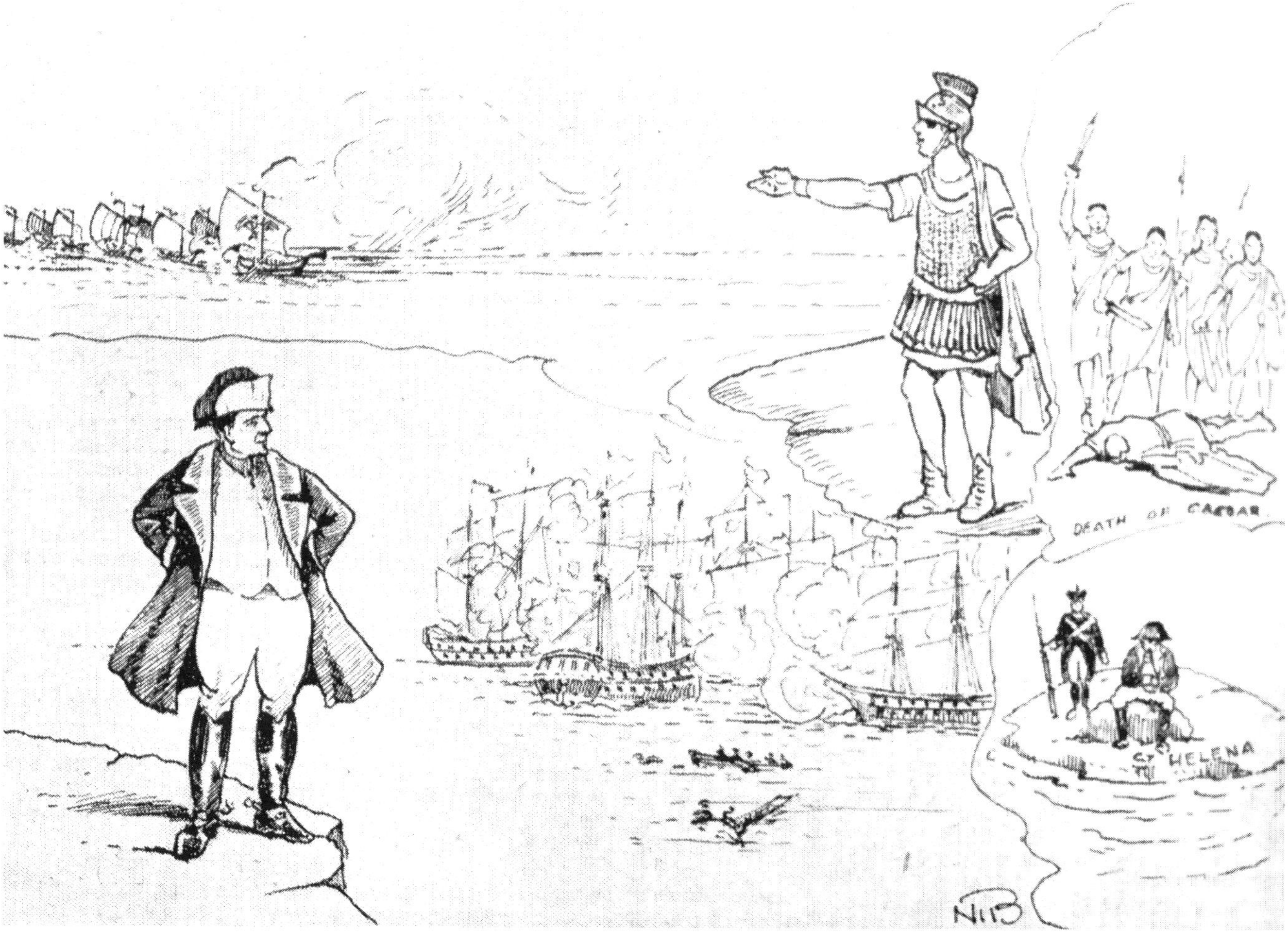
DEATH OF CAESAR
ST HELENA

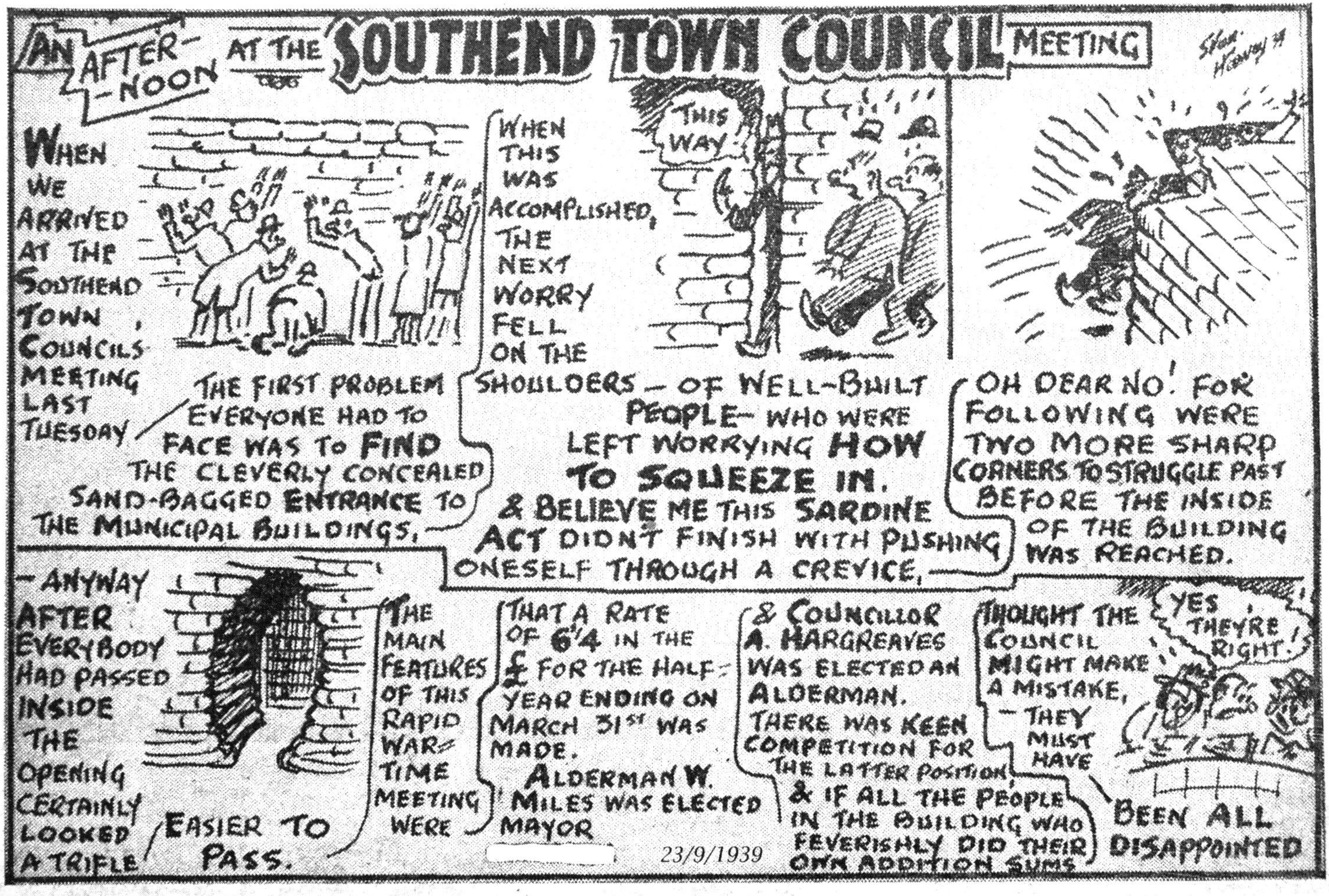
AN AFTER-NOON AT THE SOUTHEND TOWN COUNCIL MEETING
WHEN WE ARRIVED AT THE SOUTHEND TOWN COUNCILS MEETING LAST TUESDAY
THE FIRST PROBLEM EVERYONE HAD TO FACE WAS TO FIND THE CLEVERLY CONCEALED SAND-BAGGED ENTRANCE TO THE MUNICIPAL BUILDINGS,
WHEN THIS WAS ACCOMPLISHED, THE NEXT WORRY FELL ON THE SHOULDERS – OF WELL-BUILT PEOPLE – WHO WERE LEFT WORRYING HOW TO SQUEEZE IN.
THIS WAY
& BELIEVE ME THIS SARDINE ACT DIDN'T FINISH WITH PUSHING ONESELF THROUGH A CREVICE,
OH DEAR NO! FOR FOLLOWING WERE TWO MORE SHARP CORNERS TO STRUGGLE PAST BEFORE THE INSIDE OF THE BUILDING WAS REACHED.
– ANYWAY AFTER EVERYBODY HAD PASSED INSIDE THE OPENING CERTAINLY LOOKED A TRIFLE EASIER TO PASS.
THE MAIN FEATURES OF THIS RAPID WAR-TIME MEETING WERE
THAT A RATE OF 6/4 IN THE £ FOR THE HALF-YEAR ENDING ON MARCH 31ST WAS MADE.
ALDERMAN W. MILES WAS ELECTED MAYOR
& COUNCILLOR A. HARGREAVES WAS ELECTED AN ALDERMAN.
THERE WAS KEEN COMPETITION FOR THE LATTER POSITION, & IF ALL THE PEOPLE IN THE BUILDING WHO FEVERISHLY DID THEIR OWN ADDITION SUMS
THOUGHT THE COUNCIL MIGHT MAKE A MISTAKE, – THEY MUST HAVE BEEN ALL DISAPPOINTED
YES, THEY'RE RIGHT!
23/9/1939

Auxiliary Fire Brigade in action

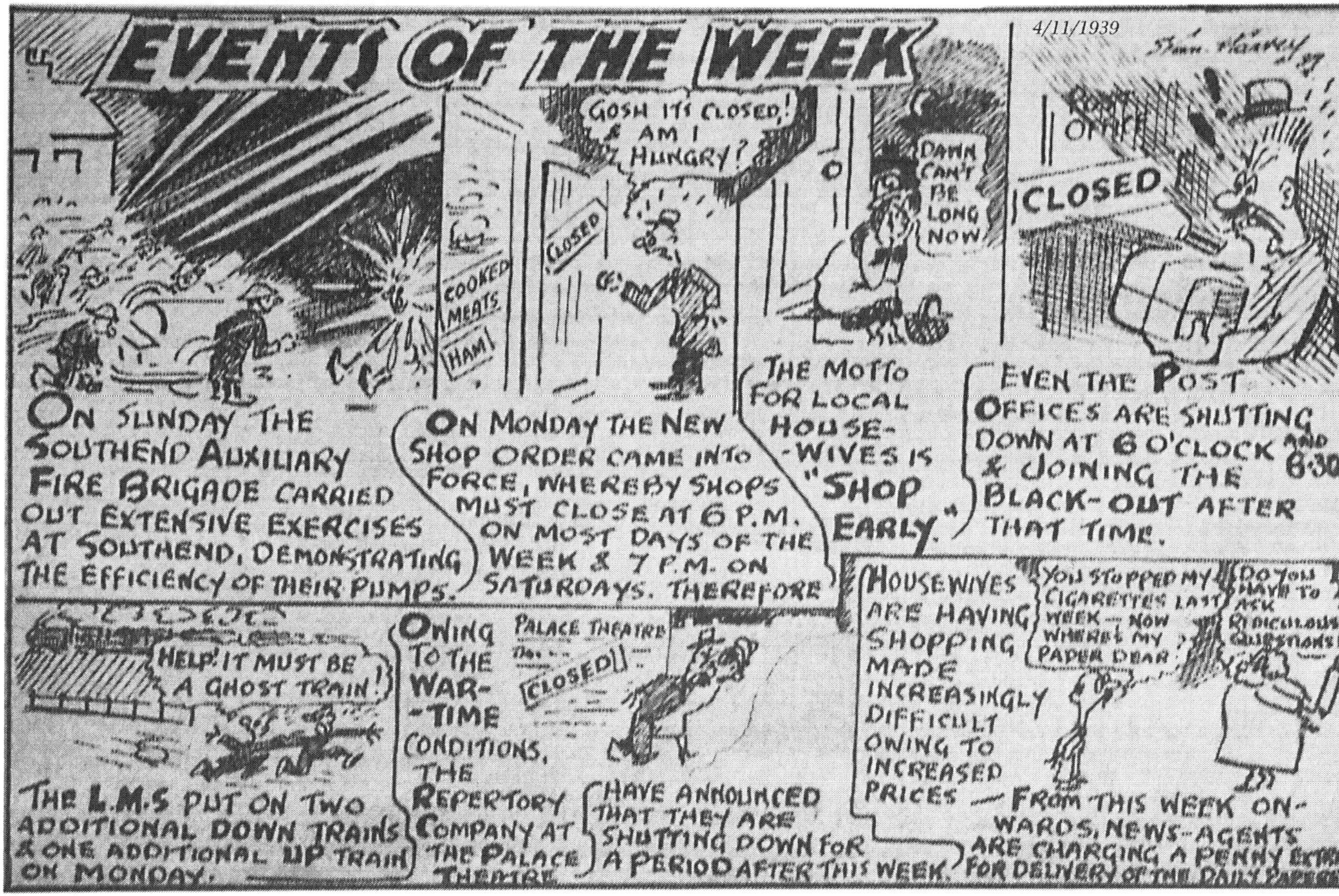

EVENTS OF THE WEEK
4/11/1939
GOSH ITS CLOSED! & AM I HUNGRY?
COOKED MEATS
HAM
CLOSED
DAMN CAN'T BE LONG NOW
CLOSED
ON SUNDAY THE SOUTHEND AUXILIARY FIRE BRIGADE CARRIED OUT EXTENSIVE EXERCISES AT SOUTHEND, DEMONSTRATING THE EFFICIENCY OF THEIR PUMPS.
ON MONDAY THE NEW SHOP ORDER CAME INTO FORCE, WHEREBY SHOPS MUST CLOSE AT 6 P.M. ON MOST DAYS OF THE WEEK & 7 P.M. ON SATURDAYS. THEREFORE
THE MOTTO FOR LOCAL HOUSE-WIVES IS "SHOP EARLY."
EVEN THE POST OFFICES ARE SHUTTING DOWN AT 6 O'CLOCK AND 6.30 & JOINING THE BLACK-OUT AFTER THAT TIME.
HELP! IT MUST BE A GHOST TRAIN!
PALACE THEATRE
CLOSED
HOUSEWIVES ARE HAVING SHOPPING MADE INCREASINGLY DIFFICULT OWING TO INCREASED PRICES
YOU STOPPED MY CIGARETTES LAST WEEK — NOW WHERE'S MY PAPER DEAR
DO YOU HAVE TO ASK RIDICULOUS QUESTIONS!
THE L.M.S PUT ON TWO ADDITIONAL DOWN TRAINS & ONE ADDITIONAL UP TRAIN ON MONDAY.
OWING TO THE WAR-TIME CONDITIONS, THE REPERTORY COMPANY AT THE PALACE THEATRE
HAVE ANNOUNCED THAT THEY ARE SHUTTING DOWN FOR A PERIOD AFTER THIS WEEK.
— FROM THIS WEEK ONWARDS, NEWS-AGENTS ARE CHARGING A PENNY EXTRA FOR DELIVERY OF THE DAILY PAPERS

The Fire Service

In October the cartoon opposite was published. Intensive bombing (the blitz) had not begun. It was the time of the so-called phoney war. Nevertheless, firefighting capacity had been greatly strengthened which led to Fred making another of his historical comparisons, writing:-

Auxiliary Fire Service. Fifty years ago Southend had only one fire engine. When a call was received horses had sometimes to be commandeered to take the engine to the scene of the fire.

The 'Alert' Southend's First Fire Engine

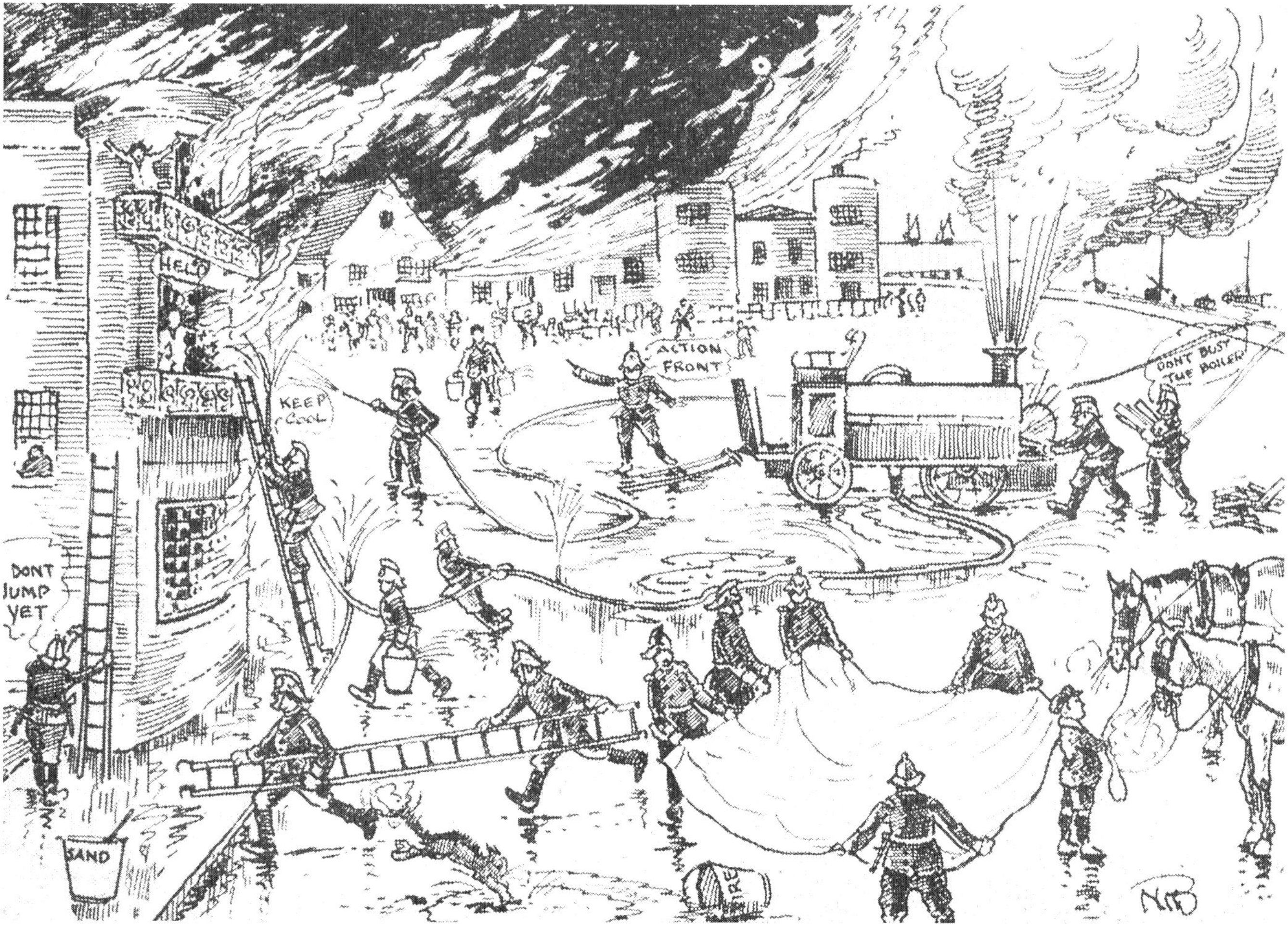
HELP
KEEP COOL
ACTION FRONT
DONT BUST THE BOILER
DONT JUMP YET
SAND

The Health Service

In November Fred turned his attention to the health service. There was no NHS in 1939. He compared the health service of 50 years previous with that of the day and added the following caption to the cartoon opposite:-

First aid in Southend a century ago was not so well developed. The new Victoria Hospital opened and dealt with the road casualties at the time.

Southend Victoria Hospital opened on Warrior Square in May 1888. By Christmas that year, it had eight beds and two cots and treated on average 61 patients a week. In 1932 the Victoria was replaced by the new Southend General Hospital, which is still located on Prittlewell Chase, Westcliff-on-Sea.

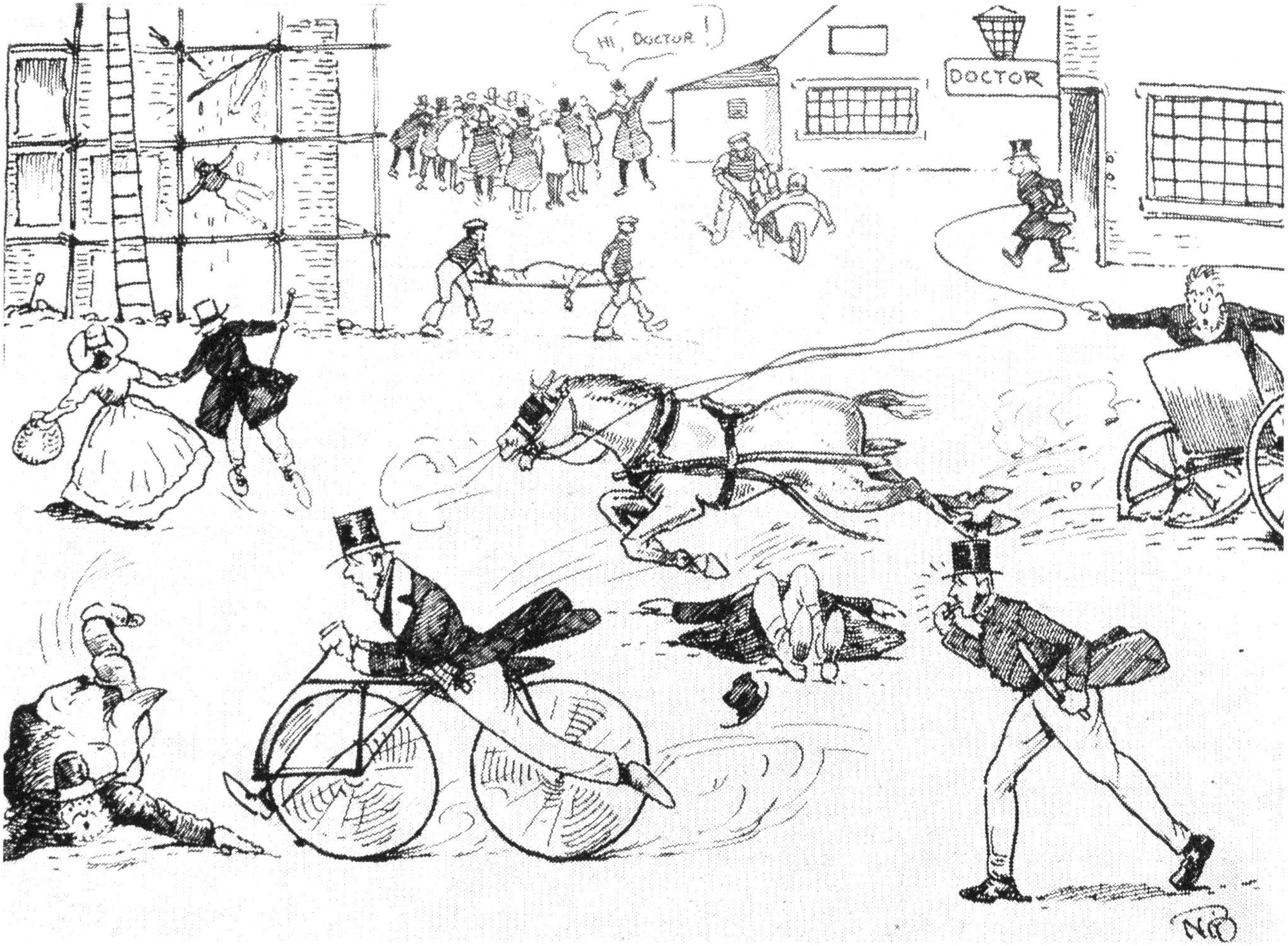
HI, DOCTOR!
DOCTOR

Christmas 1939

Are far as the cartoonists were concerned 1939 ended on a positive note. As yet the 'blitz' was still five months away although the war at sea was increasingly savage.

Despite the black-out restrictions, Stan Harvey turned his attention to Christmas shopping and the importance of shopping locally. Stan didn't do captions; his images provided all the talking.

PALACE
THEATRE . . . . . WESTCLIFF
Phone: 49138.
NOW UNDER THE "REGAL" MANAGEMENT
BOXING DAY, Dec. 26th, for 3 Weeks
Pantomime
DICK
WHITTINGTON
2.0 Twice Daily 7.15
FULL LONDON COMPANY
"A Traditional Pantomime for Old and Young."—Vide Press.
Prices of Admission - 3/- — 9d.
REGAL
VARIETY THEATRE - SOUTHEND
Phone: 67053.
BOXING DAY, Dec. 26th, for 2 Weeks
JIMMY HUNTER'S
BRIGHTON
FOLLIES
At 5.45 and 8.0
MATINEES: WED. & SAT. 2.15
NEXT WEEK ENTIRE CHANGE OF PROGRAMME
NEW
SONGS
SCENES
COSTUMES
COMEDY
SKETCHES
Prices of Admission - 2/6 — 9d.
REDUCED CHILDREN'S PRICES (HOLIDAYS & SATS. EXCEPTED)

In Southend, the pantomime *Dick Wittington* ran from Boxing Day for three weeks at the Palace Theatre and for two weeks *Jimmy Hunter's Brighton Follies* entertained at the Regal Variety Theatre. The Ritz cinema's main feature was *The Man in the Iron Mask* with Louis Hayward and Joan Bennett.

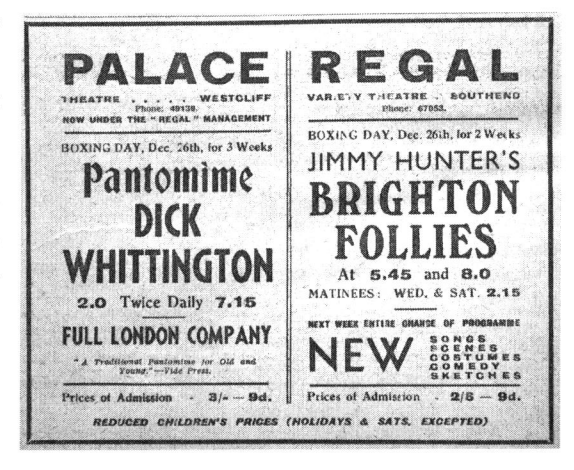

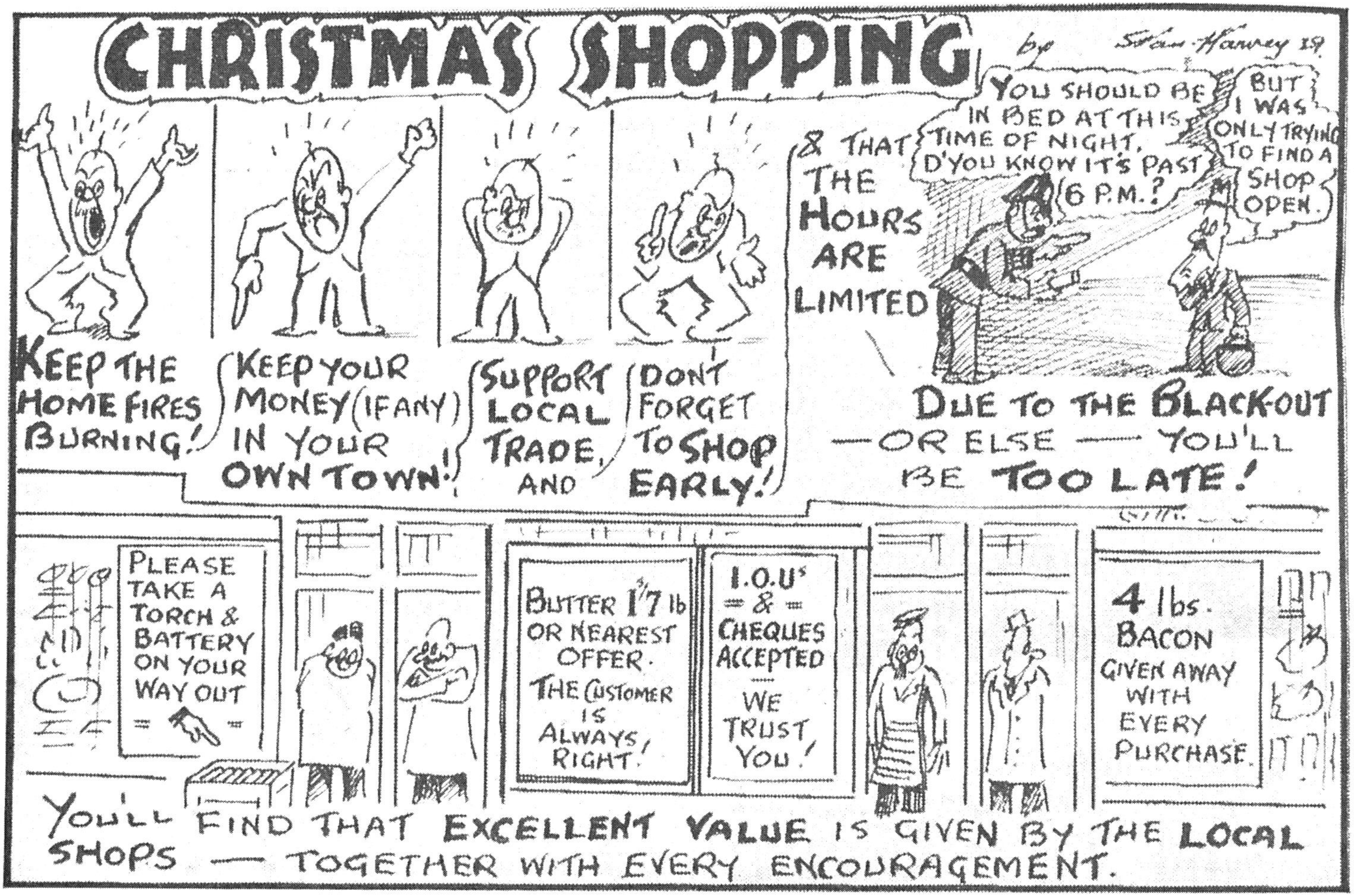
CHRISTMAS SHOPPING
by Stan Harvey 39
KEEP THE HOME FIRES BURNING!
KEEP YOUR MONEY (IF ANY) IN YOUR OWN TOWN!
SUPPORT LOCAL TRADE, AND
DON'T FORGET TO SHOP EARLY!
& THAT THE HOURS ARE LIMITED
YOU SHOULD BE IN BED AT THIS TIME OF NIGHT, D'YOU KNOW IT'S PAST 6 P.M.?
BUT I WAS ONLY TRYING TO FIND A SHOP OPEN.
DUE TO THE BLACK-OUT —OR ELSE — YOU'LL BE TOO LATE!
PLEASE TAKE A TORCH & BATTERY ON YOUR WAY OUT
BUTTER 1/7 lb OR NEAREST OFFER. THE CUSTOMER IS ALWAYS RIGHT!
I.O.U's & CHEQUES ACCEPTED WE TRUST YOU!
4 lbs. BACON GIVEN AWAY WITH EVERY PURCHASE.
YOU'LL FIND THAT EXCELLENT VALUE IS GIVEN BY THE LOCAL SHOPS — TOGETHER WITH EVERY ENCOURAGEMENT.

War or No War, Bringing the yule tide log to Southend two centuries ago.

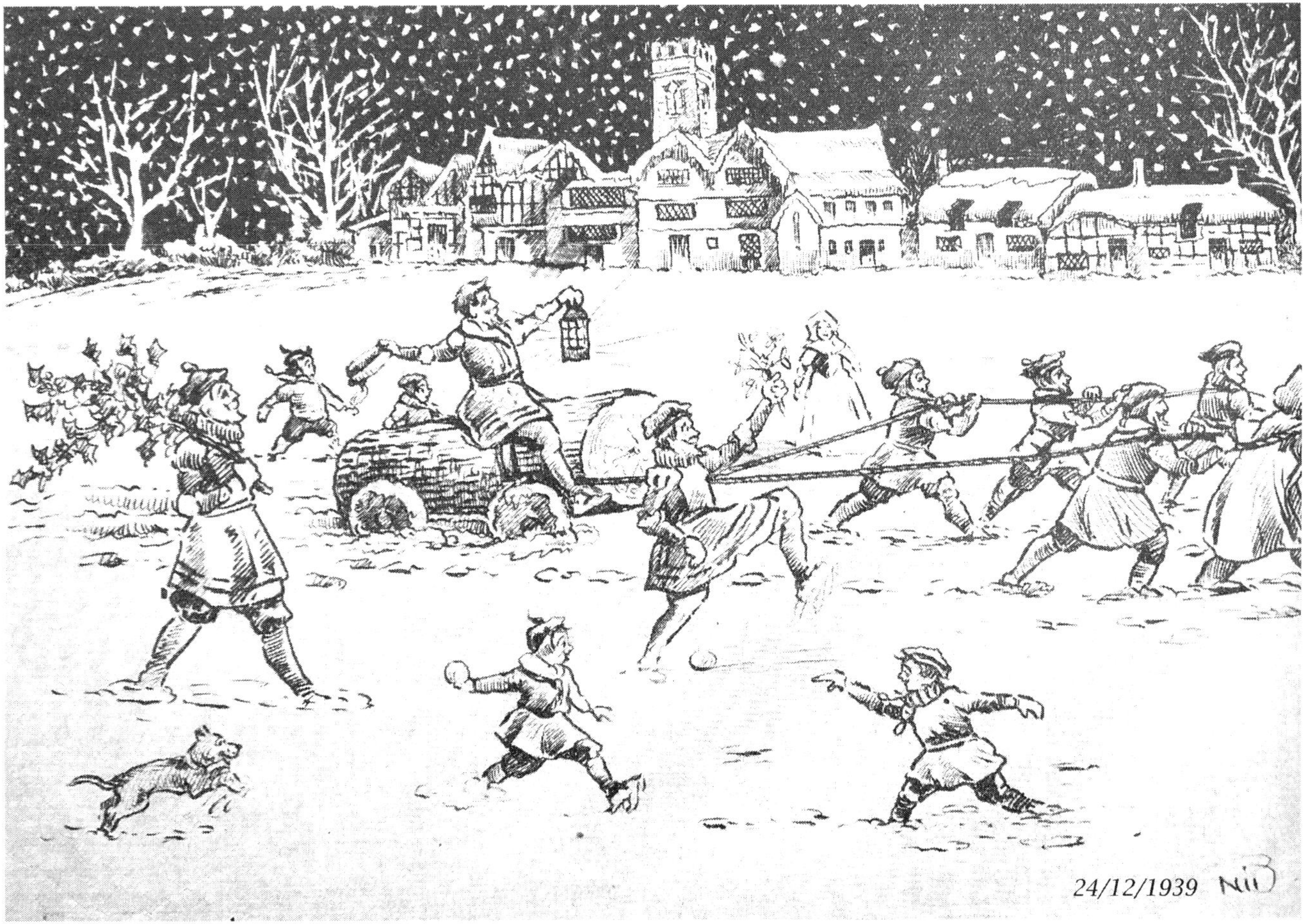
24/12/1939 NIB

We will bounce back. Promoting Southend December 1939.

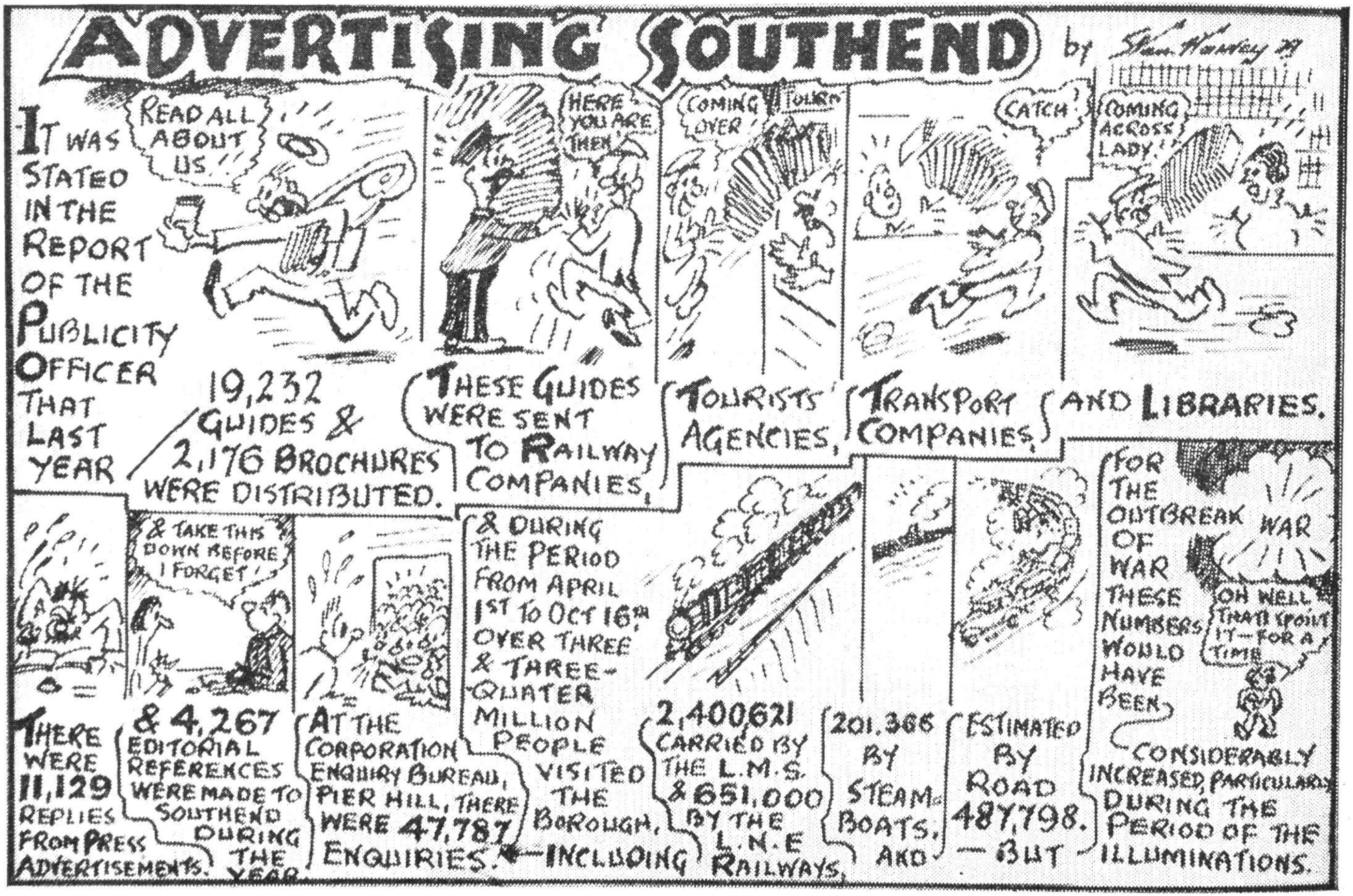
ADVERTISING SOUTHEND
by
IT WAS STATED IN THE REPORT OF THE PUBLICITY OFFICER THAT LAST YEAR
READ ALL ABOUT US
19,232 GUIDES & 2,176 BROCHURES WERE DISTRIBUTED.
HERE YOU ARE THEN
THESE GUIDES WERE SENT TO RAILWAY COMPANIES,
COMING OVER
TOURISTS' AGENCIES,
CATCH
TRANSPORT COMPANIES,
COMING ACROSS LADY
AND LIBRARIES.
THERE WERE 11,129 REPLIES FROM PRESS ADVERTISEMENTS.
& TAKE THIS DOWN BEFORE I FORGET
& 4,267 EDITORIAL REFERENCES WERE MADE TO SOUTHEND DURING THE YEAR
AT THE CORPORATION ENQUIRY BUREAU, PIER HILL, THERE WERE 47,787 ENQUIRIES.
& DURING THE PERIOD FROM APRIL 1ST TO OCT 16TH OVER THREE & THREE-QUATER MILLION PEOPLE VISITED THE BOROUGH, INCLUDING
2,400,621 CARRIED BY THE L.M.S. & 651,000 BY THE L.N.E RAILWAYS,
201,366 BY STEAM-BOATS, AND
ESTIMATED BY ROAD 487,798. — BUT
FOR THE OUTBREAK OF WAR THESE NUMBERS WOULD HAVE BEEN
WAR
OH WELL THAT'S SPOILT IT — FOR A TIME
CONSIDERABLY INCREASED, PARTICULARLY DURING THE PERIOD OF THE ILLUMINATIONS.

Stan Harvey. Foretelling the future?

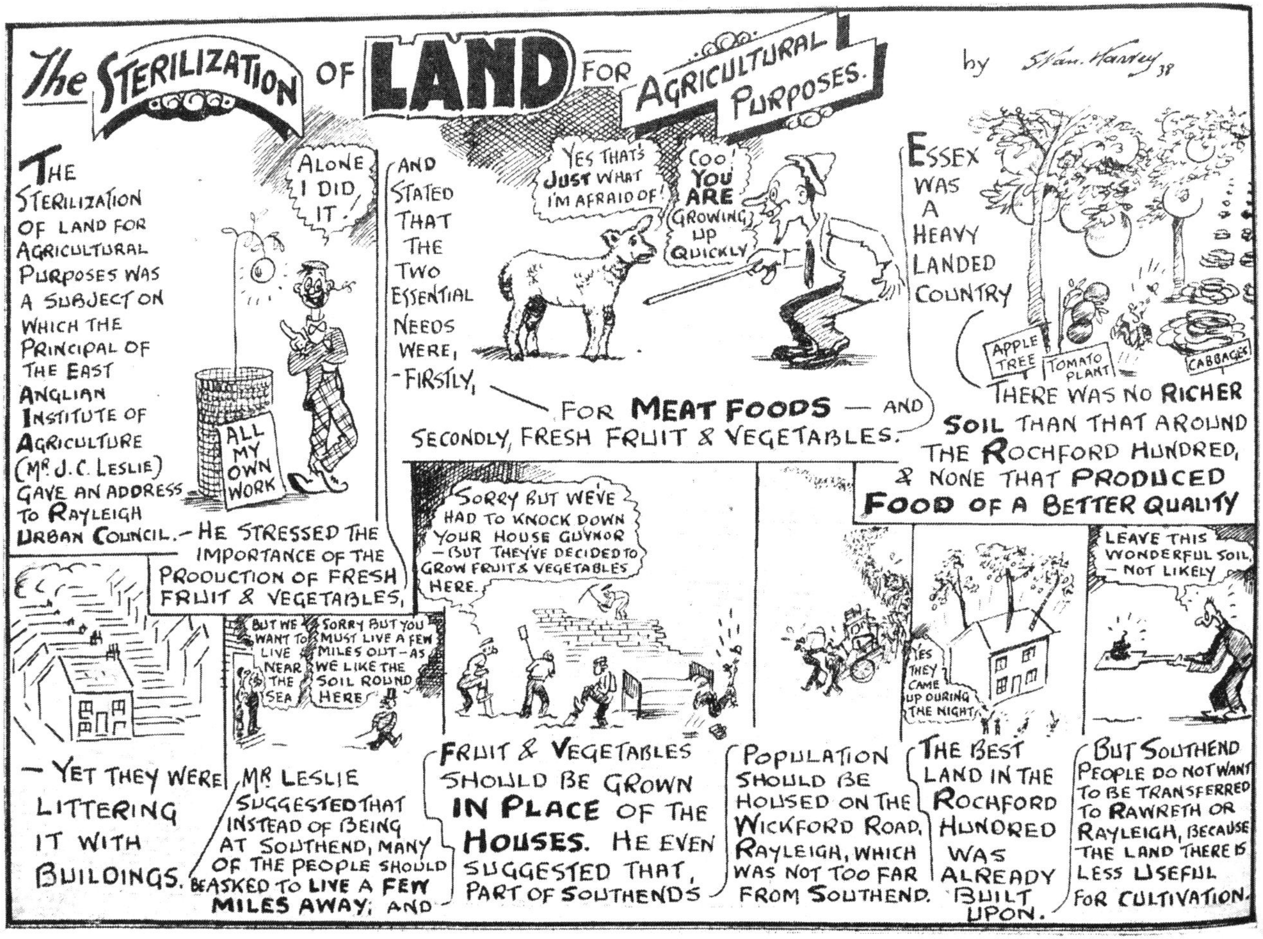
The Sterilization of LAND for Agricultural Purposes.
by Stan Harvey 38
The Sterilization of land for Agricultural Purposes was a subject on which the Principal of the East Anglian Institute of Agriculture (Mr. J.C. Leslie) gave an address to Rayleigh Urban Council. – He stressed the importance of the production of fresh fruit & vegetables,
Alone I did it.
All my own work
and stated that the two essential needs were, – firstly, for MEAT FOODS – and secondly, fresh fruit & vegetables.
Yes that's just what I'm afraid of!
Coo! You are growing up quickly
Essex was a heavy landed country
Apple tree
Tomato plant
Cabbages
There was no richer soil than that around the Rochford Hundred, & none that produced food of a better quality
– Yet they were littering it with buildings.
But we want to live near the sea
Sorry but you must live a few miles out – as we like the soil round here
Mr. Leslie suggested that instead of being at Southend, many of the people should be asked to live a few miles away; and
Sorry but we've had to knock down your house guvnor – but they've decided to grow fruit & vegetables here.
Fruit & vegetables should be grown IN PLACE of the Houses. He even suggested that, part of Southend's
Population should be housed on the Wickford Road, Rayleigh, which was not too far from Southend.
Yes they came up during the night
The best land in the Rochford Hundred was already built upon.
Leave this wonderful soil, – not likely
But Southend people do not want to be transferred to Rawreth or Rayleigh, because the land there is less useful for cultivation.

Conclusion

Unfortunately, we do not have any of the *Pictorials* for the years 1940 – 1946.

There are no digitally archived records of these newspapers either. We do have a copy of the 1947 *Southend-on-Sea & County Pictorial* but alas there were none of the cartoons that were the regular features in the pre-war years.

So, after December 1939 we didn't hear anymore from Stan Harvey or Fred Naughten. Whether they moved on or retired with the outbreak of war we just do not know.

However, we can say the magic of their cartoons will live forever.

If any reader of this book has any information on Fred and Stan we would be only too pleased to hear from you.

Andrew Summers

Andrew was born within the sound of Bow Bells, has lived in Hadleigh for the last 30 years and been married to Glenis for over 50 years. Andrew has bought books, sold books, printed books and now writes and publishes books too!

Andrew has edited *The Numbers Had to Tally,* a Second World War survival story and written *They Did Their Duty, Essex Farm* which tells the story of Essex Farm in Belgium and its connections with the Essex Regiment.

Along with his colleague John Debenham, Andrew has co-authored several books in the Essex Hundred series such as *The Essex Hundred Histories, The Essex Hundred, (The History of Essex in 100 poems), Battlefield Essex* and *Magna Carta in Essex.*

A list of Essex Hundred titles is shown on pages 161 and 162.

Also available from Essex Hundred Publications

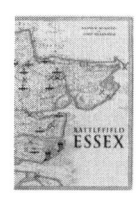

Battlefield Essex

2000 years of 'Battles' and conflicts on Essex soil.

ISBN: 9780993108341

RRP: £8.99

The Essex Hundred

The history of the county of Essex described in 100 poems and supported with historical notes and illustrations. A unique book written by Essex poets covering 2000 years of county history.

ISBN: 9780955229503

RRP: £7.99

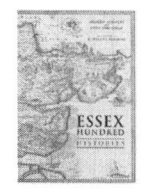

The Essex Hundred Histories

From the sacking of Roman Colchester to a dragon in Wormingford, the birth of radio and Fords of Dagenham's modern day windmills, the book reflects of the diversity of Essex over two millennia.

Reprinted ten times.

ISBN: 9780993108310

RRP: £9.99

The Essex Hundred Children's Colouring and Activity Book

The Colouring and Activity Book is another title from the Essex Hundred family aimed at children and part written by children. The book includes not only Essex information but pictures to colour in, word searches, puzzles and questions.

RRP: £3.99

ESSEX FARM
Never Forgotten

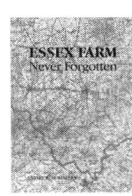

They Did Their Duty, Essex Farm, Never Forgotten by Andrew Summers

A book that tells the story of Essex Farm, a First World War cemetery in Belgium that will forever bear the county name and its connections to the Essex Regiment.

ISBN: 9780955229596

RRP: £9.99 (digital edition available).

BUFFALO BILL'S
WILD WEST

Buffalo Bill's Wild West by David Dunford

The First Reality Show in Essex.
The extraordinary story of Buffalo Bill, his Wild West show and what happened when they came to Essex in the early 1900s.

ISBN: 9780993108389

RRP: £7.99

NUMBERS
HAD TO
TALLY

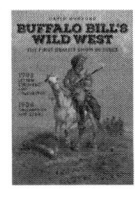

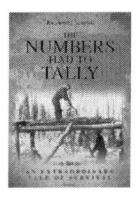

The Numbers Had to Tally by Kazimierz Szmauz

A World War II Extraordinary Tale of Survival.

ISBN: 9780955229572

RRP: £8.99 (digital edition available).

THE
LAST
FLIGHT
of
L33
and OTHER
STORIES

The Last Flight of L33 and other WWI stories (digital edition).

RRP: £2.99

Essex Hundred Publications. Books written, designed and printed in Essex.
Available from bookshops, book wholesalers, direct from the publisher or online www.essex100.com

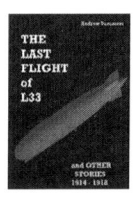